Buying Mutual Funds for *Free*

Kirk Kazanjian

Dearborn
Financial Publishing, Inc.®

DEDICATION

For my mother, Linda Kazanjian, whose continuous love and support have always made me feel immensely rich.

This publication is designed to provide accurate and authoritative information in regard to the subject matter covered. It is sold with the understanding that the publisher is not engaged in rendering legal, accounting, or other professional services. If legal advice or other expert assistance is required, the service of a competent professional person should be sought.

Executive Editor: Cynthia A. Zigmund
Managing Editor: Jack Kiburz
Interior Design: Professional Resources and Communications, Inc.
Cover Design: S. Laird Jenkins Corporation

Charts and some financial data reprinted with permission of IDD Information Services and Lipper Analytical Services. All information contained in this book was gathered from sources believed to be reliable, but accuracy is not guaranteed.

97 98 99 10 9 8 7 6 5 4 3 2 1

Library of Congress Cataloging-in-Publication Data

Kazanjian, Kirk.
Buying mutual funds for free / Kirk Kazanjian.
p. cm.
Includes index.
ISBN 0-7931-2368-2
1. Mutual funds—United States. 2. Mutual funds—United States—Purchasing. I. Title.
HG4930.K39 1997   96-48541
332.63'27—dc21   CIP

Dearborn books are available at special quantity discounts to use as premiums and sales promotions, or for use in corporate training programs. For more information, please call the Special Sales Manager at 800-621-9621, ext. 4384, or write to Dearborn Financial Publishing, Inc., 155 N. Wacker Drive, Chicago, IL 60606-1719.

CONTENTS

PREFACE

A revolution is taking place that has forever changed the way Americans buy mutual funds. It began in 1992, when discount brokerage pioneer Charles Schwab launched a service called OneSource. This program allowed customers to purchase a select group of no-load funds from several different families without paying any transaction fees. The idea was a runaway success and took the entire brokerage industry by storm. The public immediately fell in love with the concept, and there's little question as to why. After all, with a single phone call, or using a personal computer, you could buy or sell dozens of funds, have all of your holdings (including stocks, bonds, and funds) consolidated on a single statement, and let Schwab keep track of such vital tax information as the funds' cost basis, capital gains, and dividend distributions, all without any additional charges or commissions.

To no one's surprise, competitors quickly scrambled to establish similar fund supermarkets of their own. Today, Schwab has been joined by such other big players as Fidelity Investments, Jack White & Company, Muriel Siebert, Accutrade, and Waterhouse Securities, just to name a few. These programs collectively now offer close to 800 funds from 90 different families and have amassed more than $225 billion in assets in less than five years, a figure that's growing in excess of 100 percent annually.

The response from the public has been so overwhelming, even full-service firms like Smith Barney, Prudential Securities, and Merrill Lynch have joined the party by launching similar programs of their own.

Of course, even though customers pay nothing for all of these services, the brokers are still making money. How do they do it? By charging the participating funds an annual fee of between $.25 and $.35 cents for every $100 in assets under management. This money comes straight out of the fund's expense ratio, which is the same whether shareholders do business with a broker or the fund directly.

Smart investors already know that no-load funds are arguably the best investment vehicle available for accumulating wealth over time. Now, thanks to these programs, investing in no-loads is a better deal than ever. Not only are they easy to buy, but you can buy them for *free*. There is no reason to pay a sales load to purchase fund shares ever again. Nor do you need to keep tedious records and mail in checks to several different fund families. This book will show you how to take full advantage of the most exciting development to hit the brokerage industry in years.

The fact is, you can put together a top-performing, diversified portfolio of the world's finest funds by simply opening up an account with your favorite discount broker and selecting from the generous list of available no-load, no-transaction-fee offerings. Unfortunately, even though these programs reduce the amount of work required on your part to a minimum, selecting from the hundreds of available options is an overwhelming task. That's because only a handful are any good. It's great that the brokers are giving you such a wide list of options. But you want to own only the cream of the crop, and this book will teach you how to spot them. You'll even find a specific list of my handpicked All-Stars, those funds destined to remain at the head of the class as we enter the 21st century. Plus, I'll give you guidance for constructing your own wealth-building portfolio.

With so many brokers offering seemingly similar programs, how can you determine which one is right for you? And what's the best way to take full advantage of these fund supermarkets, while making sure you're getting a lot of something for nothing? You'll find the answers to these questions and many more in this, the first book ever written to focus exclusively on these exciting no-transaction-fee, or NTF, programs.

Buying Mutual Funds for Free teaches you everything you need to know to be a successful fund investor. It also provides a complete overview of what each broker offers, a thorough list of the objectives, management team, contact numbers, and past performance figures for each available fund, as well as direction for putting together a diversified portfolio of leading funds for every financial goal.

Chapter 1 reviews some of the mutual fund basics, from how they work to why they've become so popular. It's a concise, yet thorough, overview of fund fundamentals that will enlighten both novices and seasoned pros. Chapter 2 discusses the evolution of this new fund phenomenon, showing you how the no-transaction-fee programs work and explaining how to exploit them to the fullest. Chapter 3 examines and compares the major discount brokers offering these programs from the inside out. It reveals everything from the number of funds each one offers to how fast customer service representatives answer the phones. By the time you finish reading these three chapters, you'll have a good understanding of how funds operate and which broker best suits your needs.

While there are literally dozens of fantastic funds offered through these programs, including many of the nation's premier performers, only 30 are good enough to be crowned as an All-Star in its category. To earn this designation, a fund must have a proven, consistent performance record and be spearheaded by an experienced manager who is continually at the head of the pack. Every All-Star is profiled in Chapter 4, complete with up-to-date performance charts and graphs. With this exclusive information in hand, Chapter 5 then shows you how to put these funds to work in assembling your own first-rate investment plan. In addition to providing advice for determining the proper asset allocation mix based on your individual needs and preferences, four model portfolios are furnished, detailing which specific funds should be purchased and in what amounts for the following objectives: aggressive growth, long-term growth, preretirement growth, and fixed income.

Chapter 6 answers 50 of the most frequently asked questions about mutual fund investing. Among other things, you'll learn whether it ever makes sense to buy funds with sales loads, how much importance should be placed on a fund's annual expense ratio, and how long you should give a poor-performing manager before moving on.

Finally, we'll discuss the actual funds and review the mind-boggling list of available choices. Chapter 7 serves as a complete directory for about 500 of the most widely available no-transaction-fee choices. The options are laid out in an easy-to-understand chart format and categorized according to investment objective. You'll quickly see which brokers offer which funds, who the managers are, and what kind of performance numbers they have posted in the past. In general, the same funds are available through every broker. However, there are a few exceptions, and they will be clearly pointed out in this chapter. (There is also a glossary at the back containing definitions for dozens of terms you'll encounter along the way.)

Even though this book will be updated regularly, the list of available funds and leading candidates is constantly changing. Brand-new funds by seasoned managers, which tend to be top performers, are continually being launched. What's more, additional names are regularly added to my roster of All-Stars, and immediate asset allocation changes may be required to take full advantage of opportunities in the market. As a result, I've created a newsletter called *Fund Connection* that serves as a great monthly companion to the information in this book. In each issue, you'll not only get a rundown of my favorite funds for every objective (based on extensive research and the results of my proprietary computer screenings), but also my up-to-date asset allocation recommendations, exclusive interviews with leading portfolio managers, late-breaking news from the various brokers and fund families, plus other profitable news you can use to make more from your mutual fund investments. As a reader of *Buying Mutual Funds for Free*, you can subscribe to this publication at a low introductory rate, not available to the general public. You'll find the details on this special offer at the back of the book.

For now, sit back and relax as we uncover the secrets to buying mutual funds quickly, easily, and most importantly, for free.

1

MUTUAL FUNDS 101

What Are Mutual Funds?

Everybody's talking about them, and more than one in three Americans owns at least one. But what exactly are mutual funds and how do they work? Unfortunately, it seems many fund investors don't have a clue. I often hear folks say, "I can care less about what happens with the stock market because my money is safely invested in mutual funds." Talk about an oxymoron. That's why I've decided to start off by giving you the real scoop and some background into how one of the greatest investment vehicles ever invented came into being.

Mutual funds, in essence, are nothing more than large investment pools. They enable individual and institutional investors alike to put their money into one pot, which is then overseen by a professional manager. This person is in charge of making all investment decisions on behalf of the shareholders based on a specific goal, such as long-term appreciation or capital preservation.

For example, let's say you're in a growth stock fund. You've invested $1,000 of your own money, and so have many others, to the point where the fund has $1 billion in assets. The fund's manager then takes that $1 billion and buys a wide array of stocks, most likely heavily weighted in larger blue chip names, like those in the Dow Jones Industrial Average and Standard & Poor's (S&P) 500 Index. This same principle also applies to bond and money market funds. As the securities in a fund's portfolio increase in value, so does the price of your shares. Of course, the opposite is also true, meaning that when the holdings stumble, you lose money. Therefore, if you own an equity fund, and the stock market falls, your share price will too. In a mutual fund, an investor who contributes $1,000 stands to lose or gain the exact same percentage as a person putting in $1 million.

Technically, each mutual fund is an investment company in its own right charged with managing money on behalf of shareholders according to the fund's particular objective, be it growth, income, or capital preservation. The value of the shares in a fund is determined at the close of business each day and is referred to as the net asset value (NAV). This is the figure printed in the business section of your newspaper (see Figure 1.1). The NAV is calculated by taking the market price of every security in the fund's portfolio, subtracting any liabilities and dividing the result by the number of outstanding shares. That means, if the stocks, bonds, and money market instruments in a fund collectively are worth $1 million after expenses and there are 1 million shares outstanding, the NAV for the day will be $1 per share.

A Bit of History

Although mutual funds have received a lot of attention in recent years, they are certainly not new. Funds actually date back to 19th century England, when money invested in English and Scottish trusts was used to help finance the post-Civil War economy in America. The first American mutual fund, named the Massachusetts Investment Trust, was born in Boston in 1924. At that time, the industrial revolution in the United States had reached a climax and many different investment opportunities began to surface, among them mutual funds. However, shortly after these instruments gained widespread acceptance as a preferred way to invest in equities, the 1929 stock market crash hit and severely hampered the entire industry. It was not until the bull market took off again in the 1950s that equity funds enjoyed renewed popularity.

Originally, mutual funds invested almost exclusively in stocks. However, another slump emerged from 1968 to 1974, when a weak stock market, combined with rising interest rates and inflation, caused investors to seek safer havens, like bank savings accounts. Thus, the mutual fund industry got creative and developed money market funds in 1972, along

Figure 1.1 How to Read the Fine Print

The following is an example of how mutual fund tables appear in many newspapers. Note that a number of larger, metropolitan newspapers have recently expanded their mutual fund tables by providing additional information, such as investment objectives and total return figures for various time periods.

- The first column is the abbreviated fund's name. Several funds listed under a single heading indicate a family of funds.

- The second column is the net asset value (NAV) per share as of the close of the preceding business day. In some newspapers, the NAV is identified as the sell or the bid price—the amount per share you would receive if you sold your shares (less the deferred sales charge, if any). Each mutual fund determines its NAV every business day by dividing the market value of its total assets, less liabilities, by the number of shares outstanding. On any given day, you can determine the value of your holdings by multiplying the NAV by the number of shares you own.

- The third column is the offering price or, in some papers, the buy or the asked price—the price you would pay if you purchased shares. The buy price is the NAV plus any sales charges. If there are no initial sales charges, an NL for no-load appears in this column, and the buy price is the same as the NAV. To figure the sales charge percentage, divide the difference between the NAV and the offering price by the offering price. Here, for instance, the sales charge is 7.2 percent ($14.52 − $13.47 = $1.05; $1.05 ÷ $14.52 = 0.072).

- The fourth column shows the change, if any, in net asset value from the preceding quotation—in other words, the change over the most recent one-day trading period. This fund, for example, gained 8 cents per share.

- A "p" following the abbreviated name of the fund denotes a fund that charges an annual fee from assets for marketing and distribution costs, also known as a 12b-1 plan (named after the 1980 Securities and Exchange Commission rule that permits it).

- If the fund name is followed by an "r," the fund has either a contingent deferred sales charge (CDSC) or a redemption fee. A CDSC is a charge if shares are sold within a certain period; a redemption charge is a fee applied whenever shares are sold.

- A "t" designates a fund that has both a CDSC or a redemption fee and a 12b-1 fee.

- An "f" indicates a fund that habitually enters the previous day's prices, instead of the current day's.

Source: *What is a Mutual Fund?* Investment Company Institute, Washington, D.C.

with new variations of stock and bond funds, such as those investing over-seas and in gold. The concept of money market investing quickly gained wide acceptance and dramatically changed the game forever. All of a sud-den, investors with limited financial resources could enjoy higher interest rates than the banks paid by placing their hard-earned dollars in these rel-atively risk-free funds. Money markets also helped to make Americans more comfortable with the idea of mutual fund investing in general. This served to bolster the entire fund industry, as the public increasingly became willing to take on the additional risk of venturing back into stocks and bonds.

Explosive Growth

During the past decade, mutual funds have achieved the highest growth rate of all major financial intermediaries and are almost equal with commercial banks in terms of assets under management. However, investor preferences for funds have changed dramatically during this time. In 1986, the majority of all assets in the industry, 40.8 percent, were parked in money market funds, followed by bond and income funds at 36.7 percent. Equity funds accounted for a measly 22.5 percent of the total pie. But, by the end of 1995, the tables had turned. Suddenly, equity funds were on top with 45 percent, while money market funds came in dead last at 22.3 percent. Industry assets throughout this period skyrocketed from $716.3 billion at the end of 1986 to a record $2.82 trillion by year-end 1995. The figure stands well above $3 trillion today (see Figure 1.2).

Although Americans are by far the biggest fans of funds, the industry has been growing at an annual rate of 17.3 percent worldwide over the past five years, especially in Europe, Canada, and Latin America. Given that many countries, including the United States, are faced with aging populations, the need for increased private savings to fund retirement is of utmost concern. Mutual funds are the perfect vehicle for such savings, especially those invested in the stock market, since equities are the one investment class that has consistently produced the highest rates of return over the past century. As a result, the industry's record pace of expansion is expected to continue well beyond the year 2000, thanks in large part to the phenomenal growth of individual retirement accounts (IRAs) and 401(k) plans.

Who Owns Funds?

What type of people own mutual funds? In all, 38 million Americans now own shares in at least one mutual fund. That prompted the *Investment*

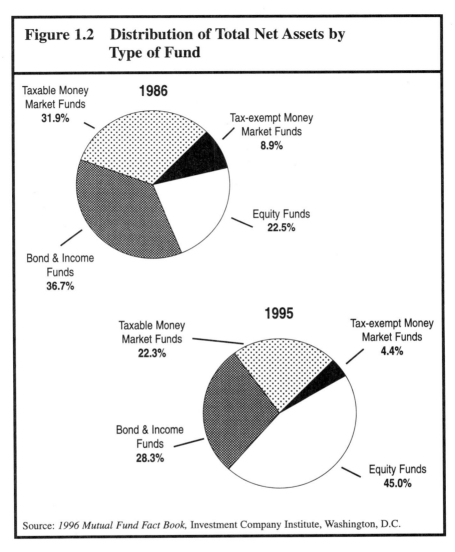

Figure 1.2 Distribution of Total Net Assets by Type of Fund

1986

Taxable Money Market Funds 31.9%

Tax-exempt Money Market Funds 8.9%

Equity Funds 22.5%

Bond & Income Funds 36.7%

1995

Taxable Money Market Funds 22.3%

Tax-exempt Money Market Funds 4.4%

Bond & Income Funds 28.3%

Equity Funds 45.0%

Source: *1996 Mutual Fund Fact Book,* Investment Company Institute, Washington, D.C.

Company Institute, the fund industry's trade organization, to conduct a survey of more than 1,000 fund shareholders nationwide to identify some basic characteristics. According to the results, the average fund investor is a member of the middle class, 44 years old, with a job, spouse, and financial assets of $50,000. The primary fund investment decision maker is most often a man (47 percent compared to 32 percent for women), while both sexes share equally in the decision-making process 21 percent of the time.

Fund investors have long-term goals. Sixty percent responded that retirement is their top objective, followed by financing a child's college education at 26 percent. The typical fund investor owns three different equity funds and more than half also own bond and income funds. Furthermore, the survey revealed some differences among the generations when it comes to fund investing. While generation X respondents (ages 18 to 30) have the lowest level of total household assets, they have the second highest percentage of those assets in funds (38 percent), just behind those aged 50 to 70 (42 percent). Not surprisingly, Generation Xers also exhibited the biggest tolerance for investment risk. While the Baby Boomers (those age 31 to 49) have roughly twice as much money in mutual funds as members of Generation X, these investments represent a small portion of their total assets (27 percent).

The Rules of the Game

All mutual funds must register under what's known as the Investment Company Act of 1940. This legislation grew out of a special study in the 1930s by the Securities and Exchange Commission (SEC) and was drafted jointly by the SEC and industry professionals. It outlines numerous rules and provisions designed to prevent any potential conflicts of interest, while providing for the safekeeping of fund assets and preventing a fund from charging excessive fees. Additionally, the law regulates a fund's performance claims and mandates that such important items as the prospectus and annual report be made readily available to shareholders.

When the law was written almost 60 years ago, there were a total 68 funds in existence. Today, there are more than 6,000. Still, mutual funds continue to operate under some of the closest scrutiny of any industry in this country. Funds are also policed in every individual state where they are sold under what are known as blue-sky laws. As a result, even though assets under management have grown from $448 million in 1940 to more than $3 trillion today, the number of problems and fund-related scandals remains relatively small.

A mutual fund, though run by an independent management company, is technically owned by its shareholders. The investment policies and objectives are determined by a board of directors, which is elected by shareholders each year. The board is responsible for hiring an adviser to manage the fund and make all of the day-to-day decisions. Policies agreed to by the board are set out in the fund's prospectus, which should be required reading before you ever invest a penny. You can get a prospectus by calling either your discount broker or the fund directly.

The Prospectus Tells All

The prospectus is designed to give current and prospective shareholders a complete disclosure of the fund's investment objectives, the types of securities it can own, the names and background of key players on the portfolio management team, the level of risk the fund pursues, and condensed financial statements going back either ten years or since inception, whichever is greater.

Yes, prospectuses can be boring and confusing. After all, most are written by lawyers. But reading them before you invest can save a lot of headaches and lost money down the line. Among the most important things to look for are the minimum initial investment (though the various discount brokers may set their own levels), the fund's investment objective, annual expense ratio, past performance numbers and risk level. This information is normally found within the first three pages. To better illustrate how to make sense of all this, Figure 1.3 shows page 2 of the prospectus for the Bonnel Growth Fund, one of my All-Stars.

This table gives a summary of the fund's fees and expenses. You'll notice the Bonnel Growth Fund has no sales load or redemption fees, but does charge $5 for exchanging assets into another fund, $10 to close an account and assesses a short-term trading fee of 0.10 percent for shares held less than 14 days. (These extra fees are meant to deter frequent in-and-out trading.) In terms of annual fund operating expenses, the Bonnel Growth Fund charges 1 percent of assets for management and administrative costs, has a 12b-1 fee of 0.25 percent, and another 1.25 percent for other expenses, bringing its total expense ratio to 2.50 percent. (Because of an increase in assets, the fund's actual expense ratio is now down to about 2 percent and will continue to fall as it gets larger.)

Toward the back of the prospectus you'll find a financial highlights table with important historical operating information. This reveals how the fund has performed in the past. Figure 1.4 shows selected per share data and ratios from the Bonnel Growth Fund prospectus.

Net asset value is the actual amount each share in the fund is worth. (As of March 31, 1996, each share in the Bonnel Growth Fund was priced at $14.81.) Net investment income or loss shows the per share amount of dividends and interest income earned on securities held by the fund after

---

Figure 1.3 Bonnel Growth Fund Summary of Fees and Expenses

Summary of Fees and Expenses

The following summary is provided to assist you in understanding the various costs and expenses a shareholder in the fund could bear directly or indirectly.

Shareholder Transaction Expenses

Maximum Sales Load ....None

Redemption Fee ....None

Administrative Exchange Fee ....$ 5

Account Closing Fee (does not apply to exchanges) ....$ 10

Short-Term Trading Fee (shares held less than 14 days)..........0.10%

Annual Fund Operating Expenses
(as a percentage of average net assets)

Management and Administrative Fees 1.00%

12b-1 Fees 0.25%

Other Expenses, including Transfer Agency and Accounting
     Services Fees (net of waivers and reimbursements) 1.25%

Total Fund Operating Expenses
     (net of waivers and reimbursements) 2.50%

Reprinted with permission of United Services Funds.

---

expenses (Bonnel posted a loss of $.07). Net gains (or losses) on investments tell you how much in capital gains the fund realized during the stated period (Bonnel earned $.89). Total investment return gives you the percentage increase (or decrease) in the value of each share in the fund over a given time horizon (Bonnel was up 5.93 percent). Ratio of expenses to average net assets represents the fund's total operating expenses divided by average net assets for the period (2 percent for Bonnel). This is a more accurate indication of what the fund's actual expense ratio is. (The numbers at the front of the prospectus generally give the maximum limit.)

Figure 1.4   Bonnel Growth Fund Selected per Share Data and Ratios

BONNEL GROWTH FUND

Notes to Financial Statements
March 31, 1996

Selected per Share Data and Ratios

Selected data for a capital share outstanding throughout each period is as follows:

	Six-month period ended March 31, 1996	Period ended (a)
Per Share Operating Performance:		
Net asset value, beginning of period	$ 14.81	$ 10.02
Net investment (loss)	(.07)	(–.07)(b)
Net realized and unrealized gain on investments (c)	.89	4.91
Total from investment operations	.82	4.84
Less dividends and distributions:		
Dividends in excess of net investment income	—	.05
Distributions from net realized gain	.65	—
Total dividends and distributions	.65	.05
Net asset value, end of period	$ 14.98	$ 14.81
Total Investment Return (d)(e)	5.93%	48.74%
Ratio/Supplemental Data:		
Net assets, end of period (in thousands)	$50,079	$24,673
Ratio of expenses to average net assets	2.00% (g)	2.48% (f)(g)
Ratio of net income to average net assets	–134% (g)	–1.46% (f)(g)
Portfolio turnover...	100%	145%
Average commission rate paid	0.0724	—

(a) For the period from October 17, 1994 (date of commencement of operations) to September 30, 1995.

(b) Net of expense reimbursements and fee waivers.

(c) Includes the effect of capital share transactions throughout the period.

(d) Total return does not reflect the effect of account fees.

(e) Total investment return is not annualized.

(f) Expense ratio is net of fee waivers. Had such reimbursements not been made, the annualized expense ratio subject to the most restrictive state limitation would have been 2.50% and the annualized net investment income ratio would have been (1.52)%.

(g) Annualized; the ratios are not necessarily indicative of 12 months of operations.

Reprinted with permission of United Services Funds.

Portfolio turnover indicates how often a manager trades around in the portfolio (Bonnel's 100 percent rate indicates a high degree of trading activities, but does not necessarily mean that every stock in the portfolio was sold).

If you need to know more than you find in the prospectus, you can either call the fund company and speak with a shareholder representative, or request a statement of additional information (SAI), which is also known as Part B of the registration statement. This document details such things as which securities the fund owned at the end of the latest fiscal year, a rundown of the fund's directors and officers, information about anyone who owns 5 percent or more of the outstanding shares and the most recent audited financial statements.

I also recommend that you review a fund's annual report before investing. This shows you exactly which companies and securities are in the portfolio, along with graphs illustrating the fund's past performance results compared to a benchmark index, such as the S&P 500 or Lehman Brothers Corporate Bond Index. That way you'll get a feel for the kind of companies the manager looks for and how he or she is doing compared to the "market." If you're considering a growth fund, and see that the portfolio is full of big names you recognize, you can assume your money will be spread across a wide array of blue chip firms. On the other hand, if none of the listed names are familiar to you, there's a good chance the fund is heavily invested in riskier, small-cap companies. There's nothing wrong with that, but you better be prepared for a higher degree of volatility. This is something essential for you to know from the start.

The annual report also breaks down what percentage of all assets are invested in various industries. Additionally, in foreign funds, you will learn how the money is divided among various countries.

Figure 1.5 shows which stocks and other investments were held by the Bonnel Growth Fund as of March 31, 1996. You'll notice the fund had 99.51 percent of its assets in common stocks, with the rest in repurchase agreements, which serve as a proxy for cash. The annual report tells you exactly which stocks are owned by the fund, broken down by industry, along with how many shares and the value of those shares on the date the report was prepared. For instance, the top of the report indicates that the Bonnel Growth Fund owned 10,000 shares of Dana Corporation, which were worth $333,750 on March 31, 1996. Dana Corporation is in the automotive parts industry. In all, Bonnel Growth had its money spread over 90 different stocks. That means if you had $5,000 invested in the fund (its minimum for regular accounts), your money would have been

Figure 1.5 Bonnel Growth Fund Annual Report

BONNEL GROWTH FUND
Portfolio of Investments in Securities
March 31, 1996

	Shares	Value
COMMON STOCKS (99.51%)		
AUTOMOTIVE PARTS (1.85%)		
Dana Corporation	10,000	$ 333,750
Gentex Corporation	20,000	595,000 (a)
		928,750
COMMERCIAL SERVICES (2.34%)		
Access Health Marketing, Inc.	22,500	871,875 (a)
Labor Ready, Inc.	12,500	300,000 (a)
		1,171,875
COMMUNICATION EQUIPMENT (8.91%)		
Brooktrout Technology, Inc.	37,500	1,293,750 (a)
California Amplifier, Inc.	40,000	1,070,000 (a)
Checkpoint Systems, Inc.	38,000	945,250 (a)
QUALCOMM Incorporated	20,000	830,000 (a)
Zoom Telephonics, Inc.	20,000	325,000 (a)
		4,464,000
COMPUTER SOFTWARE (14.26%)		
Ascend Communications, Inc.	20,000	1,077,500 (a)
BMC Software, Inc.	13,000	711,750 (a)
Computer Data Systems, Inc.	20,000	311,250
Computer Sciences Corporation	13,000	914,875 (a)
EPIC Design Technology, Inc.	7,500	229,219 (a)
Microcom, Inc.	31,000	926,125 (a)
Parametric Technology Corporation	30,000	1,173,750 (a)
Project Software & Development, Inc.	23,000	879,750 (a)
SCI Systems, Inc.	25,000	915,625 (a)
		7,139,844
COMPUTER SYSTEMS (7.45%)		
Auspex Systems, Inc.	30,000	536,250 (a)
Boca Research, Inc.	5,000	91,250 (a)
Centennial Technologies, Inc.	10,000	175,000 (a)
Inso Corporation	5,000	230,625 (a)
Iomega Corporation	35,000	896,875 (a)
Madge N.V.	19,000	762,375 (a)
Seagate Technology, Inc.	19,000	1,040,250 (a)
		3,732,625
ELECTRONICS (8.10%)		
Analog Services, Inc.	15,000	420,000 (a)
Cable Design Technologies	20,000	735,000 (a)
Cognex Corporation	11,000	281,875 (a)
Computer Products, Inc.	20,000	270,000 (a)
Cyberoptics Corporation	18,000	517,500 (a)

BONNEL GROWTH FUND
Portfolio of Investments in Securities
March 31, 1996

	Shares	Value
COMMON STOCKS (continued)		
ELECTRONICS (continued)		
Kent Electronics Corporation	30,000	$1,061,250 (a)
Maxim Integrated Products, Inc.	15,000	465,000 (a)
Nu Horizons Electronics Corp.	20,000	272,500 (a)
Reliability Incorporated	5,000	35,625 (a)
		4,058,750
FINANCIAL SERVICES (3.73%)		
The Advest Group, Inc.	10,000	96,250 (a)
A.G. Edwards, Inc.	15,000	373,125
Green Tree Financial Corporation	22,000	756,250
The Charles Schwab Corporation	25,000	640,625
		1,866,250
HEALTH CARE (12.89%)		
Chronimed, Inc.	30,000	603,750 (a)
Dura Pharmaceuticals Inc.	23,000	1,141,375 (a)
Health Management Associates, Inc.	27,000	945,000 (a)
Jones Medical Industries, Inc.	34,500	1,328,250
KV Pharmaceutical Company	15,000	211,875 (a)
Merck & Co., Inc.	10,000	622,500
Prime Medical Services, Inc.	15,000	195,000 (a)
Steris Corporation	10,000	300,000 (a)
Universal Health Services, Inc.	19,000	1,009,375 (a)
U.S. Bioscience, Inc.	15,000	98,437 (a)
		6,455,562
LEISURE TIME (1.76%)		
Action Performance Companies, Inc.	20,000	440,000 (a)
Grand Casinos Inc.	5,000	150,000 (a)
Seattle Film Works, Inc.	15,000	292,500 (a)
		882,500
MANUFACTURING (1.62%)		
Ferrofluidics Corporation	5,000	48,750 (a)
Gleason Corporation	10,000	406,250
NN Ball & Roller, Inc.	5,000	110,625
York International Corporation	5,000	245,000
		810,625
MEDICAL PRODUCTS & SUPPLIES (8.78%)		
Becton, Dickinson, and Company	10,000	818,750
Bergen Brunswig Corporation	10,000	261,250
Coherent, Inc.	22,000	935,000 (a)
Daig Corporation	14,000	337,750 (a)
Medtronic, Inc.	17,000	1,013,625
Protocol Systems, Inc.	25,000	421,875 (a)
Target Therapeutics Inc.	10,000	606,250 (a)
		4,394,500

Figure 1.5   Bonnel Growth Fund Annual Report (continued)

BONNEL GROWTH FUND
Portfolio of Investments in Securities
March 31, 1996

	Shares	Value
COMMON STOCKS (continued)		
OIL & GAS DRILLING (1.94%)		
Chesapeake Energy Corporation	10,000	$ 462,500 (a)
Rowan Companies, Inc.	40,000	510,000 (a)
		972,500
RESTAURANTS (2.70%)		
Boston Chicken, Inc.	20,000	681,250 (a)
Papa John's International, Inc.	15,000	669,375 (a)
		1,350,625
RETAIL (10.91%)		
Claire's Store, Inc.	4,500	81,563
The Gap, Inc.	8,000	443,000
Just For Feet, Inc.	3,000	124,875 (a)
Jones Apparel Group, Inc.	20,000	970,000 (a)
Kohl's Corporation	15,000	950,625 (a)
The Men's Warehouse, Inc.	11,000	346,500 (a)
OfficeMax, Inc.	8,000	194,000 (a)
Orchard Supply Hardware Stores Corporation	55,000	189,000 (a)
Pier 1 Imports, Inc.	55,000	694,375 (a)
Sears, Roebuck and Co.	16,000	780,000
Tommy Hilfiger Corporation	15,000	688,125 (a)
		5,462,063
MISCELLANEOUS (12.27%)		
Caterpillar Inc. (machinery)	6,000	408,000
The Clorox Company (household)	10,000	861,250
Hudson General Corporation (specialized services)	1,000	43,375
JLG Industries, Inc. (engineering & construction)	15,000	686,250
Level One Communications, Inc. (telecommunication)	30,000	832,500 (a)
Perceptron, Inc. (photography & imaging)	20,000	517,500 (a)
Parlux Fragrances, Inc. (cosmetics)	15,000	185,625 (a)
Pre-paid Legal Services, Inc. (insurance carriers)	30,000	446,250
Service Corporation International (funeral services)	19,000	926,250 (a)
RMI Titanium (metals)	15,000	225,000
Robert Mondavi Corporation (beverages-alcoholic)	5,000	128,750 (a)
Schult Homes Corporation (housing)	3,000	49,500
Viking Office Products, Inc. (office products)	15,000	834,375 (a)
		6,144,625
Total common stocks (cost $42,868,820)		49,835,094

BONNEL GROWTH FUND
Portfolio of Investments in Securities
March 31, 1996

	Shares	Value
COMMON STOCKS (continued)		
Joint Repurchase Agreement Account		
(cost $475,650)	$475,650	$ 475,650
Total investments (100.46%) (b)		
(cost $43,344,170)		$50,310,744

(a) Non-income producing security.
(b) The percentage shown represents the percentage of investments to net assets.

Reprinted with permission of United Services Funds.

diversified among 90 stocks. The commission to buy that many stocks on your own would be so high, it would virtually wipe out your entire investment.

Why You Should Own Mutual Funds

The reasons for investing in mutual funds are many. Three of the biggest include diversification, professional management, and liquidity.

Let's begin with diversification. You never want to put all of your eggs (or money) into one basket. By their very nature, mutual funds are a diversified investment. For as little as $100, you can buy into an equity mutual fund and instantly spread your risk over dozens or even hundreds of different stocks. What's more, because all funds have a very specific investment objective, you can specify which part of the market you want to be in, such as large-cap growth, small-cap growth, or international. That's why asset allocation, a subject we'll discuss in greater detail in Chapter 4, is so important. The key is determining where in the market you want to be, given your tolerance for risk and time horizon. Once you know that, you can go out and find funds that fit your needs.

The privilege of having your money managed by a true investment luminary used to be available only to multimillionaires. Today, some of the finest brains on Wall Street manage mutual funds, making it possible for even small investors, like you and me, to gain access to the enormous knowledge, research departments, and vast network of contacts only the best in the business have. For less than what you would pay a discount broker to trade individual shares of stock, you can hire a living investment legend to put your money to work right along with his or her own. This person will come in each day and decide on your behalf when to buy or sell securities from a broad range of industries, and you get to enjoy the fruits of their labor.

Almost 80 percent of all stock market trades currently are conducted by institutional investors. These folks are moody and their preferences are forever changing. Consequently, as Wayne Gretzky would say, if you're going to make money, you have to keep up with where the hockey puck is headed. Unless you're retired and have a lot of free time on your hands, this isn't easy. It requires tons of research and hard work. Even if you have the resources, wouldn't you rather travel or play golf instead of sitting in front of a computer screen all day watching the market? Investing is truly a full-time job. Why make it hard on yourself? Through buying mutual funds, you can tap into the profit-making potential of stocks and bonds with little work or expense on your part.

As a portfolio manager and financial writer, I am in constant contact with some of the world's greatest investors. It's interesting to note that many of the experts I talk with on a regular basis invest their own money through mutual funds. That, to me, is one the greatest testimonies I can think of to the power and benefit of funds.

A final advantage that funds offer is liquidity. With a single phone call, you can make additional investments or turn all of the shares in your account into cash. Funds are required by law to stand ready to redeem shares at the current net asset value upon demand. The proceeds must be put into your brokerage account (if you don't have one, they'll send you a check) within three days. You can also exchange money between funds with ease.

Yes, There Are Some Disadvantages

Nothing in life is perfect, and that's true with mutual funds as well. As I see it, there are two major disadvantages to mutual fund investing. To begin with, because funds are professionally managed, you have little say about the exact securities you want your manager to buy. For some people, this is a major downfall, since they always want to know exactly what they own. My uncle falls into this category. He loves to be able to walk into a store and say, "I own a part of this place, since I'm a stock-holder." I, on the other hand, see this detachment as a positive. Here's why: Mutual fund managers have a team of analysts who are constantly on the lookout for good investment ideas that the average person has never heard of. Doing this research on your own can really limit your universe of possibilities. In addition, when you know exactly which names are in your portfolio, you tend to focus on those holdings each day and might react with emotion instead of discipline when a particular stock falls or rises significantly during a short period of time. This merely adds undue stress to your life. By letting your manager make these important decisions, there's no need for you to follow the day-to-day fluctuations of the market.

Second, and arguably the biggest disadvantage to mutual fund investing, is that you must pay taxes on any capital gains a fund realizes during the calendar year, which can amount to 10 percent or more of the total investment value. When you hold individual stocks, your gains continue to accrue tax-free until you decide to sell. With funds, you can't control when your manager takes a capital gain or loss. (Obviously, this is of no concern whatsoever if your funds are held in an IRA or other tax-deferred account.) It also goes without saying that if you're in an income-oriented fund, you will have to pay taxes on any realized dividends, which are generally distributed each quarter.

By law, mutual funds are organized under Subchapter M of the Internal Revenue Code. The rules of this law require funds to distribute 90 percent of all taxable income to shareholders at the end of each year. Unlike other corporations, mutual fund income is generally taxed only once, when it is received by shareholders.

Taxation of Mutual Funds

As long as we're on the subject of taxes, let's expand on what Uncle Sam expects from you as it relates to your fund investments. It used to be that you would receive a separate year-end tax statement from each fund and be forced to keep track of your average cost basis on your own. That, fortunately, is a thing of the past. By setting up an account through one of the no-load, no-transaction-fee (NTF) programs (which we'll discuss in great detail shortly), your discount broker does all this for you, and gives you one consolidated tax statement at the end of the year, reflecting the earnings and gains from all of your funds. Your broker also provides you with a single form 1099-DIV, outlining what part of the money represents ordinary income and long-term capital gains. The distinction between the two is important because long-term gains are currently taxed at a maximum rate of 28 percent, while ordinary income is treated the same as wages. Also, capital gains can sometimes be offset by capital losses.

Reading Your 1099-DIV

Like all forms from the IRS, the 1099-DIV might look confusing at first, but it's really quite straightforward. Let's take a look at it line-by-line (see Figure 1.6).

Suffice it to say, the left side of the form contains the name and address of the fund (or your discount broker), their taxpayer identification number, your Social Security number, and your name and address. The right side of the form is where the numbers game begins. Here's a blow-by-blow look at what you'll need to transfer these data to your tax return:

Line 1a—This shows the total amount of distributions you received from your fund during the year. Known as "gross dividends," it includes ordinary dividends, capital gain distributions, and nontaxable distributions. (Remember, if this amount exceeds $400, you must attach a Schedule B to your Form 1040.)

Figure 1.6   How to Read Form 1099-DIV

Among other items, once a year, your broker will send you a Form 1099-DIV. This form contains much of the information you will need for completing your tax return.

Dividends and Distributions

OMB No. 1545-0110

Form **1099-DIV**

19**96**

Copy C For Payer

For Paperwork Reduction Act Notice and instructions for completing this form, see **Instructions for Forms 1099, 1098, 5498, and W-2G.**

Department of the Treasury - Internal Revenue Service

PAYER'S name, street address, city, state, and ZIP code
ABC Mutual Fund
235 Wall Street
New York, NY 10010

PAYER'S Federal identification number
12-3456789

RECIPIENT'S identification number
123-45-6789

RECIPIENT'S name
John Q. Investor

Street address (including apt. no.)
124 Profit Street

City, state, and ZIP code
Los Angeles, CA 90026

Account number (optional)

2nd TIN Not. ☐

Form **1099-DIV**

1a Gross dividends and other distributions on stock (Total of 1b, 1c, 1d, and 1e) $ 249.97

1b Ordinary dividends $ 186.64

1c Capital gain distributions $ 63.33

1d Nontaxable distributions $ 0.00

1e Investment expenses $

Liquidation Distributions

Cash $

2 Federal income tax withheld $ 0.00

3 Foreign tax paid $ 0.00

4 Foreign country or U.S. possession

6 Noncash (Fair market value) $

Recipient's identification number—your social security number. Failure to provide an accurate number could subject you to backup withholding.

Gross dividends and other distributions on stock—the total amount of distribution you received from the fund during the year, including ordinary dividends, capital gain distributions and nontaxable distributions. If you received a total of more than $400 in ordinary dividends from all your investments, you must attach a Schedule B to your Form 1040.

Ordinary dividends—the amount to report on Form 1040 as dividend income.

Foreign tax paid and foreign country or U.S. possession—an amount entered here represents your pro-rata share of foreign income tax paid by the fund. You may be able to take a deduction or credit on your tax return for this amount, if you take the foreign tax credit, you are required to attach Form 1116 to your Form 1040.

Capital gain distributions—the amount to report as capital gain distributions.

Nontaxable distributions—distributions that represent a return of capital; these are not taxable, but do reduce the basis in your fund shares.

Line 1b—This is the amount you must report on Form 1040 in the box marked "dividend income."

Line 1c—This is the amount in line 1a that reflects your total capital gains distributions. As you might guess, you'll want to enter this line in the "capital gains distributions" box of Form 1040.

Line 1d—If any of your distributions are exempt from federal tax, the amount will be noted in this box.

Line 1e—No, this doesn't refer to the expense ratio charged by your fund (that amount is already deducted from the share price). This line will normally be left blank.

Line 2—This is another line that will probably be blank or marked 0.00.

Line 3—This line may have an amount listed if you own an international fund. If so, you can to take a deduction or credit on your tax return, either by indicating the amount on Schedule B or by filing and attaching Form 1116. (In my experience, you almost always come out ahead filing Form 1116, though it is time-consuming and will probably only cut your tax bill by a few dollars.)

Line 4—Again, this is a box you won't need to be concerned about; ditto for Line 6.

How to Minimize Your Taxes

I've already pointed out that one of the beauties of no-load, NTF programs is that the discount broker keeps track of the cost basis for your shares. This is a real time-saver. (The broker will likely compute it under what's known as the average cost basis. There are other acceptable ways of reporting your cost basis, including first-in, first-out, and specific shares. But 99 percent of the time, you'll come out just as well with the average cost basis, so why bother with the rest?)

Still, there are a few additional things you should keep in mind to prevent Uncle Sam from hunting you down for more of your fund profits. First, don't forget that you must pay taxes on all reinvested dividends. When you exchange from one fund to another, even within the same family, it is *always* a taxable event, subject to a capital gain or loss. Many folks feel that, if they simply transfer their shares from one fund to another, they can avoid paying taxes on the increase in value. Not true. An exchange is the same as a sale in the eyes of the IRS. Also, don't forget about the "wash sale rule." Some think they can outfox the government by selling a fund with a capital loss and repurchasing it the next day. That way, they can claim the loss on their tax form, while maintaining a position in the fund. Sorry, but the government is aware of this scheme and has a law in place to prevent it. The wash sale rule states that if you sell a holding (stock, bond, or mutual fund) at a capital loss, you must wait 30 days to repurchase the same security or you can't deduct the loss. There is a way around this restriction, though. There is no law against selling one aggressive growth fund (say the ABC Fund) at a capital loss and using the proceeds to buy a similar but different aggressive growth fund (like the XYZ Fund), even if both are in the same fund family.

There are a couple of other things you should keep in mind concerning taxes. One is you need to be wary about buying shares of a fund right before it declares a year-end distribution. This event normally takes place in December. Previously, we discussed how the amount can often amount to upwards of 10 percent of the fund's net asset value. Even if you own a fund for just one day prior to the distribution, you will have to pay taxes on the entire amount. This can be costly. If you buy 100 shares of a fund selling for $10 a share, and it declares a $1 per share dividend the following day, you will immediately owe taxes on $100, even though you didn't enjoy the gains on the way up. And don't think you're getting something for nothing. Sure, you'll get that $1 dividend. But, to compensate, the fund's share price will drop by the same amount, in this case to $9. So even though you technically receive more shares when a distribution takes place, it's really a nonevent since the share price falls accordingly.

Let me emphasize once more that if you own your funds in a tax-deferred account, such as an IRA, none of this matters because you don't owe any taxes on your investment profits now anyway. We'll spend more time on this subject in Chapter 5. (We'll also discuss the pros and cons of tax-free funds, which aren't always what they're touted to be.)

If you want to learn more about the subject of taxes as they relate to mutual fund investments, you can get it straight from the horse's mouth by calling the IRS at 1-800-TAX-FORM and requesting Publications 550 (Investment Income and Expenses), 551 (Basis of Assets), and 564 (Mutual Fund Distributions).

Load versus No-Load

There are two basic types of mutual funds: load and no-load. Both operate in a similar way under the exact same guidelines. However, load funds charge you a fee, from 1 percent to 8 percent, either up-front or when you decide to sell. This "load" is really a commission that goes directly into the pocket of the person who peddles the fund, usually a stockbroker or financial planner. As a result, if you invest $1,000 in a fund with an 8 percent load, $80 of your investment immediately disappears.

Some funds are both front- and back-end loaded, meaning you pay a fee on the way in and out. Therefore, if you wind up buying a poor-performing load fund, and later decide to move into another one, it could be very expensive.

All funds, both load and no-load, earn money by charging an annual expense fee. This is generally between 1 and 2 percent of assets for stock funds, and under 1 percent for bond and money market funds. Don't forget, the exact management charges, referred to as the expense ratio, can be found at the front of your fund's prospectus. The fees are about the same for both load and no-loads, making loaded funds almost always a more expensive way to go. The truth is, I can't imagine ever paying a load to buy a fund, unless you absolutely don't want to do any research on your own and prefer to walk blindly into the hands of a salesperson who may not have your best interests at heart. In terms of performance, there is no proof that a loaded fund will perform any better than a no-load one. To be honest, many of the most popular loaded funds are real dogs.

It's important to point out that both some load and no-load funds charge what are known as 12b-1 fees, so named for the 1980 SEC rule that authorized them. This charge is reflected in the annual expense ratio, and the money is used for marketing and distribution costs. The National Association of Securities Dealers recently put a cap on these fees, mandating that they be no higher than 0.75 percent (though an additional 0.25 percent can be tacked on to compensate brokers or other salespeople for providing ongoing advice). I obviously prefer funds without 12b-1 fees, though this expense in itself won't prevent me from becoming a shareholder as long as the fund continues to provide superior returns.

All of the funds in this book are not only no-loads, but can also be purchased through any of the listed discount brokers without paying any transaction fees. It's the closest thing you'll ever find to a free lunch on Wall Street!

Closed-End Funds

There aren't any closed-end funds available without transaction fees through the various supermarket programs. However, I want to spend a little time discussing them, since many investors are confused about what makes them different from the traditional open-ended funds that this book focuses on.

There are many similarities. Both open- and closed-end funds invest a pool of money in various securities based on a stated objective. Likewise, closed-end funds are professionally managed, often by investment pros who run similar open-end funds as well. But the major difference rests with how the shares are traded.

An open-end fund, by definition, can issue an unlimited number of shares. As more money comes in, additional shares are created. Of course, some funds decide to close to new investors at a given dollar amount, but this doesn't happen often. In addition, open-end funds are not traded on any stock exchange and can be bought and sold at the actual net asset value either directly from the fund or through a discount broker of your choice. By contrast, closed-end funds begin as initial public offerings, in which a set amount of shares are offered to the public, just like individual stocks. Since the funds are publicly traded on an exchange, you must go through a stockbroker and pay a commission to buy or sell shares.

Finally, as I just pointed out, open-end funds trade at the actual NAV. That's not true with closed-end funds. Instead, share prices are based on supply and demand. Therefore, closed-end funds often sell at either a premium or discount to their actual value. If a fund has a net asset value of $20 but is trading for $16, it is said to be selling at a 20 percent discount. Conversely, if this same fund trades for $24, it is being peddled at a 20 percent premium. In recent years, most new closed-end funds have traded at discounts to their initial offering prices shortly after going public, so they rarely make good investments out of the starting gate.

With so many great no-load, NTF open-end funds available, I can only think of three reasons why anyone would ever consider a closed-end fund. The first is elementary: you want access to a manager who doesn't manage a similar open-end fund, which is rare. Second, if you spot a good closed-fund selling at a significant discount, this is another valid reason to choose it over an open-ended version. Finally, if you're seeking to invest in a certain region and want to spread your risk around, there are many good single-country, closed-end funds available, though the number of similar open-ended funds with identical investment objectives is rapidly increasing.

The bottom line is that you can construct a great portfolio without ever buying a closed-end fund. I personally have never owned one, and don't think I ever will. But at least you know the difference now and can understand why these investment vehicles are so popular in some circles.

Understanding Fund Expenses

All other things being equal, I prefer funds with low expense ratios. Unfortunately, in the financial services industry, everything isn't equal.

Therefore, you would be foolish to choose a fund solely on the basis of how much it costs.

Let's first talk about bond and money market funds. Because these funds offer a low yield and small chance of price appreciation to begin with, expense ratios are more important than they are with stock funds. If you're looking for a short-term bond or mortgage-backed securities fund, you would be wise to shop around for one with the lowest expense ratio, since any fees will eat directly into your returns. (I bet when you check on past performance, you'll find that those with lower fees consistently do better.)

Stock funds, in my opinion, are a different story. In this case, *performance* is everything. Let me ask you a question. Would you rather buy a fund with a 3 percent or a 1 percent expense ratio? Unless you have more money than you know what to do with or a couple of loose screws, you'll probably agree the 1 percent fee is more attractive. But, what if I told you the fund with a 3 percent fee produced a 20 percent annualized gain over the past five years, while the fund charging just 1 percent posted a 15 percent return over that period? That changes everything, doesn't it? All of a sudden, the more expensive fund looks exceedingly more attractive.

There's no question that expense ratios can weigh down a fund's performance. If the market is only up a few percentage points for the year, every little bit helps. But in the final analysis, I would argue that a fund's performance record and future potential is more important than its overall expense ratio. Again, this doesn't mean you should concentrate on high expense funds. I have a blanket rule whereby I almost always avoid any stock fund with an expense ratio higher than 2 percent. My point is, if there's one fund charging 1 percent and another 2 percent, I won't automatically buy the 1 percent fund because it's cheaper. As with anything else in life, you sometimes get what you pay for.

Choosing the Best Funds

Obviously, the expense ratio is only one factor to consider when buying a fund. In Chapter 4, I have profiled 30 funds for various objectives and crowned them as All-Stars. This means they have been consistent performers, are spearheaded by top-notch managers, and are positioned to outshine all others in their respective categories for years to come. In other words, they're the kinds of funds I put my own money in. These funds, and all others in this book, are closely monitored each month in my newsletter *Fund Connection.*

How do I choose funds for my own portfolio and those of my clients? I begin with the most important aspect of putting a portfolio together— asset allocation. That means figuring out where in the market I want to be and to what extent. In other words, how much do I want in stocks and bonds? Beyond that, I must pinpoint which specific areas of the market I want to focus on. Do I want to keep most of my money in small-cap growth stocks, large-cap value holdings, U.S. Treasuries or international issues? This is a variable that is constantly changing, depending on my outlook for the market and such important factors as the economy and interest rates.

Once these determinations have been made, I begin the process of picking funds that meet my objectives by looking through a proprietary database containing hundreds of funds offered through the different supermarkets and ranking them based on both intermediate and long-term past performance compared to their peers and various benchmark indexes. One line I guarantee you'll find in every fund prospectus is that "past performance is no guarantee of future results." I couldn't agree more. I often say that the biggest mistake investors make is putting their money in yesterday's big winner that has just been profiled in a leading personal finance magazine. Chasing that kind of short-term performance is a loser's game. Some of these funds will rack up even greater gains. But more often than not, their success is due to short-term luck and won't be sustained. Nevertheless, history is the only indicator we have for what the future might hold. My philosophy is that if a fund has been a long-term, consistent winner, it will likely continue to do well in the future. If it is a regular loser, I can't think of any reason why it would suddenly change and start to shine. Therefore, the first step in my screening process involves compiling a list of those funds that routinely make the grade compared to their peers in various categories, both in up and down markets.

Next, I look at the people behind the performance. I want to make sure the manager who achieved the record in front of me is still in place. Otherwise, the numbers are meaningless. Then I often talk with the manager to see where he or she is investing right now and whether I agree with his or her philosophy. Since I am continually speaking with the financial world's leading minds, I have a good sense as to where the smart money is going and want to see if the manager I am considering is equally as plugged in. In essence, the past performance numbers serve as a resume and our personal conversation is the interview to determine whether I want to hire this person to manage money for me.

Once a fund is selected, I watch it like a hawk, in terms of both monitoring performance and staying in touch with the manager. This isn't to say that I trade around all the time. I prefer to stick with a manager for as long as possible. But even the best skippers can lose touch with what's working on Wall Street, and I am always prepared to move on when that happens. In addition, fund managers are constantly changing. I strongly believe that you should invest in *managers,* not *funds.* In other words, the Robertson Stephens Growth & Income fund made my All-Star list because it is spearheaded by John Wallace, who is one of the most brilliant managers and consistent performers in the business. It was not selected because it's part of the Robertson Stephens family. It wasn't chosen for its name either. I simply wanted to hire Wallace, and this happens to be the fund he manages. If Wallace moves to another firm, I will probably sell the fund and follow him.

2

THE NEW MUTUAL FUND REVOLUTION

The Old Way of Buying Funds

Imagine you want to buy shares in a stock mutual fund you have carefully researched and determined is perfect for your portfolio. It's Saturday, and you discover an extra $1,000 sitting in your savings account. Since the market has just experienced a significant correction, you want to get that money invested right away. So on Monday, you call the mutual fund company and ask for a prospectus and application. The representative tells you she'll send it right out. You finally receive it on Friday. That weekend, you answer all of the essential questions, make out a check to the fund, and mail it on Monday. The fund receives your application on Friday and opens your account on the following Monday. In all, it has taken two full weeks from the time you first decided to buy the fund for you to actually become a shareholder. During that period, the market has jumped 200 points. You're annoyed that you didn't get in when the idea first came to you because you've missed out on all of these interim profits. You also realize it could take another full week for you to make additional investments, since your checks have to be mailed to the fund's transfer agent, which is located across the country. If you redeem your shares and want to buy into another fund, that time line increases exponentially. Not only do you have to wait for your redemption check to arrive from the first fund, but you must also hold off on sending in a deposit to the new one until your check clears.

Or perhaps you've been investing in mutual funds for years and own ten funds from several different families. While you know funds are the best way to go, you're overwhelmed by the enormous amount of paperwork involved in keeping such a highly diversified portfolio. One of your fund families has tried to convince you that life would be easier if you would just turn all your money over to them and choose from their limited menu. But you know the rest of their fund offerings are mediocre and want the freedom to choose top-performers from other quality companies. Nevertheless, you begin to rethink your decision come April, as you struggle to put together a dozen different tax forms, not to mention figuring out the cost basis for each of your holdings.

Regardless of which boat you're in, either situation is unquestionably a nightmare. Yes, mutual funds are the easiest and best way for investors to get money working in the stock, bond, and money markets. But, until now, you were forced to put up with these time-consuming and frustrating hassles. Thanks to some of America's leading discount brokers, these pitfalls have become a thing of the past.

A Faster, Cheaper, More Convenient Way

While Charles Schwab generally gets most of the credit, it was California discount broker Jack White who first allowed customers to trade no-load funds in their brokerage accounts back in 1984. Schwab started a similar program weeks later. Each offered about 150 no-loads that could be traded for a minimal transaction fee, similar to the commission paid on stocks. The programs offered a variety of services that were never before available, such as having all transactions consolidated on one statement and the ability to purchase shares on the same day a request was made. However, initial public reaction to this concept was lukewarm. It seemed many were reluctant to pay for buying no-loads. "We knew the transaction fee was a big stumbling block for people because they could purchase fund shares free by going direct," admits Jeffrey Lyons, senior vice-president of mutual fund marketing for Charles Schwab & Co. "For many people, the convenience of having their funds all in one place was not enough to overcome the $30 to $50 transaction fee."

In 1990, Charles Schwab himself began working on a plan to get the fund companies to pay this charge so it would cost his customers nothing.

"This whole thing was really Chuck's baby," Lyons tells me. "He knew this was a huge opportunity, but realized he couldn't realize its full potential unless he got rid of the transaction fees. That, in a sense, is how OneSource was born in 1992." Just as he transformed the way people bought stocks 17 years earlier, Schwab dramatically changed the distribution channel for mutual funds in one move with the launch of OneSource. From the start, this program allowed clients to purchase and sell shares of hundreds of no-load funds absolutely free of any commissions. In essence, Schwab created a virtual supermarket of funds. Now, instead of being forced to stick with one fund family to enjoy such conveniences as statement consolidation and the ease of exchanging from one offering to another, you could establish a single account with Schwab and trade among dozens of families without incurring any additional charges. If you invested in individual stocks, those positions could also be lumped together, giving you a complete look at what you were worth each month. Then, at the end of the year, all of your gains would be presented on one easy-to-read statement. Tons of paperwork instantly became a thing of the past.

How Discount Brokers Make Money

Of course, Schwab's intention all along was to make money from the concept, and a lot of it. Even though customers didn't have to pay a dime to trade the funds, Schwab planned to charge the funds themselves an annual management fee of $.25 to $.35 for every $100 in assets held at the brokerage firm. This would serve as a distribution and marketing fee. Since the funds would save the cost of performing these functions on their own, the argument was it was actually a cheaper way for them to go. At first, the program didn't receive a very enthusiastic response from the fund companies. "There was a lot of resistance in the beginning," Lyons recalls. "This was a new concept for the no-load fund companies. There was a great deal of jockeying back and forth. Many fund companies decided to test the water saying, 'If we go, will somebody else go?' Everyone was playing their cards very close to the chest." Schwab succeeded in getting eight big behemoths to sign on for the launch, including Berger, Dreyfus, Federated, Founders, Invesco, Janus, Neuberger & Berman, and Stein Roe.

Jack White quickly introduced a similar program, although he admits he had his doubts about whether it would survive for the long-run. "I didn't think the fund companies would endorse the program," he concedes.

"I doubted they would be willing to pay us 25 or 35 basis points for distribution. I knew a lot of these fund managers personally and thought they'd say, 'Why should I pay a broker for distributing my shares when chances are that broker is going to attract customers who will trade in and out all the time, knowing there aren't any fees for doing so?' I figured that was the last thing they would want. But it didn't work out that way."

Instead, the concept spread like wildfire, and one fund family after another started courting Schwab and Jack White for a piece of the action. "The marketplace was expanding so fast, these fund companies, driven by greed, wanted the cash flow," White adds. "They could care less about the in-and-out trading because that was all on the broker's books. They couldn't afford to be left out." Within a year, Schwab had signed up 25 fund families. The other major discount brokers, including Fidelity Investments, Muriel Siebert, Accutrade, and Waterhouse Securities quickly followed suit by starting NTF programs of their own. The strategy paid off. These six firms alone now house more than $225 billion in no-load, NTF assets, a figure that has been doubling each year.

Interestingly enough, all of the brokers maintain that, while these programs are incredibly popular, they're not very profitable yet on a stand-alone basis. Nevertheless, they bring in a lot of new business and, in the end, do generate a substantial amount of added revenue. "We really look at it more from the perspective of what it takes to get that relationship," Lyons offers. "Although we may not be making any money on OneSource, we are making money on the total customer relationship." Accordingly, as the number of funds and customer accounts continues to increase, so does the profitability of these programs.

What You Get Out of It

The benefits to you as a discount brokerage client are obvious: With one phone call, you can buy and sell, or just receive a prospectus for hundreds of high-quality funds from dozens of different families. These programs also allow you to buy into funds that were formerly only available to powerful institutional investors. You can even purchase funds with high minimum investment requirements of from $100,000 to $1 million for as little as $1,000 when you invest through select brokers. Whether you open a regular or IRA account, you can keep all of your free cash in a central money market fund and make purchases or redemptions on any day you choose. If the market plummets 200 points and you want to buy some shares that same day, a phone call is all it takes. Forget about waiting up to a week for the post office to deliver your request. Redemptions are equally as easy. You also won't have to worry about securing a notarized signature in order to get your money back.

Furthermore, you no longer have to keep track of several accounts or fill out a separate application each time you want to buy a new fund. All mutual fund transactions and positions are concentrated on one statement, along with any other financial assets you own, including stocks and bonds. Your dividends and capital gains can be reinvested without charge. In many cases, you'll have 24-hour, 7-day-a-week access to a representative to discuss your account. You can order outside objective research material on the funds you are considering, often at little or no cost. If you're computer-savvy, or prefer not to deal with humans, you're able to track your holdings and make trades online with software provided by your broker. (That's something none of the fund families currently offer, with the exception of Internet sites.) If you want to exchange from one fund to another, even within different families, it's as easy as picking up the phone. Your work in satisfying Uncle Sam is brought down to a bare minimum, since the discount brokers do most of the work by putting all of the important tax numbers (like capital gains distributions, dividends, and cost basis data) together on a single form. Other advantages include the ability to trade on margin, sell fund shares short (at Jack White), and gain instant check writing access to your money.

Now for the Drawbacks

Yes, there are a few disadvantages to doing business with the brokers. First, since the fund families won't know about you (your investment is lumped into an account registered in the name of your broker), chances are you won't get much promotional mail from them touting new product offerings. (I'll let you decide whether that's good or bad.) When it comes time to mail a report, prospectus, or promotional newsletter, Schwab will only provide the names and addresses of shareholders to a fund company through a third-party mailing center. "We're very protective of our customers," Lyons maintains. The fund families aren't very happy about that policy. "We like to know who our shareholders are," reveals Eli Suarez of San Antonio-based United Services Funds. "We conduct seminars across the country and like to be able to tell those who own our funds about them." Nevertheless, United Services participates in most of the programs. Another drawback is that representatives of the discount brokers aren't going to be as intimately familiar with the funds you're interested in as the fund employees themselves. This stands to reason since the brokers are responsible for so many different offerings. The simple solution for this is to call the fund directly with any specific questions you might have, such as getting the current top holdings and learning when the next distribution will be paid.

Beyond that, most brokers have enacted short-term trading rules, which require you to pay a transaction fee if you sell out of a fund position before a given period of time, usually 90 days. This is designed to discourage frequent switching around.

All in all, the downfalls are relatively minor, and I can't imagine why anyone would want to buy shares straight from the funds ever again. In fact, the whole concept has become so popular, several full-service brokerage firms, which formerly were famous for cursing no-loads, are now joining the bandwagon to stem the flow of lost assets.

Why Some Funds Love No-Transaction-Fee Discounters

One additional negative for the fund companies is that money flowing through the NTF supermarkets tends to be "hotter" than normal. This means it comes in and out faster than when purchased directly from the fund. "I think that's because it's so easy to just call and place a trade and move from one fund to another," suggests Peter Kris, managing partner of the highly successful Van Wagoner Funds. "Shareholders look at us more as a number and don't really develop a relationship with us. Besides, the discount broker's aren't going to talk with you about what's going on in the fund and give you information helpful in making your decisions. They probably don't even know."

Nevertheless, when Kris teamed up with star fund manager Garrett Van Wagoner to start a new fund company at the end of 1995, their first line of attack was to meet with the discount brokers to see what they needed to do to become part of the NTF programs. "We knew participation was essential to our success," he tells me. "We structured our funds around these programs because they're a great source of distribution. If clients have all of their money with Schwab or Fidelity, for example, and your fund isn't part of the program, they probably won't invest with you because they like to see all of their information on a consolidated statement."

Even though Van Wagoner's name was well-known from his days at Govett Smaller Companies fund, and he received a lot of media attention for his chart-topping performance, he believes being part of the NTF programs at Schwab, Fidelity, and Jack White allowed his company to zoom from zero to more than $1.2 billion in assets in less than six months, becoming the fastest growing mutual fund family in history. "It takes awhile for a new fund group to get their back office up and going," Kris maintains. "The brokers were very helpful in allowing us to collect assets quickly." Today, more than half of Van Wagoner's assets come in through the NTF supermarkets, and Kris expects that number to grow dramatically in the years to come.

Independent financial advisers have embraced the NTF programs from the start and are their biggest source of assets. It's truly a dream come true for the small guys who want to be in business for themselves without having to affiliate with or be under the sales pressure of a full-service brokerage firm. Instead, they can place client assets into an account with one of the discounters and trade around in participating no-loads as they please without incurring any commissions. Independent advisers make their money by charging an annual fee of from 1 to 2 percent of assets under management for their "professional" guidance in determining which funds to be in at any given time.

NTF Programs Are a Bargain for Funds

When you break it down, the no-load, NTF programs are a real bargain for the fund companies as well. In return for the small fee they pay, the brokers take care of setting up accounts and mailing out all statements and other required documents, such as the prospectus and proxy statements. In fact, the fund families themselves probably won't even know you exist, since your account will be listed under the name of the broker. "Even after paying the distribution fee, it's cheaper for us to get assets from a broker than to attract them on our own," United Services' Suarez points out. "You have to think in terms of what you must spend to get a new investor. When we go through a broker, we don't have to field any calls or handle trades. We also have a marketing channel that we wouldn't otherwise have."

In addition, more and more funds are now being run by former managers of bigger firms who have gone out on their own and are operating on bare-bones budgets. These folks can't spend much on hiring representatives to answer the phones and handle shareholder requests. By joining forces with the discount brokers, they can instantly tap into an established network of professionals able to handle client questions around-the-clock, both on the phone and in person, for much less than they could do it on their own. "The money they receive from Schwab is operationally easy for them because we simply set up one omnibus account and internally keep track of how many shares each customer owns," Lyons points out.

"In a sense, what we're providing is all of the shareholder servicing that a customer would receive going directly to the fund. We provide statements, the ability to buy, sell, and exchange shares, plus all of the shareholder reports."

What's more, with these programs becoming so popular, many investors are wisely concentrating exclusively on funds available through the NTF programs. So, if you're not a member of the team, chances are you will lose out on a tremendous amount of business. "The logistics of gathering in customers are much better when they come in through a broker," White contends. "But I would still maintain that the public's response to a fund will be based on its performance and what type of public relations work it has done to get the word out. Then, once the public wants to buy shares in the fund, using a broker as a conduit is so much easier."

The Reason Some Funds Spurn NTF Discounters

For the most part, fund families have been clamoring to be part of these programs, though not all are accepted. While each broker has a different policy, Schwab claims to be the pickiest about who it lets in. "We look at customer demand issues," Lyons explains. "If there's demand for a fund, we will definitely consider having them in the program. We also look at funds of a certain size and like to see a track record. It's obviously not free for us to add funds to our system. There are a lot of operational issues we need to consider before adding one."

But some fund companies have flatly refused to sign up. Low-cost fund distributor The Vanguard Group claims its current expense ratios are so low, it would lose money if it had to pay brokers even a relatively modest 25 to 35 basis points. Others want to preserve the right to call themselves "one-stop fund supermarkets" in their own right. As White puts it, "T. Rowe Price and Vanguard will say there's no reason for an investor to go beyond the many funds they offer. They claim they have enough choices to meet your every need, be it growth or income. But, of course, when you look at performance, you can always do better by spreading your assets among different families instead of just sticking with one group."

Schwab agrees and is convinced these fund supermarkets are the wave of the future where those who refuse to join will suffer. "Customers really want to have easy access to their investments," Lyons insists. "I think most fund companies are open to this 'open architecture.' They want their products open to as many distribution channels as possible. Open architecture has worked for Microsoft and Intel. Obviously, closed architecture didn't work for Apple. We believe this ubiquity and omnipresence availability of products is what clients are looking for."

Avoid the No-Loads That Aren't Free

In addition to the hundreds of NTF funds, the discount brokers also allow you to trade virtually all other no-loads for a transaction fee that's similar to a stock commission. As I previously mentioned, that's how these programs initially started. However, I highly recommend that you stick exclusively with the NTF selections and avoid ever paying a commission to make a trade. Here's why: Let's say you buy $1,000 worth of a given fund at Charles Schwab that's not part of the NTF program. Schwab will charge you a $39 fee when you buy it and another $39 when you sell, for a total of $78, or 7.8 percent of the total investment. That's like paying a 7.8 percent load! Of course, the impact of transaction fees diminishes as the value of your investments increase. In this case, a $5,000 investment at Schwab carries the same commission of $78, which only represents 1.56 percent of the total. But that's still more than I want you to pay. Remember, I'm going to teach you how to buy mutual funds for free. In almost every case, for each fund you show me that either carries a load or isn't a part of these programs, I can find another one that's just as good, if not better, available without a transaction fee.

Welcome to the Future

The fact is, you can now put together a top-performing, diversified portfolio of the finest funds in the country simply by opening an account at one of the participating discount brokers and choosing from the generous list of available no-load, NTF offerings. Forget about paying loads or other commissions. Those days are gone. Unfortunately, selecting from the hundreds of options is an overwhelming task. That's because only a handful are any good. Plus, with so many brokers offering seemingly identical programs, how can you figure out which funds are right for you? And what's the best way to take full advantage of these supermarkets? I'll answer those questions and more in the coming chapters.

3

HOW THE TOP DISCOUNT BROKERS STACK UP

Getting Started with the Major Players

Your first step toward taking advantage of these no-load, NTF programs is to call one or more of the participating discount brokers and request a new customer information kit. Inside, you'll find a brochure detailing the services offered, an account application, and a directory of funds available through the given supermarket. You will also learn such things as the minimum investment requirement for each fund (both in regular and IRA accounts), along with the cut-off times for purchases and redemptions to take place on the same day. While around a dozen discount brokers now offer commission-free funds, only six presently have a large enough selection to make them worthwhile. On the following pages, I have profiled these firms in alphabetical order. They are Accutrade, Charles Schwab & Co., Fidelity Investments, Jack White & Company, Muriel Siebert & Co., and Waterhouse Securities. You will learn about the features offered by each, from how many funds they have to how fast their representatives answer the phone. This will give you a good idea as to which firm can best suit your needs. Still, I recommend that you request an information kit from each of the "big six," since the list of funds and services changes almost daily, and this will give you an updated look at what they're up to.

Which Broker Is Best for You?

This is an impossible question to answer without knowing your individual needs and preferences. Let's say you prefer to do all of your trading online. While all of the brokers offer computerized trading programs and/or Internet sites, Schwab and Accutrade currently have the most sophisticated products. On the other hand, if you desire personal face-to-face service, Schwab and Fidelity are the only firms with convenient branch offices across the country. Accutrade and Jack White have none. This requirement alone will help to narrow your list of possibilities significantly. (Personally, I conduct all of my trades either on the phone or by computer, so the fact that a firm doesn't have a lot of branch offices wouldn't deter me from doing business with them.)

From here, you can look at some of the smaller details. For example, I think Fidelity has by far the best-looking monthly account statements, but Schwab's representatives are generally more knowledgeable and faster at answering calls. Meantime, Jack White offers the most funds (754), and Waterhouse is the only broker that doesn't charge for using the ATM debit card that comes with its money market account (the other brokers charge up to $2 per transaction).

Free Checking and Cash Management Services, Too

Speaking of ATM cards, when you open an account at every broker except Accutrade, you in essence establish an entire cash management program, which not only links all of your funds and other investments together, but also gives you easy access to an interest-bearing money market account in which all of your free cash is swept into. You can then write as many checks as you want in any amount or can use a debit card to tap into automated teller machines around the world. For all intents and purposes, you could make this your primary checking account, and would be well advised to do so. That's because you'll earn a much higher rate of interest than you'll ever find at your local bank. Simply send your paycheck to your broker instead of your local bank, which probably isn't paying a penny in interest. This will also make it easy for you to dollar-cost-average into your favorite funds on a regular basis. One word of warning to the wise who take this advice: don't be tempted to redeem shares from your funds to pay for unnecessary extras. If having your long-term investments so close to your everyday checkbook will prove deadly to your financial health, you're better off skipping this option and letting your bank continue to enjoy a free ride with your cash. In the end, you'll be much better off.

Since the beauty of these NTF programs is that they cost you nothing, the requirements for getting these free services should also be an important consideration. What I mean by that is, at Fidelity, for example, you are charged a $12 annual fee for each fund that falls below $2,500. If you can't keep your balance that high, look elsewhere. On the other hand, Fidelity doesn't charge you for selling fund positions you own less than 90 days and waives IRA fees for balances more than $2,500. Jack White and Schwab impose commissions on short-term trades (held less than 90 days) from the start and require you to keep $10,000 in your IRA to avoid annual service charges. Alternatively, Accutrade and Waterhouse offer free IRAs with no minimums, but they don't have service representatives available around the clock to answer your questions, like Schwab and Jack White.

Questions to Ask Brokers

Now you understand why it's impossible to say which broker is best for you. It all depends on what you're looking for. Here's what I recommend: First, call each broker and ask for a new account kit. Then, on paper, map out which services you're looking for. Next, determine which broker(s) offers most of the things on your list. Here are some examples, with the strongest brokers in each category listed in parenthesis:

- No-fee IRA, even for low balances (Accutrade, Fidelity, and Waterhouse)
- Knowledgeable telephone representatives available 24 hours a day, 7 days a week (Fidelity, Jack White, and Schwab)
- Easy-to-read account statements that list your cost basis each month (Fidelity)
- A broker with branch offices in most major cities across the nation (Fidelity and Schwab)
- The longest roster of available funds (Jack White)
- An asset management account that comes with a fee-free ATM debit card (Waterhouse)
- The lowest brokerage commissions for trading stocks and funds not offered in the NTF programs (Accutrade and Waterhouse)
- Strong computerized trading programs (Accutrade, Fidelity, and Schwab)

You Can't Go Wrong

I think you get the idea. While I'm not pinpointing any particular broker as my absolute favorite, I will say all six of the following firms have fine reputations and I would feel comfortable doing business with any one. The truth is, you might want to establish accounts with more than one, based on your needs. I have done that with my own personal portfolio. I have my IRA housed with one broker and my regular account with another. Of course, the goal here is to consolidate things and make your life easier, so I wouldn't open a lot of different accounts. Just don't feel like you have to choose a single broker. And by all means, if you are dissatisfied with the service you receive after you open an account, you can easily switch to another firm with a simple phone call. Simply ask your new broker to do a direct transfer of all the holdings in your old account. It's another one of the services that makes NTF programs so attractive.

Opening Your Account

While each broker requires a different minimum opening deposit, you have two ways of getting cash into your account at the start. If you're a new investor, you can simply mail in a check for your opening deposit. If you have an account with a full-service broker and want to switch it over to a discount broker, just give that information to your discount broker and he or she will take it from there. (This type of switch could take a couple of months, since full-service brokers often take their time in transferring accounts.)

Also, if you're cashing in all of your investments for cash, you will have to pay taxes on any capital gains. This often keeps people from making such a bold move. Quite honestly, if your gains are substantial, and I mean really substantial to the point where you'll owe Uncle Sam a considerable amount, you might want to leave your account with the full-service broker and invest only new money through the NTF program. If the gain isn't all that much, make the transfer and be done with it. My guess is your returns from the discount broker will be so much higher that, in the end, the extra taxes won't even matter.

Another possible scenario is that you could already own a portfolio of funds directly with one or more families. In this case, you have three choices. If the fund participates in the NTF program at the broker you've decided on, you can have the shares in your fund simply transferred in kind. That way, they won't be redeemed, they will simply show a change in ownership (to the broker). This is *not* a taxable event. If the fund isn't part of the NTF program, but is offered by the broker, you can still transfer it in kind without charge, though you will have to pay the broker's standard transaction fee when you sell. This is an appropriate option when you have a fund you love with substantial built-in capital gains. I think it's worthwhile to transfer the fund into the program, since you can consolidate it with all of your other holdings and make your life easier. The final option for handling funds you currently own is to redeem them and have the cash proceeds mailed to you or your broker. Then, you can use this money to purchase shares in one of the fine NTF offerings.

Profiles of Top Discount Brokers

Each of the following profiles begins with the name of the brokerage firm, along with its contact address and phone number. After a brief background on the company and some of the stand-out features of its NTF program, I have included a number of key statistics that will help in your overall evaluation. You will uncover such revealing data as the year the firm was founded, total brokerage assets, year it began offering NTF funds, total assets in the NTF program, number of NTF funds offered, minimum amount required to open an account, short-term trading policies, commission charged for trading all other funds, stock commissions, total number of branch offices around the country, number of registered representatives on staff, customer service hours of operation, number of customers on file, and IRA fees. (All data is as of September 1996 unless otherwise indicated.) Next, I conducted a survey over a two-week period to see both how fast representatives answered calls, along with how knowledgeable they were. I called at various times during the day and took an average of the length of time it took to be connected to a human voice. Based on the responses to basic questions I asked about the NTF programs and the market in general, I assigned each firm a "knowledge rating" of either high, average, or low. I queried the reps on such basic items as which funds were offered without a transaction fee, what the underlying investment objective was for several funds selected at random, and what types of securities these funds held.

Furthermore, I evaluated all of the computerized trading programs being offered (both in disk form and on the Internet) and have summarized the highlights and downfalls of each. Every profile ends with a look at the major strengths and weakness of the firm, along with "the bottom line."

ACCUTRADE

4211 South 102nd Street
PO Box 2227
Omaha, NE 68103-2227
800-882-4887

Not Your Father's Discount Broker

If you treasure personal service and human hand-holding, Accutrade is probably not the broker for you. That's because the firm has always been at the forefront of using technology to execute trades and keep costs down. It introduced the industry's first touch-tone trading product in 1988, has both a DOS and Windows-based software investment program (available at no cost), and recently unveiled a service allowing individuals to get quotes, place orders, and check their account balances by connecting Sharp's 8.5-ounce Zaurus personal digital assistant unit to any telephone. "This thing will fit in your suit pocket," explains Accutrade's vice-president and general manager Michael Anderson. "It has a modem built into it and allows you to take it on a trip, plug it in at the hotel, and download your positions in a matter of seconds." As with all of its online services, each account is allotted a given number of free quotes, and you earn more with each trade. After you've used up the freebies, there is an additional charge.

An Interesting History

Accutrade's roots date back to 1975, when it was known as First Omaha Securities. In the beginning, the company offered to trade 100 shares of stock for $25, which was an absurdly low price at the time. A year later, the firm changed its name to First National Brokerage. Today, it is a wholly owned subsidiary of TransTerra Co., which also controls K. Aufhauser, Ceres Securities, and All-American Brokers (aka eBroker). In 1993, the company introduced a PC trading product called Accutrade, which was heavily promoted and received a tremendous response. "We'd answer the phone, 'First National Brokerage,'" and callers would say, 'Oh, I was looking for Accutrade,' and hang up," Anderson recalls. "So we decided that since this product was so successful and well-known, we'd go ahead and change the name of our entire company to Accutrade."

The Formation of a Fantastic Freebie

Accutrade's no-load, NTF program was born in 1994, primarily to keep up with the tremendous growth being experienced by Schwab and Fidelity. "We needed to add the program to maintain our competitive stance," Anderson admits. "When we decided to start it, our chairman Joe Ricketts said he wanted to offer the most funds of any program in the industry." He has come close to accomplishing that goal and now boasts 662 offerings. However, many of the largest fund companies, including Janus, Stein Roe, and Strong, are noticeably absent from Accutrade's roster, while they are available through most of the other brokers. The reason? "We're not as big as Schwab or Fidelity and don't do enough business for these large families to pay us for the transactions," Anderson concedes. "That's why we can only trade funds that assess a 12b-1 marketing fee without charge, since that 12b-1 is paid directly to us." Mutual funds that aren't part of Accutrade's NTF program can still be bought or sold for just $27, regardless of the transaction size.

Non-Techies Welcome

Clearly, Accutrade is after clients who are techno-literate, though they do have humans manning the phones as well. "We sometimes surprise people when we tell them we have real-life brokers who take trades and a customer service department to boot," Anderson chuckles. Still, 82 percent of Accutrade's business is conducted electronically. "People are too busy to spend a lot of time schmoozing with a full-service broker trying to get good ideas, especially when the broker's ideas often aren't very good," he maintains. "They know there's much more information out there than there was ten years ago, and you can do so many incredible things with technology."

Take the firm's Windows trading product, for example. It not only keeps track of your holdings, taxable gains, and portfolio performance, but also allows you to create your own program for tracking securities or executing buy and sell orders for stocks, options, and mutual funds when the market reaches a specified point, even if you're not in front of the computer. "Let's say you have a cut-off time of noon every day on a fund you're wanting to buy," Anderson explains. "You can set the program up to check the market at 11:45AM and execute the purchase if the Dow is at or below a certain level. You can actually set it up on what we call 'scripts,' so it will execute even if you're in a meeting or out playing golf."

Client Profiles

The average Accutrade customer earns less than $100,000 per year, is in the market for speculation or growth, owns a computer, and is between 36 and 45 years old. "They're people who are entrepreneurs and own their own businesses,"

Anderson adds. "They're not afraid to use a technological device to place a trade. Frankly, they're most interested in finding ways to make money with their money."

Accutrade

Year Founded: 1975

Total Assets: Won't reveal

Number of Clients: 70,000

Year Began Offering NTF Program: 1994

Total Assets in NTF Program: $187 million

Number of NTF Funds Offered: 662

Minimum Required to Open an Account: $5,000

Short-Term Trading Policy: Shares held less than six months subject to a $27 service charge

Commission for Trading Nonparticipating Funds: $27, regardless of transaction size

Stock Commissions: $28 plus $.02 per share, regardless of stock price for automated trades; $35 plus $.02 per share for trades executed through a live representative

Number of Branch Offices: None

Total Number of Registered Reps: 23

Customer Service Hours of Operation: 7:30AM–5:00PM (CST) Monday through Friday

IRA Fees: $0 (no minimum balance)

Average Time for Broker to Answer Phone: Ten seconds

Knowledge of Brokers: Average

Computerized Trading Program: Accutrade for Windows (no charge)

Internet Site: Home page located at http://www.accutrade.com. Gives information on the firm and lets you print out a new account application, but does not offer Internet trading.

Major Strengths: Strong on using technology to execute trades, has a large number of NTF funds, charges just $27 to buy all other no-loads, and offers free IRA accounts, even for small investors

Major Weaknesses: No branch offices, small staff of brokers, customer service department only open during the day, doesn't offer a cash management account allowing you to write checks on available balances (though money can be transferred electronically into your bank account at no charge), and many funds in NTF program are mediocre performers (the company will accept any fund that pays a 12b-1 marketing fee, but lacks a lot of the big names).

Bottom Line: If you're the kind of person who prefers to conduct all of your trades by computer and you almost never need to talk to anyone in person, Accutrade may be just what you're looking for. However, if you like human contact and do most of your investing at night or on the weekend, you'll probably be unhappy here, since compared to other brokers, its office hours are relatively limited.

CHARLES SCHWAB & CO.

101 Montgomery Street
San Francisco, CA 94104
(branch offices located across the United States)
800-845-1714

A Real Pioneer

Charles Schwab is clearly the grandfather of all discount brokers. When the SEC abolished fixed-rate brokerage commissions, in May 1975, clearing the way for brokers to charge lower fees for executing trades, Schwab immediately opened the first branch office of his discount brokerage firm in Sacramento, California. In 1980, he established a 24-hour quotation service and shortly thereafter began offering around-the-clock customer service by phone. With 500,000 client accounts under his belt, Schwab sold his firm to BankAmerica for $55 million in 1983, only to buy it back or $280 million four years later. By then, the publicly traded company had 1 million customers and 100 branch offices, with assets of $14.3 billion.

Always at the Forefront

It seems Schwab is a master at seeing the future. Realizing that investors were increasingly favoring mutual funds over individual stocks, he began selling no-loads to the public for a commission similar to what he charged for trading stocks in 1984. The service was called Mutual Fund Marketplace. He then launched his own mutual fund in 1991, Schwab 1000, and took the investment world by storm by offering to trade dozens of funds from different families with no transaction charges in 1992. Schwab himself claims he does most of his own investing through funds.

Today, OneSource offers close to 600 funds from more than 45 well-known companies. It is by far the largest program, in terms of assets under management, in the industry. Schwab makes a tidy profit on the service by charging the fund companies a distribution fee of 25 to 35 basis points a year for all assets under management. Unlike some of his competitors, Schwab claims he'll only allow top-performing funds that pass a strict screening process into the program. That doesn't mean there aren't any dogs in the pack though. Truth be told, there are more losers than winners in his stable, so as always, you shouldn't choose from the options blindly.

Services Aplenty

As discount brokers go, Schwab arguably offers more services than anyone else. In addition to providing telephone access to registered representatives 24 hours a day, he offers the "StreetSmart" computerized trading program for both Windows and Macintosh ($39), TeleBroker touch-tone trading, and most recently e.Schwab—another online-only trading program offering low commission rates that rival even the deepest discounters in exchange for fewer services. It is estimated that 70 percent of all Americans live or work near one of Schwab's 235 branch offices, and he claims most clients open their accounts in person. "They still want a bricks-and-mortar lifeline and someone to talk to when things go wrong," he has said. "The branch office is still important."

Schwab's plethora of offerings is so comprehensive, some argue he often blurs the line of what a discount broker should be. For example, while his competitors make it clear they're not in the business of giving advice, Schwab not only publishes many different guides and a list of top-performing funds, he also peddles an impressive retirement planning software program that guides you through a series of questions, suggests an investment mix, and then recommends Schwab-offered funds to be considered for purchase. The firm also recently began offering several "fund or funds" comprised on OneSource offerings (none of which I recommend), which automatically do all of the asset allocating for you.

The Good, the Bad, the OK

Schwab's brokers are generally quite knowledgeable, and the firm's overall service is commendable. However, Schwab's monthly statements leave a lot to be desired. They aren't very attractive to read and contain far less information than you'll find on Fidelity's or Jack White's. Year-end summaries and tax forms are much more impressive.

If you opt to do business with Schwab, you'll want to open a Schwab One Asset Management Account, which requires a $5,000 minimum deposit and comes with unlimited check writing and a no-fee Visa debit card. If you have a lower balance, you can open a regular Schwab Account with as little as $1,000, but the available services are more limited.

Keep the Costs Down

When Schwab's program was first introduced, you could make unlimited exchanges and redemptions. Unfortunately, too many people took advantage of the program. Now Schwab's policy is to charge a commission for selling NTF funds that are held for less than 90 days, and the fees are among the highest in the business. Therefore, if you doubt you'll be able to follow the rules, or plan to buy funds outside of the NTF universe, I recommend you set up an account elsewhere to avoid being eaten alive by commissions.

Charles Schwab & Co.

Year Founded: 1973

Total Assets: $216.7 billion

Number of Clients: 3.4 million

Year Began Offering NTF Program: 1992

Total Assets in NTF Program: $33.5 billion

Number of NTF Funds Offered: 580

Minimum Required to Open an Account: $1,000

Short-Term Trading Policy: Shares held less than 90 days are subject to a sliding scale transaction fee when sold, with an overriding minimum of $39. Also, a maximum of 15 short-term redemptions are allowed per year.

Commission for Trading Nonparticipating Funds: Sliding scale with overriding minimum of $39

Stock Commissions: $30 plus 1.7 percent of principal up to $2,499; $56 plus 0.66 percent of principal from $2,500 to $6,249; $76 plus 0.34 percent of principal from $6,250 to $19,999; $100 plus 0.22 percent of principal from $20,000 to $49,999; overriding minimum of $39 (10 percent discount offered for StreetSmart online trading, along with a flat fee of $29.95 for transactions of up to 1,000 shares placed through e.Schwab)

Number of Branch Offices: 235

Total Number of Registered Reps: 4,800

Customer Service Hours of Operation: 24 hours a day, 7 days a week

IRA Fees: $29 per year, waived for accounts more than $10,000

Average Time for Broker to Answer Phone: 26 seconds (including the time it takes to get through automated touch-tone voice prompts)

Knowledge of Brokers: High

Computerized Trading Program: StreetSmart for Windows and Macintosh ($39) and e.Schwab (no charge)

Internet Site: www.schwab.com (allows for trading and provides background information on the firm)

Major Strengths: Branch offices around the country, knowledge-able representatives available around-the-clock, impressive computer programs, plenty of free investment planning material available, convenient cash management program, and always introducing new innovative products

Major Weaknesses: Unimpressive monthly statements, charges for computer software, smaller list of NTF funds than some competitors, and high commissions for short-term trades/buying nonparticipating funds

Bottom Line: Schwab is clearly one of the top discount brokers in the industry. You'll be happy here regardless of whether you prefer to deal with brokers in person, on the phone, or online. The list of available services is second-to-none. The major downfall is that if you have to pay commissions for either stock or mutual fund trades, or don't qualify for a free IRA, you'll pay more in fees at Schwab than at almost any other discount broker.

FIDELITY INVESTMENTS

82 Devonshire Street
Boston, MA 02109
(branch offices located across the United States)
800-544-9697

The King of Fund Companies

It has been 50 years since Edward C. Johnson II founded Fidelity Management & Research Company to act as the investment adviser to the Fidelity Fund, which was formed in Boston in 1930. Back then, the firm's total fund assets stood at $5 million. Today, Fidelity has more than $407 billion in its 232 proprietary funds, with another $192 billion in discount brokerage accounts. Fidelity is by far the best known name in the mutual fund industry. Its most widely recognized fund, Magellan, is also the world's largest. Johnson's son, Edward III (Ned), now serves as chairman of the privately held company, which has regional centers strategically placed across the country, along with branch offices in most major U.S. cities.

The Johnson Legacy Begins

Edward Johnson II, known to employees and associates simply as Mister Johnson, was a lawyer by training. He grew fascinated with the market after reading Edwin Lefevre's classic *Reminiscences of a Stock Operator* in the 1920s. Much of the money Mister Johnson managed in the early days came from a family trust. Between 1947 and 1970, Mister Johnson launched 13 different stock funds, earning a reputation for superior performance. His policy was to give the responsibility of fund management to individuals, instead of committees, a trend that continues at the firm today.

Fund Fever

Mutual funds were enormously popular during the mid-1960s, and Fidelity was a major beneficiary. Many of its funds favored super-growth stocks that weren't closely followed by Wall Street. By 1974, following a brutal bear market, the public's appetite for funds soured. All of a sudden, nobody was buying stocks or stock funds. So Ned Johnson introduced the first money market fund with a unique added feature: check writing. He reasoned that if you made it easy for investors to get their money out, they'd be more likely to put a lot of it in. The idea worked and money quickly came through the doors.

Taking a Load Off

Up to this time, all of Fidelity's funds were sold through full-service brokers with 8 percent loads. But, in order to keep the money market fund's yield high, Ned decided it was more cost-effective to sell shares directly to the public by advertising a toll-free number. He began this new marketing strategy with one telephone line. The calls came in so fast, more lines were immediately added and soon Fidelity began offering most of its stock funds load-free through this channel. It also introduced a computerized telephone system to provide price and yield quotes 24 hours a day.

Birth of the Brokerage

Fidelity's discount brokerage arm was formed in 1978. Ned's idea was that if investors were buying Fidelity funds without the advice of a broker, they would probably do the same with individual securities. This is also when Fidelity started to build its nationwide network of walk-in centers for retail customers. Even while the company's own stable of in-house funds was growing in 1988, the brokerage arm began offering clients a chance to buy and sell funds from other families through its FundsNetwork program. While it originally charged a transaction fee for such trades, it too became a fee-free supermarket in late 1992.

A Protective Parent

Although Fidelity is constantly courting other fund companies to join its FundsNetwork program, it has not allowed any other broker to offer its funds without a transaction fee. In fact, in 1996, it told Schwab it could no longer sell Fidelity funds at all. Therefore, if you are a fan of Fidelity funds, this is the only broker that will allow you to trade these investments without a transaction fee. That means if you know you want to own some Fidelity funds, this is the broker you should establish an account with. (Because Fidelity funds aren't offered through any other supermarket, and none of their funds made my All-Star list, they are not included in the directory in Chapter 4. However, Fidelity would be happy to send you a list of its funds and their past performance figures upon request.)

An Ultra Opportunity

If you send Fidelity an initial opening deposit of at least $10,000, you will be placed in an Ultra Service account, which comes with unlimited free check writing. You'll also receive what I view as the best monthly account statement offered by any of the discount brokers. It's easy to read and keeps track of your cost basis and changes in investment value from month-to-month, so you always know how well you're doing. You need at least $2,500 to open an account, which is the same amount you need to establish a position in a fund (even if the fund family has a lower minimum). If you fall below this minimum, you are charged a $12 annual service fee per fund. IRA fees are waived if you maintain a $2,500 balance, though if you transfer your IRA to another broker down the line, you'll be hit with a hefty $50 closing fee.

Fidelity Investments

Year Founded: 1946

Total Assets: $197.4 billion (in brokerage division)

Number of Clients: 4.5 million

Year Began Offering NTF Program: 1993

Total Assets in NTF Program: $8 billion

Number of NTF Funds Offered: 600+

Minimum Required to Open an Account: $2,500

Short-Term Trading Policy: Allows short-term trades, but says after doing five in one year, you may be subject to transaction fees in the future

Commission for Trading Nonparticipating Funds: Maximum of $35

Stock Commissions: $29.50 plus 1.7 percent of principal up to $2,500; $55.50 + 0.66 percent of principal from $2,501 to $6,000; $75.50 plus 0.34 percent of principal from $6,001 to $22,000; $99.50 plus 0.22 percent of principal from $22,001 to $50,000; $154.50 plus 0.11 percent of principal from $50,001 to $500,000; overriding minimum of $38 for all transactions (10 percent off all trades placed electronically)

Number of Branch Offices: 232

Total Number of Registered Reps: 3,320

Customer Service Hours of Operation: 24 hours a day, 7 days a week

IRA Fees: $12 per year, waived for accounts more than $2,500

Average Time for Broker to Answer Phone: 44 seconds (including time it takes to get through automated voice prompts)

Knowledge of Brokers: Average

Computerized Trading Program: Fox for DOS and Windows ($49.95)

Internet Site: www.fid-inv.com (features information about Fidelity and the FundsNetwork program)

Major Strengths: Impressive monthly statements, branch offices around the country, representatives available around-the-clock, computerized trading programs, ability to trade Fidelity funds, convenient cash management program, and no charge for short-term trades

Major Weaknesses: Representatives ask too many personal questions before giving out information, charges steep close-out fee for IRAs, requires $2,500 minimum opening investment for all funds (except those that have higher minimums anyway), charges a $12 annual service fee if you fall below that threshold, and some representatives are not very knowledgeable.

Bottom Line: We've come to expect superior service from Fidelity, and its brokerage arm delivers. Impressive statements and generous trading policies make it a real standout, but higher minimums and hefty hidden fees may make this a more costly alternative for some.

JACK WHITE & COMPANY

9191 Towne Centre Drive, 2nd Floor
San Diego, CA 92122
800-233-3411

Who Is This Guy?

If you haven't heard of Jack White & Company by now, you must not read any of the personal finance magazines. The firm has done a lot of advertising to increase both business and its chairman's name recognition in recent years. While the firm has grown significantly and offers the largest NTF program among the discount brokers, it is still small enough to give personal attention to each customer. In fact, if you want to speak with Jack White himself, you'll probably be able to get through by simply asking the representative who answers the phone to put him on the line.

The Instigator

White set up the first discount brokerage firm on the west coast, the second in the nation, after moving to California in 1973. He was in business even before chief competitor Charles Schwab. It was 11 years later that he emerged as the first to trade what at the time attracted a relative small piece of the investment pie, no-load mutual funds. "The reason I have always been so active in offering no-loads is because I have a no-load fund background and know a lot of people in the industry," White tells me. "I have always felt funds were the trend of the future."

A Fund of Opportunity

In fact, his fund experience is what led him to get into the discount brokerage business to begin with. He started out as a commodities broker before becoming president of the top-performing Comsec Fund in the late 1960s. "Ninety percent of the assets were invested in securities," he recalls. "The remaining 10 percent was put into commodities. Thus, we called it Comsec. We got a special ruling from the IRS that allowed us to take any earnings and profits from the commodity subsidiaries and, using the fund as a conduit, pass them through to shareholders as dividends. We had what we thought was the ultimate structure to pay out high dividends, while keeping $.90 out of every $1 invested for growth. We were the number one fund in the country during most of a two-year period."

Good-Bye Fund, Hello Discount Brokerage Industry

Sadly, the fund started at the tail end of the stock market's "go-go" days, and despite excellent performance, White found it difficult to attract cash. So he sold out to an insurance company in the early 1970s. While contemplating what to do next, he remembered that the fund was able to keep commissions down to almost nothing by taking part in third-market trading. "If I wanted to buy 1,000 shares of IBM, for instance, I wouldn't go to the local Merrill Lynch office," he reveals. "I would go to an institution or dealer and line up the trade to avoid paying a commission. That way I could enhance my overall performance by as much as 100 basis points, especially back in those days, since commissions were so high." He figured he could transfer that same principle over to the retail side of the business, by allowing individual investors to enjoy similar savings. That's how Jack White & Company came into being.

A Plethora of Services

White has deliberately kept his firm simple. All of his 300 employees work out of a single-story building in San Diego. He has no branch offices and doesn't plan to open any, yet he offers more services than any other discount broker. In addition to stocks, bonds, and funds, Jack White allows you to trade commodities, options, and precious metals. He also sells variable annuities and life insurance, and some of his money market funds enable you to earn frequent-flier miles on American Airlines. His representatives are available 24 hours a day, seven days a week. He has also cooked up a plan to let individual investors trade after hours through electronic crossing networks, a service not available through any other firm. What's more, his Connect program matches buyers and sellers of loaded funds to save money.

More about Jack's NTF Program

Jack White has 821 mutual funds in his NTF program, more than any other firm. He's also the only broker who allows you to sell funds short, subject to availability. "It's a special service for sophisticated investors who understand the risks and rewards of volatile markets," White points out. The man himself is very fond of funds, and not just because he has such an experienced background in the industry. "Funds are a very efficient way to buy professional management," he explains. "You not only get diversification and a wide variety of options, but the overall expense ratio is often less than 1 percent, which includes the cost of management and all of the trades. You can't beat that." I agree.

For the Electronically Inclined

Jack White has also kept up with the times by creating several electronic trading options. First there's TelePATH, an automated telephone trading service that enables you to place trades, receive real-time quotes, and review cash balances. Then there's ComputerPATH, White's proprietary Windows-based PC software program that allows you to execute trades, access account holdings, get real-time quotes, and manage your portfolio. If you're connected to the Internet, you can punch up PATH On-Line, White's Internet site, at http://pawws.com/jwc. Here you can open an account, place trades, view positions, and consolidate all of your investments into one account.

Cash Management

With a deposit of at least $10,000, you'll receive free check writing, a MasterCard debit card, and access to an automatic bill-paying service (for an additional fee) through White's ProCash Plus program. It only takes $500 to open an account.

Jack White & Company

Year Founded: 1973

Total Assets: $8 billion

Number of Clients: 100,000

Year Began Offering NTF Program: 1992

Total Assets in NTF Program: $3.5 billion

Number of NTF Funds Offered: 821

Minimum Required to Open an Account: $500

Short-Term Trading Policy: Charges regular transaction fee of $27 to $50 for funds sold less than 90 days after purchase. Fees depend on the amount of the trade. Customers who make 15 or more short-term redemptions in a calendar year are charged transaction fees on all purchases and redemptions for the rest of the year.

Commission for Trading Nonparticipating Funds: $27 for transactions up to $5,000, $35 from $5,000 to $25,000, and $50 for trades more than $25,001

Stock Commissions: $33 plus $.03 per share (drops to $.02 per share more than 2,000 shares), with a 10 percent discount for using the ComputerPATH software or Internet site

Number of Branch Offices: None

Total Number of Registered Reps: 200

Customer Service Hours of Operation: 24 hours a day, 7 days a week

IRA Fees: $35 per year (waived for accounts more than $10,000)

Average Time for Broker to Answer Phone: 54 seconds (including time to get through automated voice prompts)

Knowledge of Brokers: High

Computerized Trading Program: ComputerPATH PC software ($29.95) and PATH On-Line Internet site

Internet Site: http://pawws.com/jwc

Major Strengths: Offers widest selection of NTF funds, provides excellent customer service, has many electronic trading options (including Internet site), and is always at forefront of offering new programs

Major Weaknesses: No branch offices

Bottom Line: If you don't need face-to-face interaction with your discount broker, Jack White & Company offers all of the same services as the big boys from one central location. I trust the name Jack White will become as common as Charles Schwab in the coming years.

MURIEL SIEBERT & CO.

885 Third Avenue, 17th Floor
New York, NY 10022-4082
(offices also in Boca Raton, Naples, and Los Angeles)
800-872-0711

A Classy CEO

I remember the first time I met Muriel Siebert. She was the keynote speaker at a conference for women executives in California in the early 1990s. I was working as a television news business reporter at the time and was assigned to cover her appearance. From the moment she walked into the press room, I was immediately impressed. She was dashingly dressed, well-spoken, highly opinionated and clearly knew the equities markets like the back of her hand. There was good reason for that. Siebert was the first woman ever to become a member of the New York Stock Exchange. But her journey to the top is even more remarkable once you know how she got there.

From Cleveland to the Big Apple

Siebert came to New York from Cleveland in 1954, having dropped out of college after only two-and-a-half years. She had $500 to her name and tried to get a job at the United Nations. Unfortunately, she only spoke English, and the United Nations required employees to be fluent in at least two languages. She then applied for work at Merrill Lynch. "They asked if I had a college degree, and I said no," Siebert recalls. "They said no degree, no job. So I went over to Bache. When they asked if I had a college degree, I said yes. I kept that going until I put my bid card in for a seat on the stock exchange."

For more than a decade, Siebert worked as a successful securities analyst, specializing in the aviation industry. At one point, her studies on Lockheed were credited with saving the company. By 1966, she was making close to $400,000 a year, an enormous sum back in those days. Three years later, on December 28, 1968, Siebert made the New York Stock Exchange coed by becoming the first woman to buy a seat. It cost her $445,000.

Shaking Up the Kettle

At first, Siebert wasn't exactly given a warm welcome by her male colleagues. "To begin with, I was delightfully outnumbered," she explains. "For ten years, I could say the Exchange was comprised of 1,365 men and me." Many gave her a hard time. "What I quickly learned is that when you change a tradition that old, not everyone is going to love you," she confides. "People like the status quo, and I was changing it. However, I found that for every stinker, there was also someone great." Today this college dropout is one of the most successful women on the Street and holds ten honorary doctorates.

Going Discount

Siebert's firm originally specialized in research for institutional investors. That all changed on May 1, 1975, known in the industry as D-Day or May Day because it was the first day regulators allowed brokers to charge lower commissions for trades. She immediately turned her firm into a discount brokerage, first targeting institutions, and later turning her attention to the retail market, which is where the bulk of her business comes from today. "I immediately made the switch because I believed the industry as it stood back then was finished for awhile," she says. "It turned out I was right."

Focusing on Funds

Siebert started her own no-load, NTF mutual fund program three years ago. "New investors are definitely using funds. They have propelled this market," Siebert observes. "Some of our older and wealthier customers will always be in individual stocks. Others, especially those who only hold a handful of stocks, will increasingly gravitate toward funds since they're so much easier to buy and sell thanks to NTF programs like ours. It's really a no-brainer."

What Sets Siebert Apart

Why should you do business with Muriel Siebert & Co. instead of her competitors? When I asked Siebert herself, she quickly responded, "Because we're nicer and cheaper than Schwab and Fidelity." (Did I mention she's also quite modest?)

At any rate, Siebert has four branch offices across the country, in New York, Boca Raton, Los Angeles, and Naples. She doesn't have an Internet site (yet), but recently introduced her own computerized trading program, Siebert OnLine, which offers toll-free trading, real-time account information, and late-breaking quotes for up to 20 securities. Siebert also has a touch-tone trading line, charges no fees for IRA accounts with balances above $10,000, provides free check writing with no minimum check amount, and boasts close to 500 fund offerings in her supermarket.

Like Jack White, Muriel Siebert & Co. is large enough to offer a wide array of services, yet small enough to give you direct access to the president. If this extra level of personal service and accessibility is something you cherish, Siebert is worth considering. What's more, if you also trade stocks, Siebert's policy is that if you're ever dissatisfied with a trade, for any reason, you don't pay for it.

Muriel Siebert & Co.

Year Founded: 1967

Total Assets: Won't reveal

Number of Client Accounts: Won't reveal

Year Began Offering NTF Program: 1993

Total Assets in NTF Program: Won't reveal

Number of NTF Funds Offered: 474

Minimum Required to Open an Account: None

Short-Term Trading Policy: No restrictions, as long as funds are available in the account, though Siebert reserves the right to change this policy at any time.

Commission for Trading Nonparticipating Funds: $17.50 plus 0.8 percent of principal up to $5,000; $29.50 plus 0.4 percent of principal between $5,000 and $10,000; $39.50 plus 0.2 percent of principal between $10,001 and $25,000; $67.50 plus 0.1 percent of principal from $25,001 and $100,000; and $157.50 + 0.08 percent of principal for transactions more than $100,000. All transactions subject to an overriding minimum fee of $39.50.

Stock Commissions: Based on dollar volume with an overriding minimum of $39.50

Number of Branch Offices: Four

Total Number of Registered Reps: 50

Customer Service Hours of Operation: 7:30AM–7:30PM (EST), Monday through Friday

IRA Fees: $25 per year (waived for accounts more than $10,000)

Average Time for Broker to Answer Phone: 68 seconds

Knowledge of Brokers: Average

Computerized Trading Program: Siebert OnLine (no charge)

Internet Site: None

Major Strengths: Smaller firm with an emphasis on customer service, and no short-term trading restrictions

Major Weaknesses: Few branch offices, longest wait time to reach a broker by phone, high commissions for trading funds outside of the NTF program, and limited computerized trading capabilities

Bottom Line: Muriel Siebert & Co. offers a respectable array of funds and quality customer service. Since the firm doesn't charge a fee for short-term trading of funds in the NTF program, this is the discount broker you want if you plan to switch around frequently. (Let me emphasize that I recommend against this. But, Siebert is clearly the best place for short-term traders.)

WATERHOUSE SECURITIES

100 Wall Street
New York, NY 10005
(branch offices located across the country)
800-934-4443

All in the Family

When money manager Larry Waterhouse and his partner Ed Nicoll formed Waterhouse Securities in 1979, it was designed to be a small family business with a limited clientele and reputation for superior service. Now, 86 branches and 1,500 employees later, the firm isn't all that tiny but still tries to convey that "family" feel. For example, when you open a new account, it is assigned to a specific broker at your nearest branch office to handle. This is the person you're supposed to contact each time you want to place a trade. However, on busy market days, you might not be able to get through to that person, so you will often be working with other members of your so-called account team. (I'm also told by some Waterhouse customers that the firm has a high degree of turnover, meaning your assigned rep is likely to change frequently.)

A Little Behind These Electronic Times

Although Waterhouse Securities offers a touch-tone telephone trading service, at press time it was the only one of the major discount brokers without a computerized trading product. This is one of the company's major downfalls, given the large number of people who like to trade online. Waterhouse just launched an Internet site, but it serves as more of an advertisement than anything else and doesn't offer any trading capabilities. Randy Miller, Waterhouse's executive vice-president of marketing, admits, "As far as product development is concerned, we're usually a follower not a leader. We like to take a look at what everyone else has done and see the mistakes they've made. Then we hope to make it a little bit better and cheaper."

In Waterhouse's defense, many of the smaller discount brokers that offer such services are able to tap into existing programs offered by their clearing houses. They simply put their name on the product. Waterhouse, on the other hand, is self-clearing and isn't able to take advantage of this type of alliance.

The Big Acquisition

That may change soon now that Waterhouse has been acquired by Toronto Dominion Bank for $535 million. (Until September of 1996, Waterhouse was a publicly traded independent company.) "Toronto Dominion is a very large bank holding company in Canada," Miller explains. "It's an $85 billion organization. They have the capability of infusing capital into the company as needed. Also, from a technological standpoint, they have some pretty good systems in place that we can leverage."

Growing Funds

Clearly, stock trades are the lifeblood of Waterhouse's business. But its no-load, NTF program is coming on strong. Launched in 1994, it now features 400 participating funds and assets are growing in excess of 100 percent a year. You can open an account with as little as $1,000, and IRAs are offered free of charge, regardless of your balance. Another advantage is that all of your available cash is swept into an interest-earning money market account, which comes with checks and a debit card allowing up to five withdrawals per month from ATM machines without any transaction fees. (Most other brokers charge from $1 to $2 each time you use an ATM.)

Lots of Additional Freebies

The long list of free services is something that truly sets Waterhouse apart from the pack. "We provide stock guides, stock reports, stock screens, retirement guides, and mutual fund performance guides," Miller points out. "You name it, we give it away." A notable exception is Morningstar mutual fund research reports. The first one is complimentary, but after that you have to pay $3 each.

Other Available Services

In addition to offering stocks and funds, Waterhouse allows you to trade options and bonds. You can buy securities (including mutual funds) on margin, and there is no charge to have stock certificates issued in your name, nor any other hidden expenses other than the standard commission.

Making a Statement

I must say that I am impressed with the monthly statements sent out by Waterhouse. Although they don't include the cost basis figure, like Fidelity, they do contain a column called "Estimated Annual Income," which guesses how much you'll receive in dividends and/or interest every year from each investment. This is helpful for those of you relying on investment income to pay your monthly bills. Of course, this is only an estimate, and the actual figure may be quite different.

Waterhouse Securities

Year Founded: 1974

Total Assets: Won't reveal

Number of Clients: 500,000

Year Began Offering NTF Program: 1993

Total Assets in NTF Program: Won't reveal

Number of NTF Funds Offered: 400+

Minimum Required to Open an Account: $250

Short-Term Trading Policy: Allows up to five short-term trades in a one-year period. Once that limit is exceeded, you can no longer be a part of the NTF program. (Short-term trade is defined as selling shares that are held for six months or less.)

Commission for Trading Nonparticipating Funds: $25 for transactions up to $4,999, $35 from $5,000 to $9,999, $45 from $10,000 to $14,999, and $55 for trades more than $15,000.

Stock Commissions: Based on a published schedule that starts at $35 and varies based on the number of shares and amount of purchase.

Number of Branch Offices: 88

Total Number of Registered Reps: 800

Customer Service Hours of Operation: Normal hours are 8:30AM–5:30PM (EST) Monday through Friday, but representatives are available by phone 24 hours a day, 7 days a week.

IRA Fees: None (although there is a $25 termination fee)

Average Time for Broker to Answer Phone: Five seconds

Knowledge of Brokers: High

Computerized Trading Program: None offered at press time, though the firm plans to introduce one in 1997.

Internet Site: www.waterhouse.com (gives information on the firm and provides a new account application, but no online trading at present)

Major Strengths: Offers personal service, branch offices located in major metropolitan areas, and provides many free services.

Major Weaknesses: No computerized trading program (at press time), is a follower instead of a leader in terms of technology and new product offerings, and representatives not easily accessible after business hours (your assigned account executive only works Monday through Friday and may not be reachable during busy times).

Bottom Line: You can expect to receive a higher degree of service and free products through Waterhouse than most any of the other major discount brokers. If you trade stocks as well, the firm's commissions are competitive and it provides a plethora of complementary research material. The downside is that historically Waterhouse has been behind its competitors in unveiling new offerings. This may change, however, now that the firm has been bought out by Toronto Dominion Bank.

The Discount Brokers at Large

Broker	# of Funds in NTF Program	# of Branch Offices	Min. Req'd. to Open Acct.	Min. Req'd. for Free IRA	Hours of Operation	Computerized Trading?	Internet Trading?
Accutrade	662	0	$5,000	$0	7:30AM–5:00PM (CST) M–F	Yes	Yes
Schwab	580	235	$1,000	$10,000	24 hours/7 days	Yes	Yes
Fidelity	600+	232	$2,500	$2,500	24 hours/7 days	Yes	No
Jack White	980	0	$500	$10,000	24 hours/7 days	Yes	Yes
Siebert	474	4	$0	$10,000	7:30AM–7:30PM (EST) M–F	Yes	No
Waterhouse	400+	88	$250	$0	8:30AM–5:30PM (EST) M–F	No	No

Other Discounters

The discount brokers are quickly learning that not having some type of no-load, NTF program in place is costly in more ways than one, both in terms of losing existing customers and failing to attract new ones. That's why smaller operators, like those below, are increasingly beginning to offer NTF funds to customers. While the number of players grows each month, the following discounters, listed in alphabetical order, are aggressively trying to upgrade their stable of offerings. (Please note that, at this time, the services and number of selections offered by these firms are too few to merit a recommendation on my part. But stay tuned. I'll let you know if anything changes in future editions of this book and in my monthly newsletter *Fund Connection.*)

American Express Financial Direct
PO Box 59196
Minneapolis, MN 55459-9801
800-297-2007

Kennedy, Cabot & Co.
9470 Wilshire Blvd.
Beverly Hills, CA 90212
800-252-0090

Lombard Institutional Brokerage
595 Market Street, Suite 780
San Francisco, CA 94105
800-688-6896

National Discount Brokers
50 Broadway, 18th Floor
New York, NY 10004
800-888-3999

4

THE ALL-STAR FUNDS

Once again, I must warn you that even though these discount broker-age programs offer hundreds of no-load funds without transaction fees, only a handful of the available funds are any good. The sad truth is that most are mediocre performers. In this chapter, I will lead you to the most profitable funds spearheaded by Wall Street's savviest minds, regardless of whether you seek long-term capital appreciation or monthly income.

The All-Stars

After carefully analyzing more than 500 NTF funds, I have narrowed down the list to 30 of the very best for various investment objectives, from aggressive growth to income producing. I call these my 30 All-Stars, since they are proven achievers spearheaded by experienced managers. They are, quite simply, the cream of the mutual fund crop.

You will find several top stock funds for each of the following areas: Aggressive Growth, Growth, Small Company Growth, Growth and Income, Equity Income, Global Stock, International Equity, Balanced, and Flexible Portfolio. On the conservative fixed-income side of the equation, I have chosen top bond funds in each of these categories: Short/Intermediate-Term General Corporates, Long-Term General Corporates, High-Quality Corporates, High Yield Corporates, Short/Intermediate-Term Government,

Long-Term Government, Mortgage-Backed Government, International/ Global Bond, and Long-Term Municipals. (For definitions of these various categories, please turn to the directory in Chapter 7.)

All-Stars Do Change

Keep in mind that these represent my list of All-Stars at the time this book is being written. Since new funds are always being formed and managers are constantly moving around, this list will certainly change over time. I will keep you updated on new additions and deletions each month in *Fund Connection*, as well as in future updated editions of this book. But I'm confident you won't go wrong adding any of these funds to your portfolio.

Meet the All-Stars

For now, get yourself acquainted with these fantastic funds. Then, in Chapter 5, I'll show you how to put them together to form your own All-Star portfolio.

AGGRESSIVE GROWTH

MONTGOMERY SELECT 50

Managers: John Brown, Oscar Castro, Roger Honour, Andrew Pratt, and Angeline Ee

There are several funds from Montgomery Securities that have made my All-Star list, and we begin with what you might call their "best of the best" product. Montgomery Select 50 brings together the firm's leading managers from five separate investment disciplines. The team includes John Brown (who also heads the All-Star Montgomery Equity Income fund), Oscar Castro (an international expert), Roger Honour (U.S. growth stock manager), Andrew Pratt (an experienced U.S. micro-cap analyst), and Angeline Ee (part of the firm's emerging markets group).

Each manager is asked to choose ten favorite stocks from the other portfolios he or she oversees for inclusion in Montgomery Select 50. The end result is a fund full of securities from around the world representing companies of various sizes, industries, and geographic locations. The fund's general policy is to keep assets spread among at least three different countries, including the United States, and each holding represents about 2 percent of the total pie.

What I especially like is that most portfolio managers would probably admit they're only passionate about a dozen of their holdings. With this fund, you get nothing but prime picks from five of the finest pros in the field. Insiders tell me the portfolio managers have a friendly competition going on and are constantly trying to outdo their colleagues in selecting great stocks. I like having that kind of enthusiasm on my side. This fund also gives you one-stop global diversification, which can reduce the overall volatility of this otherwise aggressive offering.

Fund Contact Information:

Montgomery Funds
101 California Street
San Francisco, CA 94111
800-572-3863

Montgomery Select 50
Symbol: MNSFX

Value of $1000

(cumulative, monthly beginning Oct. 31, 1995 through Nov. 30, 1996))

— MNSFX
▒ S&P 500

Value of $1000	Investment Period		
	1 Year	3 Years	5 Years
MNSFX	$1276.34	N.A.	N.A.
S&P 500	$1252.94	$1730.46	$2257.76
Total Return	1 Year	3 Years*	5 Years*
MNSFX	27.63%	N.A.	N.A.
S&P 500	25.29%	20.06%	17.69%

* - Total Return percentages for periods greater than 1 year are annualized.
Source: IDD Information Services

Top 10 Holdings
as of October 31, 1996

Ericsson (Sweden)
Gucci (Italy)
AccuStaff (U.S.)
DMCI Holdings (Philippines)
Safeco (U.S.)

Caribiner Intl. (U.S.)
Northern Telecom (U.S.)
HA-LO Industries (U.S.)
Eidos (U.K.)
Bristol-Myers Squibb (U.S.)

Key Statistics

Assets:	$83.6 mil.	Dividend Yield:	0.37%
Expense Ratio:	1.80%	Turnover Ratio:	105.98%
12b-1 Fee:	0.00%	Beta:	N/A

AGGRESSIVE GROWTH

NAVELLIER AGGRESSIVE GROWTH PORTFOLIO

Managers: Louis Navellier and Alan Alpers

In the late 1970s, as a finance student at California State University, Hayward, Louis Navellier developed several computer models to prove the stock market wasn't always efficient. He concluded there are inefficiently priced stocks that offer the potential for excess returns by taking on increased risk. It is a strategy he still follows today. Specifically, he focuses on quantitative calculations of alpha (excess return uncorrelated to the stock market) and standard deviation (volatility). By screening a database consisting of almost every actively traded stock in the United States, he tries to uncover ideas with the strongest appreciation potential and, by back-testing, figures out which investment techniques are presently working best on Wall Street.

It's a complicated procedure, not easily replicated by the average GI. That's why so many people subscribe to Navellier's monthly *MPT Review* newsletter, which uncovers those stocks that make the cut. How have his picks done in the past? *The Hulbert Financial Digest*, a newsletter-rating service, claims *MPT Review* is the top-performing investment newsletter over the past ten years.

Now we can tap into this same winning database by buying Navellier's Aggressive Growth Portfolio, the first in a new series of high-performance funds. However, this fund poses one major risk. Navellier manages more than $1.2 billion in funds and private accounts. His list of recommended stocks for all of this money is very similar, meaning his various accounts will often be fighting for the same shares. This could create a potential illiquidity problem, should he try to sell everything at once. Without question, this fund is the most volatile pick of my All-Stars and should outshine the rest when the market does well and fall the hardest when it goes down.

Fund Contact Information:

Navellier Securities
1 East Liberty, Third Floor
Reno, NV 89501
800-887-8671

Navellier Aggressive Growth Portfolio
Symbol: NPFGX

Value of $1000
(cumulative, monthly beginning Apr. 30, 1996 through Nov. 30, 1996)

1996

Value of $1000	Investment Period		
	1 Year	3 Years	5 Years
NPFGX	N.A.	N.A.	N.A.
S&P 500	$1252.94	$1730.46	$2257.76
Total Return	**1 Year**	**3 Years***	**5 Years***
NPFGX	N.A.	N.A.	N.A.
S&P 500	25.29%	20.06%	17.69%

* - Total Return percentages for periods greater than 1 year are annualized.
Source: IDD Information Services

Top 10 Holdings
as of July 5, 1996

PMT Services	Jones Medical Inds.
Hologic Inc.	U.S. Office Products
ATC Communications	Prime Medical
Natures Sunshine	ABR Information
Ross Stores	WPI Group

Key Statistics

Assets:	$100 mil.	Dividend Yield:	N/A
Expense Ratio:	2.00%	Turnover Ratio:	N/A
12b-1 Fee:	0.25%	Beta:	N/A

AGGRESSIVE GROWTH

PBHG EMERGING GROWTH

Managers: Christine Baxter and Gary Pilgrim

Gary Pilgrim's record at the PBHG Growth fund is outstanding. It's the best-performing fund in the entire industry over the past ten years, up a whopping 605 percent. Under most circumstances, PBHG Growth, which was designed to invest in small-cap stocks, would have made my list of All-Stars. Unfortunately, I feel that fund's best days are behind it. Pilgrim has allowed the fund to grow to almost $5 billion in assets, making it an entirely different creature. He closed the fund in 1995 at around $2 billion, only to open it up again, allowing it to more than double in size. As aggressive funds like this get bigger, their returns tend to fall. That's because being large makes it tough to navigate through the more illiquid over-the-counter market.

PBHG Emerging Growth is closer to what PBHG Growth used to be, although it borders on being too large as well. (It also closed, only to reopen several months later.) Nevertheless, given Pilgrim's brilliant record and prowess at finding fast-growing companies, you should have him on your team. Pilgrim practices what's known as an "earnings momentum" strategy. That means he buys companies with rapidly growing earnings, and sells them as soon as that trend begins to reverse. PBHG Emerging Growth's prospectus says it seeks stocks with market capitalizations below $500 million, but that threshold has been raised along with the increase in assets.

While both Pilgrim and Christine Baxter are listed as portfolio managers, the two claim Baxter, who is the daughter of the management firm's cofounder, makes most of the day-to-day decisions. In any case, she follows the same discipline Pilgrim has perfected over the years, which is one that has made his shareholders very rich.

Fund Contact Information:

PBHG Funds
680 E. Swedesford Road
Wayne, PA 19087-1658
800-433-0051

PBHG Emerging Growth
Symbol: PBEGX

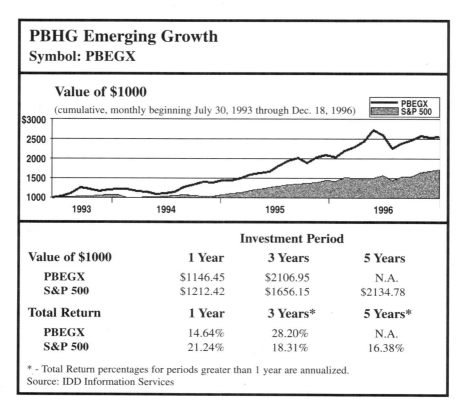

Value of $1000
(cumulative, monthly beginning July 30, 1993 through Dec. 18, 1996)

Legend: PBEGX, S&P 500

		Investment Period	
Value of $1000	**1 Year**	**3 Years**	**5 Years**
PBEGX	$1146.45	$2106.95	N.A.
S&P 500	$1212.42	$1656.15	$2134.78
Total Return	**1 Year**	**3 Years***	**5 Years***
PBEGX	14.64%	28.20%	N.A.
S&P 500	21.24%	18.31%	16.38%

* - Total Return percentages for periods greater than 1 year are annualized.
Source: IDD Information Services

Top 10 Holdings
as of September 30, 1996

Legato Systems	U.S. Office Products
Aspen Technology	ABR Information Services
Papa John's International	Inso
Vantive	Eagle USA Airfreight
Video Server	Wind River Systems

Key Statistics

Assets:	$1.4 bil.	Dividend Yield:	0.00%
Expense Ratio:	1.47%	Turnover Ratio:	97.05%
12b-1 Fee:	0.00%	Beta:	0.97

GROWTH

BONNEL GROWTH FUND
Manager: Art Bonnel

If a company's earnings aren't growing, even at a modest rate, it won't make it into the Bonnel Growth Fund's portfolio. Manager Art Bonnel looks for stocks with market capitalizations of around $1 billion, making it technically a mid-cap fund. However, he doesn't limit himself to any particular size and holds a wide array of large and small names.

Bonnel runs the portfolio for United Services Funds from his home in Reno, Nevada. He's assisted by wife Wanda, who holds an accounting degree. She looks through earnings reports in search of companies that meet her husband's strict criteria. He then goes through and conducts further analysis to see if the company is worth buying.

In addition to growing earnings, Art Bonnel likes to see such fundamental characteristics as high insider ownership and a strong management team. He also demands a sustainable price-earnings (PE) ratio and likes to see a current ratio (current assets divided by current liabilities) of around 2-to-1. He spends so much time on balance sheet analysis because he believes the numbers tell the most accurate story of what's going on. Though corporate officers may lie, the numbers don't. His technical considerations include stock price movement and the magnitude of trading volume.

Although this fund was launched at the end of 1994, Bonnel has one of the best long-term track records in the business. He's been managing money since 1970 and previously navigated the MIM Stock Appreciation Fund to an 18 percent annualized gain during the five years he was there.

Fund Contact Information:

United Services Funds
PO Box 781234
San Antonio, TX 78278-1234
800-426-6635

Bonnel Growth Fund
Symbol: ACBGX

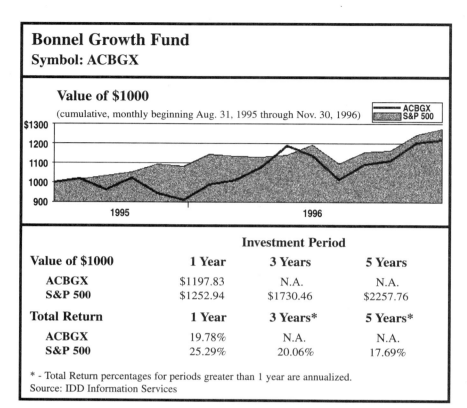

Value of $1000
(cumulative, monthly beginning Aug. 31, 1995 through Nov. 30, 1996)

	Investment Period		
Value of $1000	**1 Year**	**3 Years**	**5 Years**
ACBGX	$1197.83	N.A.	N.A.
S&P 500	$1252.94	$1730.46	$2257.76
Total Return	**1 Year**	**3 Years***	**5 Years***
ACBGX	19.78%	N.A.	N.A.
S&P 500	25.29%	20.06%	17.69%

* - Total Return percentages for periods greater than 1 year are annualized.
Source: IDD Information Services

Top 10 Holdings
as of September 30, 1996

Jones Medical Industries	Uniphase
BMC Software	Aspect Telecommunications
PeopleSoft	PairGain Technologies
Compuware	Nautica Enterprises
ADC Telecommunications	Gateway 2000

Key Statistics

Assets:	$90.7 mil.	Dividend Yield:	0.00%
Expense Ratio:	2.48%	Turnover Ratio:	145%
12b-1 Fee:	0.25%	Beta:	N/A

GROWTH

STRONG GROWTH FUND

Manager: Ronald Ognar

Strong Growth Fund manager Ronald Ognar looks for the best growth stocks in the strongest industries, regardless of size. What's unique is that if Ognar feels the market is in danger of a steep fall, he can invest as much of the portfolio as he wants in cash and short-term fixed-income securities as a defensive measure. He is also allowed to put up to 25 percent of the fund's assets in foreign stocks.

Ognar likes to bet on companies whose earnings are in a strong uptrend. To identify these gems, he looks for such characteristics as over-all financial strength (including sound financial and accounting policies, and a solid balance sheet); something that gives the company a competitive edge (such as innovative products and services); signs that invested capital is producing a high return; clear indications of favorable prospects for continued above-average sales and earnings growth; an effective research, marketing, and product development department; and stable, capable management.

Ognar is presently overweighted in small- and mid-cap issues. That's because the valuations of these equities compared to their growth rates are more attractive to him than many of their larger brethren. He also expects small- and medium-size stocks to outperform the market on a longer term basis, especially if there's a reduction in the capital gains tax rate.

What's more, Ognar adheres to a strict valuation discipline, which calls for buying stocks at significant discounts to their projected growth rates and selling them when those valuations become excessive or better opportunities are found elsewhere.

Fund Contact Information:

Strong Funds
PO Box 2936
Milwaukee, WI 53201-2936
800-368-1030

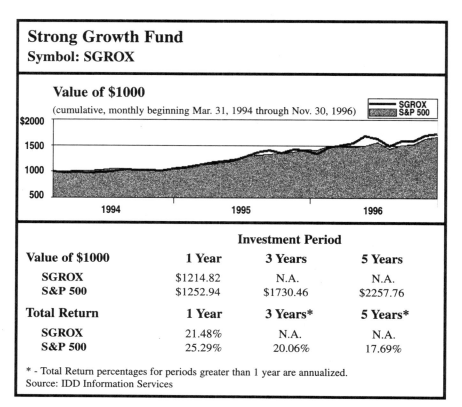

Strong Growth Fund
Symbol: SGROX

Value of $1000
(cumulative, monthly beginning Mar. 31, 1994 through Nov. 30, 1996)

Legend: SGROX / S&P 500

Chart y-axis: $2000, 1500, 1000, 500
Chart x-axis: 1994, 1995, 1996

	Investment Period		
Value of $1000	**1 Year**	**3 Years**	**5 Years**
SGROX	$1214.82	N.A.	N.A.
S&P 500	$1252.94	$1730.46	$2257.76
Total Return	**1 Year**	**3 Years***	**5 Years***
SGROX	21.48%	N.A.	N.A.
S&P 500	25.29%	20.06%	17.69%

* - Total Return percentages for periods greater than 1 year are annualized.
Source: IDD Information Services

Top 10 Holdings
as of September 30, 1996

Danka Business Systems (ADR)   ADC Telecommunications
Cisco Systems   Sykes Enterprises
Intel   Uniphase
Accustaff   McAfee Associates
COREstaff   Clear Channel Communications

Key Statistics

Assets:	$1.29 bil.	Dividend Yield:	0.16%
Expense Ratio:	1.40%	Turnover Ratio:	321%
12b-1 Fee:	0.00%	Beta:	N/A

GROWTH

YACKTMAN FUND

Manager: Donald Yacktman

You might call Donald Yacktman the comeback kid. After successfully managing money for other funds, including Selected American Shares, he decided to go out on his own in 1992, one year after *Morningstar* named him "Portfolio Manager of the Year." His first 12 months working solo were a nightmare. His self-named fund lost 6.58 during that period, making it one of the top ten worst-performing funds in the country. When asked by the press, "What happened?" Yacktman replied that he didn't know and if people didn't like him anymore, they could take their money out of the fund because he wasn't changing his management style. Those who left have been sorry ever since. In recent years, Yacktman has once again proved that he knows what he's doing.

His strategy is to buy primarily big, financially strong blue chip stocks when they are out of favor and trading at a discount. Yacktman's not afraid to take large positions in his favorite picks and likes to hold on for the long haul. He tells me there are three main traits every company in his portfolio must have: a good business, shareholder-oriented management, and a low initial purchase price.

Yacktman further seeks out firms that earn high returns on tangible assets, with management teams willing to do whatever it takes to build the company's private market value. He then likes to see the stock selling for less than what a rational person would pay for the entire business if it were put up for sale. It's what he refers to as "growth at a price."

Don't expect the Yacktman Fund to be at the top of any short-term performance charts. But, over time, you can count on it to make you a lot of money.

Fund Contact Information:

Yacktman Fund
303 West Madison Street, Suite 1925
Chicago, IL 60606
800-525-8258

Yacktman Fund
Symbol: YACKX

Value of $1000
(cumulative, monthly beginning Sep. 30, 1992 through Nov. 30, 1996)

Value of $1000	Investment Period		
	1 Year	3 Years	5 Years
YACKX	$1273.92	$1739.84	N.A.
S&P 500	$1252.94	$1730.46	$2257.76
Total Return	**1 Year**	**3 Years***	**5 Years***
YACKX	27.39%	20.27%	N.A.
S&P 500	25.29%	20.06%	17.69%

* - Total Return percentages for periods greater than 1 year are annualized.
Source: IDD Information Services

Top 10 Holdings
as of May 31, 1996

Philip Morris
Reebok International
Clorox
Bristol-Myers Squibb
Salomon

United Asset Management
Whitman
UST
Fruit of the Loom
Torchmark

Key Statistics

Assets:	$684.4 mil.	Dividend Yield:	1.51%
Expense Ratio:	0.91%	Turnover Ratio:	55.37%
12b-1 Fee:	0.25%	Beta:	0.82

GROWTH-COLLEGE SAVINGS

STEIN ROE YOUNG INVESTOR FUND

Managers: David Brady, Erik Gustafson, and Arthur McQueen

If you've been searching for the perfect vehicle to save money to fund the college education of that special child in your life, look no further than the Stein Roe Young Investor Fund. This fund is perfect for a number of reasons. It has consistently ranked among the top growth funds in the country. It holds an impressive array of both large and small stocks. And its goal is to excite children about the world of investing.

Because managing money for youngsters is the fund's primary objective, portfolio managers prepare their annual report with this target audience in mind. Everything is explained in simple terms so children can understand how their money is being put to work and which companies they own. In one recent report, there was a discussion about the impact inflation has on the market, in which the writers clearly defined what the term meant and showed how it was calculated by the government, complete with big letters and illustrations. Wouldn't it be nice if all reports made understanding this financial jargon so easy? Stein Roe even prints special publications just for kids who own shares in the fund.

Young Investor's portfolio managers encourage shareholders to send in possible investment ideas and suggestions. Not surprisingly, many of the names in this diverse portfolio are familiar to children, like Mattel, Nike, Wrigley, Hershey, The Home Depot, Walgreens, and Coca-Cola. My expectation is that this fund will not only make your child's money grow, but also get them excited about investing. (Be sure to ask your broker about setting up this account under the Uniform Gift Trust to Minors Act to save taxes. Also keep in mind that the fund is equally appropriate for grown-ups as well.)

Fund Contact Information:

Stein Roe Mutual Funds
PO Box 804058
Chicago, IL 60680
800-338-2550

Stein Roe Young Investor Fund
Symbol: SRYIX

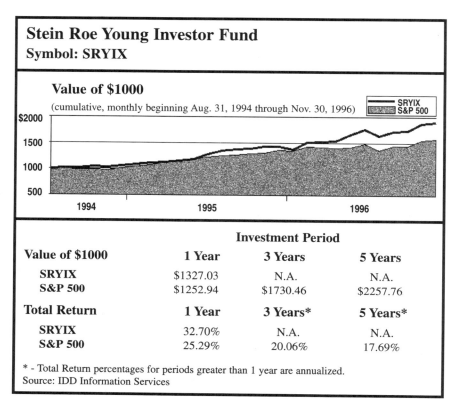

Value of $1000
(cumulative, monthly beginning Aug. 31, 1994 through Nov. 30, 1996)

	Investment Period		
Value of $1000	**1 Year**	**3 Years**	**5 Years**
SRYIX	$1327.03	N.A.	N.A.
S&P 500	$1252.94	$1730.46	$2257.76
Total Return	**1 Year**	**3 Years***	**5 Years***
SRYIX	32.70%	N.A.	N.A.
S&P 500	25.29%	20.06%	17.69%

* - Total Return percentages for periods greater than 1 year are annualized.
Source: IDD Information Services

Top 10 Holdings
as of March 31, 1996

Apollo Group
Sitel
StrataCom
Procter & Gamble
Sterling Commerce

Sandoz (ADR)
Nabisco Holdings Class A
Fed. Home Loan Mortgage Corp.
American Express
Nike Class B

Key Statistics

Assets:	$177.6 mil.	Dividend Yield:	0.25%
Expense Ratio:	0.99%	Turnover Ratio:	55%
12b-1 Fee:	0.00%	Beta:	N/A

SMALL COMPANY GROWTH

BERGER SMALL COMPANY GROWTH
Manager: William Keithler

William Keithler's small company stock-picking record is impressive. Before being recruited by Berger Associates to head up their Small Company Growth fund, he managed the Invesco Dynamics and Emerging Growth portfolios, which posted chart-topping returns. Therefore, it came as no surprise when Keithler continued his winning ways at Berger, producing a gain of almost 14 percent in 1994, the fund's inaugural year and one in which the major market indexes were barely above water.

Keithler mines for stocks with market capitalizations below $1 billion at the time of initial purchase that have favorable long-term prospects. He tries to find companies with either a dominant position in an emerging sector or growing market share in a larger fragmented industry.

Like all funds in the Berger group, investment decisions are based on the belief that it's best to seek out companies that are already proven successes because they are more likely to become profitable investments. Keithler therefore finds his ideas by analyzing information such as industry economic trends, earnings expectations, and fundamental valuation factors to identify companies that are most likely to have predictable, above average earnings growth, regardless of the company's geographic location. This means he's not afraid to put his money overseas if that's where his research leads him. Keithler also looks at management and innovations in products and services in an effort to estimate the company's potential future earnings growth. In recent times, he has found most of his buys in the areas of health care, outsourcing, retailing, and, to a much smaller degree, technology.

Fund Contact Information:

The Berger Funds
210 University Blvd., Suite 900
Denver, CO 80206
800-333-1001

Berger Small Company Growth
Symbol: BESCX

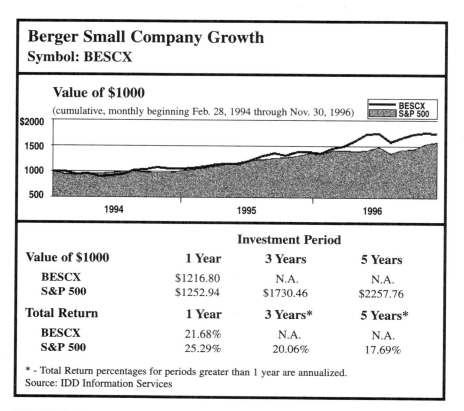

Value of $1000

(cumulative, monthly beginning Feb. 28, 1994 through Nov. 30, 1996)

	Investment Period		
Value of $1000	**1 Year**	**3 Years**	**5 Years**
BESCX	$1216.80	N.A.	N.A.
S&P 500	$1252.94	$1730.46	$2257.76
Total Return	**1 Year**	**3 Years***	**5 Years***
BESCX	21.68%	N.A.	N.A.
S&P 500	25.29%	20.06%	17.69%

* - Total Return percentages for periods greater than 1 year are annualized.
Source: IDD Information Services

Top 10 Holdings
as of September 30, 1996

ACC
Wet Seal Cl A
Orthodontic Centers of America
Technology Solutions
PAREXEL International

VIASOFT
Eagle Hardware & Garden
PairGain Technologies
Cascade Communications
Total Renal Care Holdings

Key Statistics

Assets:	$830.2 mil.	Dividend Yield:	0.00%
Expense Ratio:	1.89%	Turnover Ratio:	109%
12b-1 Fee:	0.25%	Beta:	N/A

SMALL COMPANY GROWTH

TURNER SMALL CAP

Manager: William Chenoweth

Turner Small Cap is one of those funds that most of you would never be able to buy were it not for these wonderful no-load, NTF programs. That's because the fund's minimum investment for direct investments is $10,000. However, through participating discount brokers, you can get in for as little as $1,000. This is yet another example of why it pays to be a part of these plans.

Manager William Chenoweth diversifies his portfolio among stocks with market capitalizations of less than $1 billion that his computer shows to have superior earnings growth potential and reasonable valuations. Although the fund has only been around for two years, Chenoweth's performance has been outstanding, especially when you consider that he maintains sector weightings similar to those of the Russell 2500, the fund's benchmark index. In other words, he doesn't put all of his money into one or two "hot" areas, like technology or health care, which is how many similar funds earn their short-term standout numbers. Given his savvy for good stock picking over a broad range of industries, I feel confident that Chenoweth will continue to post impressive numbers, and that his excellent showing thus far isn't just a fluke.

Another thing I like is how Chenoweth watches his portfolio like a hawk. He and his analysts continually check the flow of money into and out of their stocks, to get a measure of market support for their holdings based on price and volume trends. As soon as investors begin to pull money out of one of his holdings, he asks why and follows them to the exits if he doesn't like the answer. Furthermore, Chenoweth keeps an eye on earnings estimates and tries to sell any holdings that might disappoint before they get hit.

Fund Contact Information:

Turner Funds
680 E. Swedesford Road
Wayne, PA 19087-1658
800-932-7781

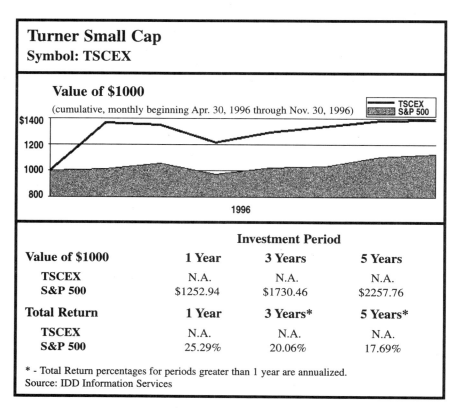

Turner Small Cap
Symbol: TSCEX

Value of $1000
(cumulative, monthly beginning Apr. 30, 1996 through Nov. 30, 1996)

	Investment Period		
Value of $1000	**1 Year**	**3 Years**	**5 Years**
TSCEX	N.A.	N.A.	N.A.
S&P 500	$1252.94	$1730.46	$2257.76
Total Return	**1 Year**	**3 Years***	**5 Years***
TSCEX	N.A.	N.A.	N.A.
S&P 500	25.29%	20.06%	17.69%

* - Total Return percentages for periods greater than 1 year are annualized.
Source: IDD Information Services

Top 10 Holdings
as of June 30, 1996

Waters	PMT Services
Citrix Systems	Sitel
Imperial Credit Industries	Concord EFS
Arbor Software	HNC Software
Aames Financial	NOVA

Key Statistics

Assets:	$68.4 mil.	Dividend Yield:	0.00%
Expense Ratio:	1.25%	Turnover Ratio:	183%
12b-1 Fee:	0.00%	Beta:	N/A

SMALL COMPANY GROWTH

WARBURG PINCUS SMALL COMPANY VALUE

Managers: George Wyper and Kyle Frey

Unlike the Berger and Turner funds, Warburg Pincus Small Company Value doesn't chase fast-growing stocks on the way up. Instead, managers George Wyper and Kyle Frey look for those firms with market capitalizations below $1 billion that they deem to be undervalued based on a variety of different measures. Among the statistics they look at are PE ratios, price-to-book ratios, price-to-cash flow ratios, earnings growth rates, and debt-to-capital ratios. Other important factors, such as the worth of a company's underlying assets, its franchise value, and quality of management are also considered.

Investing in small company stocks of any kind involves a heightened amount of risk. These securities normally have a limited number of outstanding shares, haven't been in business all that long, and are more illiquid than large capitalization issues. However, because of this fund's strict value parameters, I expect it to be far less volatile than other similar funds. It's the perfect complement to a higher-octane pick, like Turner Small Cap or Berger Small Company Growth.

Having said that, you should be aware that this fund is allowed to buy nonpublicly traded securities, which are illiquid and can result in either substantial losses or gains, depending on what happens with the company. It can also engage in strategies involving options, futures, currency transactions, and foreign securities. I doubt that these activities will ever play a substantial role in the fund's overall operation, but you should know that the managers have the prerogative to engage in them if they wish.

Fund Contact Information:

Warburg Pincus Funds
466 Lexington Avenue
New York, NY 10017-3147
800-927-2874

Warburg Pincus Small Company Value
Symbol: WPSVX

Value of $1000
(cumulative, monthly beginning May 31, 1996 through Nov. 30, 1996)

Value of $1000	Investment Period		
	1 Year	**3 Years**	**5 Years**
WPSVX	N.A.	N.A.	N.A.
S&P 500	$1252.94	$1730.46	$2257.76
Total Return	**1 Year**	**3 Years***	**5 Years***
WPSVX	N.A.	N.A.	N.A.
S&P 500	25.29%	20.06%	17.69%

* - Total Return percentages for periods greater than 1 year are annualized.
Source: IDD Information Services

Top 10 Holdings
as of September 30, 1996

Larson-Davis Inc.
Cole National Cl A
Transport Holdings Cl A
Tracor
MTL

Schnitzer Steel Cl A
Scotts Cl A
Westpoint Stevens Cl A
Nuevo Energy
Universal Stainless & Alloy

Key Statistics

Assets:	$83.8 mil.	Dividend Yield:	N/A
Expense Ratio:	1.75%	Turnover Ratio:	N/A
12b-1 Fee:	0.25%	Beta:	N/A

GROWTH AND INCOME

BABSON VALUE

Manager: Roland Whitridge

Roland Whitridge hates to pay top dollar for anything. "I resist paying full price for automobiles, suits, or appliances," he says. "I believe that if you're patient you can always find a good value." That's the same mantra this contrarian has followed when picking investments for his Babson Value Fund, ever since he began managing it in 1984. Whitridge seeks long-term growth by buying stocks when they are unpopular on Wall Street and undervalued based on earnings, assets, or dividends. His goal is to find ideas that offer an above-average potential for growth in principal and income, while assuming a lower degree of market risk.

One important factor in Whitridge's selection process is a company's financial strength. He wants to make sure there's enough money on the balance sheet to give key members of management time to turn things around. The prospectus restricts him to buying only stocks he believes are backed by sound businesses with good future potential and the ability to eventually gain greater favor among investors. This usually means they must be rated B- or better by S&P. Whitridge keeps his portfolio fully invested almost at all times and gives equal weighting to the 40 or so holdings inside.

Babson Value's overall PE ratio is usually 20 percent lower than the S&P 500. This stands to reason, given its value bent. Whitridge likes to hold on to a stock until the share price fully reflects his target price. Since this often takes some time (and there's no guarantee it will ever happen), the fund's turnover is relatively miniscule, which should help to lower its year-end taxable distributions.

Fund Contact Information:

Jones & Babson Mutual Funds
2440 Pershing Road
Kansas City, MO 64108-2518
800-422-2766

Babson Value
Symbol: BVALX

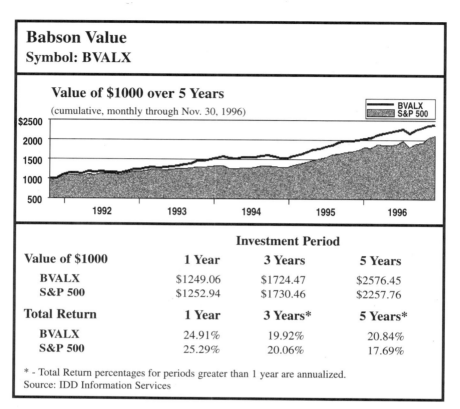

Value of $1000 over 5 Years
(cumulative, monthly through Nov. 30, 1996)

Value of $1000	Investment Period		
	1 Year	**3 Years**	**5 Years**
BVALX	$1249.06	$1724.47	$2576.45
S&P 500	$1252.94	$1730.46	$2257.76
Total Return	**1 Year**	**3 Years***	**5 Years***
BVALX	24.91%	19.92%	20.84%
S&P 500	25.29%	20.06%	17.69%

* - Total Return percentages for periods greater than 1 year are annualized.
Source: IDD Information Services

Top 10 Holdings
as of September 30, 1996

Apple Computer	United Healthcare
SLMA	Allstate
Boeing	IBM
National City	Grand Metropolitan (ADR)
Chase Manhattan	Harcourt General

Key Statistics

Assets:	$678.8 mil.	Dividend Yield:	1.54%
Expense Ratio:	0.98%	Turnover Ratio:	6%
12b-1 Fee:	0.00%	Beta:	0.84

GROWTH AND INCOME

BARON GROWTH & INCOME

Manager: Ronald Baron

Baron Growth & Income is a very unique fund. Instead of loading up on big blue chips, like most funds in this category, manager Ron Baron fills the portfolio with small- and medium-sized, lesser known or misperceived companies with favorable growth prospects. It's the same formula he has successfully used for his flagship high-octane Baron Asset Fund, which has consistently ranked in the top 2 percent of all taxable mutual funds since it was born in 1987. Asset has rewarded its shareholders with an annualized return of 22 percent over the past five years.

Baron Growth & Income was launched in January of 1995. In its rookie year, it skyrocketed 53 percent. While this fund might be new, Ron Baron has 22 years of investment management experience. He looks for stocks he believes can jump at least 50 percent within two years in industries where new jobs are being created. His goal is to achieve a 15 to 25 percent annual return for shareholders.

While both Growth & Income and Asset contain many similar names, Baron seeks to reduce this fund's volatility by including a chunk of income-producing assets, like real estate investment trusts, convertible bonds, and dividend paying equities. Baron Growth & Income gives you a chance to tap into the small-cap growth of Asset with less risk. Also, this fund is smaller, which is an advantage.

Before Baron will buy a stock, he meets with company management and follows up with them at least once a year. He remains fully invested at all times and is quick to unload shares when there's a fundamental change in any of his businesses. This fund gives conservative investors a more aggressive way to grow their capital.

Fund Contact Information:

The Baron Funds
767 Fifth Avenue, 24th Floor
New York, NY 10153
800-992-2766

Baron Growth & Income
Symbol: BGINX

Value of $1000

(cumulative, monthly beginning Aug. 31, 1995 through Nov. 30, 1996)

	Investment Period		
Value of $1000	**1 Year**	**3 Years**	**5 Years**
BGINX	$1269.47	N.A.	N.A.
S&P 500	$1252.94	$1730.46	$2257.76
Total Return	**1 Year**	**3 Years***	**5 Years***
BGINX	26.95%	N.A.	N.A.
S&P 500	25.29%	20.06%	17.69%

* - Total Return percentages for periods greater than 1 year are annualized.
Source: IDD Information Services

Top 10 Holdings
as of March 31, 1996

Charles Schwab & Co.
Manor Care
Sun Communities
Scandinavian Broadcasting Conv. 7.25%
Smart & Final

Waterhouse Inv. Svcs. Conv. 6%
Intl. CableTel. Conv. 7.25%
Saga Communications
Leucadia National Conv. 5.25%
Robert Half International

Key Statistics

Assets:	$221.7 mil.	Dividend Yield:	0.20%
Expense Ratio:	2.00%	Turnover Ratio:	N/A
12b-1 Fee:	0.25%	Beta:	N/A

GROWTH AND INCOME

ROBERTSON STEPHENS GROWTH & INCOME

Manager: John L. Wallace

This fund is similar to Baron Growth & Income in that it concentrates its investments in small- and mid-cap companies. What's different is the way manager John Wallace picks his stocks and structures his portfolio. He tries to keep the fund's risk profile similar to other growth and income funds, while giving himself better upside potential by placing 75 to 80 percent of his money in stocks and the rest in income-producing instruments, such as preferreds, convertibles, and bonds. Wallace calls this his "barbell" strategy. It allows him to take purportedly higher risk on the equity side without significantly raising the fund's overall volatility.

Wallace searches for companies with above-average growth potential and/or current income. He begins his bottom-up process by conducting fundamental analysis, namely looking at company management, demand for its products, and the overall business plan. He then evaluates such technical considerations as the stock's price-earnings multiple compared to the growth rate and cash flow. Most importantly, Wallace wants to uncover some catalyst that will drive earnings growth even higher. He pays little attention to what's happening with the overall market.

Portfolio holdings are sold when they reach Wallace's price objective. It's a strategy that has worked well for him in the past. Before joining Robertson Stephens in 1995, Wallace managed the Oppenheimer Main Street Income & Growth fund, producing a total return of 236 percent from 1991–1995, compared to the S&P's 88 percent. That put the Oppenheimer fund in the top 10 percent of all equity funds during that period.

Fund Contact Information:

Robertson Stephens & Company
555 California Street, Suite 2600
San Francisco, CA 94104
800-766-3863

Robertson Stephens Growth & Income
Symbol: RSGIX

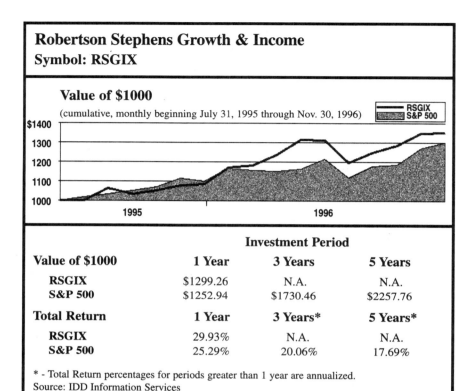

Value of $1000

(cumulative, monthly beginning July 31, 1995 through Nov. 30, 1996)

	Investment Period		
Value of $1000	**1 Year**	**3 Years**	**5 Years**
RSGIX	$1299.26	N.A.	N.A.
S&P 500	$1252.94	$1730.46	$2257.76
Total Return	**1 Year**	**3 Years***	**5 Years***
RSGIX	29.93%	N.A.	N.A.
S&P 500	25.29%	20.06%	17.69%

* - Total Return percentages for periods greater than 1 year are annualized.
Source: IDD Information Services

Top 10 Holdings
as of September 30, 1996

Skyline Corporation   National Education
BMC Software   Compuware
Vans   Fisher Scientific Intl.
Transocean Offshore   Monsanto
Vanstar   Smith International

Key Statistics

Assets:	$301 mil.	Dividend Yield:	N/A
Expense Ratio:	1.85%	Turnover Ratio:	N/A
12b-1 Fee:	0.25%	Beta:	N/A

EQUITY INCOME

HOTCHKIS AND WILEY
EQUITY INCOME

Managers: George Wiley and Gail Bardin

The folks at Hotchkis and Wiley focus on large-cap value stocks with high dividend yields. Their search process starts off by filtering through a universe of 7,000 domestic securities that are screened on three initial criteria. First, each stock must have a dividend yield greater than the S&P 500. Second, candidates are required to sport earnings yields at least 3 percent greater than that of long-term bonds. Finally, every company under consideration must be financially strong.

Only 150 to 400 stocks will pass these tests, depending on market conditions. Then, the Equity Income fund's eight-member management team, led by George Wiley and Gail Bardin, begin to perform quantitative and qualitative analysis on each security. They want to determine every company's competitive and strategic position within its industry. This is done by talking with customers, competitors, and research analysts. Wiley and Bardin also like to meet with senior management before making a purchase.

On the quantitative side of the equation, they look at cash flows, return on equity, and the sustainability of projected growth. Hotchkis and Wiley has developed several proprietary valuation models that further help managers figure out whether something is a compelling bargain.

Wiley and Bardin fill their fund with equities, including common stocks, convertibles, preferreds, and warrants, and remain fully invested most of the time. They'll sell a position for several reasons, including when it appears to be fully valued, to maintain portfolio diversification, or if price appreciation causes its dividend yield to fall 1 percent or more below that of the S&P 500.

Fund Contact Information:

Hotchkis and Wiley
800 West Sixth Street, Fifth Floor
Los Angeles, CA 90017
800-346-7301

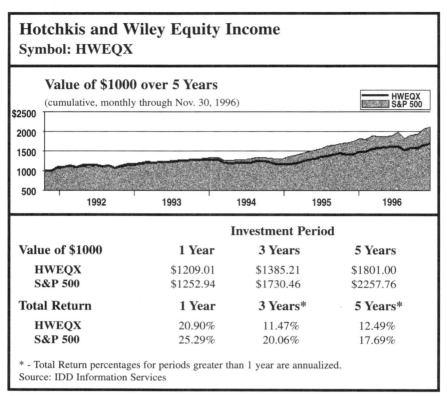

Hotchkis and Wiley Equity Income
Symbol: HWEQX

Value of $1000 over 5 Years
(cumulative, monthly through Nov. 30, 1996)

	Investment Period		
Value of $1000	**1 Year**	**3 Years**	**5 Years**
HWEQX	$1209.01	$1385.21	$1801.00
S&P 500	$1252.94	$1730.46	$2257.76
Total Return	**1 Year**	**3 Years***	**5 Years***
HWEQX	20.90%	11.47%	12.49%
S&P 500	25.29%	20.06%	17.69%

* - Total Return percentages for periods greater than 1 year are annualized.
Source: IDD Information Services

Top 10 Holdings
as of September 30, 1996

Allegheny Teledyne	American Brands
General Motors	Ford Motor Co.
Browning-Ferris Industries	Aon Corp.
Tenneco	Georgia Pacific
Household International	Eastern Enterprises

Key Statistics

Assets:	$180.3 mil.	Dividend Yield:	3.20%
Expense Ratio:	0.96%	Turnover Ratio:	50%
12b-1 Fee:	0.00%	Beta:	0.95

EQUITY INCOME

MONTGOMERY EQUITY INCOME
Manager: John Brown

Montgomery Equity Income is designed to provide current income and capital appreciation by investing in dividend-rich domestic stocks with market capitalizations above $1 billion. It rarely holds preferreds, bonds, low-yielding equities, or foreign securities. Manager John Brown says his goal is to generate a significantly greater yield than the S&P 500, while maintaining a low level of price volatility.

The fund remains almost fully invested at all times. Brown targets companies with favorable long-term fundamental characteristics and current relative yields at the upper end of their historical range. He identifies potential candidates by having his computer search for stocks that meet these criteria. He then targets those firms with yields that are at least 140 percent of the average paid by components of the S&P 500.

Predictably, the companies he finds are usually in the maturing stages of development or involved in slower growth areas of the economy. They also generally have conservative accounting practices, strong cash flows (to maintain dividends), low financial leverage, and market leadership.

Brown tries to keep turnover low, hanging on to his average holding from two to four years. He begins to cut back on a position as its price moves up and yield drops to the lower end of its historical range. A stock will also be sold if it reduces or eliminates its dividend, or is in jeopardy of doing so.

Even though the fund is usually concentrated in stocks, Brown can put up to 35 percent of his portfolio in debt instruments. When he does, he normally emphasizes cash equivalents, which throw off interest and keep volatility down.

Fund Contact Information:

Montgomery Funds
101 California Street
San Francisco, CA 94111
800-572-3863

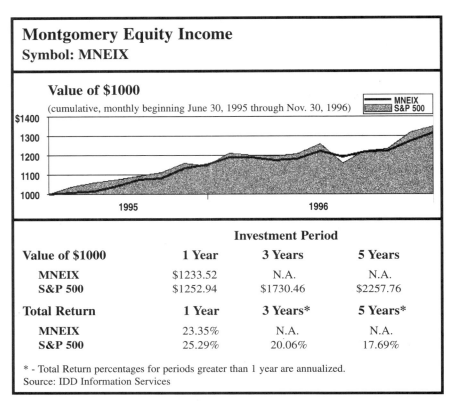

Montgomery Equity Income
Symbol: MNEIX

Value of $1000
(cumulative, monthly beginning June 30, 1995 through Nov. 30, 1996)

— MNEIX
▓ S&P 500

Value of $1000	1 Year	3 Years	5 Years
	Investment Period		
MNEIX	$1233.52	N.A.	N.A.
S&P 500	$1252.94	$1730.46	$2257.76
Total Return	**1 Year**	**3 Years***	**5 Years***
MNEIX	23.35%	N.A.	N.A.
S&P 500	25.29%	20.06%	17.69%

* - Total Return percentages for periods greater than 1 year are annualized.
Source: IDD Information Services

Top 10 Holdings
as of June 30, 1995

Philip Morris	UST
Bristol-Myers Squibb	AMOCO
Anheuser-Busch	Baltimore Gas & Electric
Wachovia	SAFECO
Exxon	JC Penney

Key Statistics

Assets:	$23.3 mil.	Dividend Yield:	2.62%
Expense Ratio:	0.84%	Turnover Ratio:	N/A
12b-1 Fee:	0.00%	Beta:	N/A

GLOBAL STOCK

JANUS WORLDWIDE

Manager: Helen Young Hayes

Janus Worldwide has the flexibility to invest in companies of any size around the globe. While it normally holds securities from at least five different countries, including the United States, it can put all of its money into just one, if manager Helen Young Hayes thinks that's the right thing to do. She can also invest in preferred stocks, warrants, government securities, and corporate debt, and is able to use derivatives as a way to hedge risk or enhance returns.

Hayes joined Janus Capital in 1987. She also manages the group's Overseas Fund. She holds a Bachelor of Arts degree in economics from Yale University and is a Chartered Financial Analyst.

To give you some insight into how she thinks, in mid-1996, she had her portfolio invested 93 percent in equities. Of that, 48.6 percent of the assets rested in European stocks, 20.2 percent in the Pacific Rim, 14.5 percent in Japan, and 14 percent in the United States (excluding short-term securities). The stocks were concentrated in four main industries: pharmaceuticals, information technology, outsourcing, and telecommunications.

The remaining 7 percent was spread among preferred stocks, along with U.S. corporate bonds, government obligations, and time deposits.

This fund can add a substantial amount of diversification to your portfolio. You can also tell from its beta of 0.84 that it has historically been less volatile than the S&P 500, making it appropriate for both aggressive and more conservative investors alike.

Fund Contact Information:

Janus Group
100 Fillmore Street, Suite 300
Denver, CO 80206-4923
800-525-8983

Janus Worldwide
Symbol: JAWWX

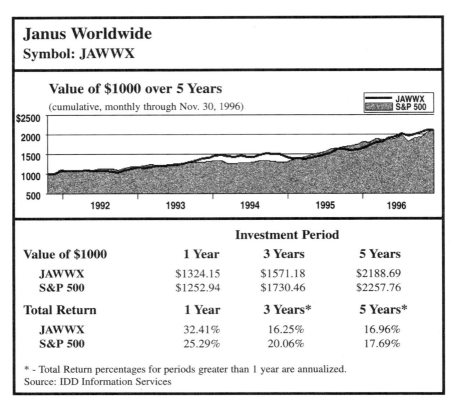

Value of $1000 over 5 Years
(cumulative, monthly through Nov. 30, 1996)

Value of $1000		Investment Period	
	1 Year	3 Years	5 Years
JAWWX	$1324.15	$1571.18	$2188.69
S&P 500	$1252.94	$1730.46	$2257.76
Total Return	**1 Year**	**3 Years***	**5 Years***
JAWWX	32.41%	16.25%	16.96%
S&P 500	25.29%	20.06%	17.69%

* - Total Return percentages for periods greater than 1 year are annualized.
Source: IDD Information Services

Top 10 Holdings
as of September 30, 1996

Rentokil Group	Hays
Securitas CIB Free	Nutricia Verenigde Bedrijren
Getronics	Adidas
Ciba-Geigy	Kinnevik CI B
Wolters Kluwer	Lagardere Groupe

Key Statistics

Assets:	$4.45 bil.	Dividend Yield:	N/A
Expense Ratio:	1.24%	Turnover Ratio:	142%
12b-1 Fee:	0.00%	Beta:	0.84

GLOBAL STOCK

FOUNDERS WORLDWIDE GROWTH

Manager: Michael Gerding

Founders Worldwide Growth uses a company-by-company approach to investing around the world. Instead of making decisions about which countries he wants to be in, manager Michael Gerding searches for equities with solid fundamentals, plus growing revenues and earnings, wherever they might be on the face of the planet, including the United States. (By contrast, strict international funds stick to firms outside of the United States.)

Gerding buys stocks of both emerging and established companies, as long as they have proven performance records and strong market positions. He always keeps at least 65 percent of his assets in three or more countries and won't put more than 25 percent of his portfolio into any single company.

Even with slowing economic growth around the world, Gerding is still finding companies that are flourishing in virtually every country. He attributes.that to his emphasis on company and not country fundamentals. He further notes that many overseas corporations are following the lead of their American counterparts by restructuring and becoming more competitive. Founders Worldwide has profited from this trend in more ways than one. In addition to investing in companies that are cutting back and turning more profitable, the fund owns the shares of several technology outfits that have been major beneficiaries. That's because when corporations reduce their workforce, they often replace it with technology.

Gerding has been with Founders for six years and is in charge of all of the firm's overseas funds.

Fund Contact Information:

Founders Funds
2930 E. Third Avenue
Denver, CO 80206
800-525-2440

Founders Worldwide Growth
Symbol: FWWGX

Value of $1000 over 5 Years
(cumulative, monthly through Nov. 30, 1996)

		Investment Period	
Value of $1000	**1 Year**	**3 Years**	**5 Years**
FWWGX	$1134.98	$1451.38	$1892.56
S&P 500	$1252.94	$1730.46	$2257.76
Total Return	**1 Year**	**3 Years***	**5 Years***
FWWGX	13.50%	13.22%	13.61%
S&P 500	25.29%	20.06%	17.69%

* - Total Return percentages for periods greater than 1 year are annualized.
Source: IDD Information Services

Top 10 Holdings
as of September 30, 1996

Ladbroke Group	Autoliv
Wolters Kluwer	Verenigde Nederland Vitgever
OCE—Van der Grinten	Total CI B
Hoya	HSBC Holdings
Dixons Group	Singapore Airlines

Key Statistics

Assets:	$334.8 mil.	Dividend Yield:	0.38%
Expense Ratio:	1.56%	Turnover Ratio:	54%
12b-1 Fee:	0.25%	Beta:	0.93

INTERNATIONAL EQUITY

ARTISAN INTERNATIONAL

Manager: Mark Yockey

Artisan International is a new fund, but manager Mark Yockey has plenty of experience searching the globe for quality investments. He managed the United International Growth fund from 1990 through 1995, producing an annualized return of 13.7 percent, outpacing the group's average by almost four percentage points.

While he spends some time deciding which specific countries he wants to be in, most of Yockey's effort goes toward picking individual stocks. He looks for well-managed companies with dominant or increasing market positions in strong industries. He will only buy stocks selling for reasonable PE ratios. Financially speaking, he demands a strong balance sheet and accelerating earnings.

Yockey has often been called a contrarian who likes to do the opposite of the crowd. He prefers to find under-researched companies, hoping to take positions in them before they become overly popular. His portfolio has historically had a significant exposure to small-cap issues because of his growth bent and desire to get up-close with management.

Artisan International can be expected to remain broadly diversified in an effort to reduce risk. Individual positions will never exceed 5 percent of the total portfolio and the fund generally holds 80 to 100 different names. Yockey works with one analyst and spends part of his time traveling to meet with companies he currently owns, while searching for promising new ones. This fund offers a great opportunity to tap into the brainpower of an experienced manager with a long-term investment record who has just taken over a new fund that is still small enough to allow him to be very flexible.

Fund Contact Information:

Artisan Funds
1000 N. Water Street, Suite 1770
Milwaukee, WI 53202
800-344-1770

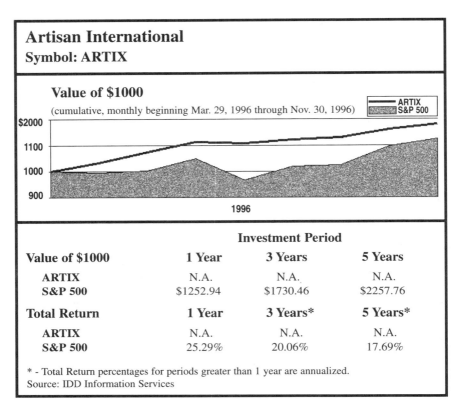

Artisan International
Symbol: ARTIX

Value of $1000
(cumulative, monthly beginning Mar. 29, 1996 through Nov. 30, 1996)

Legend: ARTIX, S&P 500

	Investment Period		
Value of $1000	**1 Year**	**3 Years**	**5 Years**
ARTIX	N.A.	N.A.	N.A.
S&P 500	$1252.94	$1730.46	$2257.76
Total Return	**1 Year**	**3 Years***	**5 Years***
ARTIX	N.A.	N.A.	N.A.
S&P 500	25.29%	20.06%	17.69%

* - Total Return percentages for periods greater than 1 year are annualized.
Source: IDD Information Services

Top 10 Holdings
as of June 30, 1996

Sondagsavisen (Denmark)   TT Tieto (Finland)
Sonae Investments (Portugal)   Argentaria (Spain)
Marseille Kliniken (Germany)   Circle K (Japan)
Autobacs Seven (Japan)   Se-Banken (Sweden)
Xebio (Japan)   Bankard Inc. (Philippines)

Key Statistics

Assets:	$126.1 mil.	Dividend Yield:	N/A
Expense Ratio:	2.10%	Turnover Ratio:	N/A
12b-1 Fee:	0.00%	Beta:	N/A

INTERNATIONAL EQUITY

WARBURG PINCUS INTERNATIONAL

Manager: Richard King

Warburg Pincus International is a more aggressively managed overseas fund that generally spreads a third of its assets equally throughout Europe, Japan, and the Pacific Basin, although it is not tied down to such restrictions. It tries to achieve long-term capital appreciation by investing in a broadly diversified portfolio of stocks in companies located outside of the United States.

It tends to buy larger companies than Artisan International that are financially strong, undervalued, and capable of earnings growth. The fund also keeps a respectable portion of its assets in the fast-growing emerging markets of the world, such as Hong Kong, Israel, Brazil, and Chile. In fact, manager Richard King also runs a very successful emerging markets fund for Warburg Pincus.

King has been International Equity's skipper since inception in 1989. He's the former chief investment officer at Fiduciary Trust Company International S.A. in London, responsible for all international equity management and investment strategy. His present staff at Warburg Pincus includes several equally seasoned analysts.

As with all international investments, the fund's returns will be dependent on currency fluctuations. That's why King believes in hedging his exposure to select currencies as a defensive measure. One main advantage to holding this fund in tandem with Artisan International is that you get exposure to almost every market in the world. For example, Artisan was recently heavily weighted in Europe and had only minor exposure to Japan. The composition of Warburg Pincus International, on the other hand, was almost exactly the opposite.

Fund Contact Information:

Warburg Pincus Funds
466 Lexington Avenue
New York, NY 10017-3147
800-927-2784

Warburg Pincus International*
Symbol: CUIEX

Value of $1000 over 5 Years
(cumulative, monthly through Nov. 30, 1996)

	CUIEX
	S&P 500

	Investment Period		
Value of $1000	**1 Year**	**3 Years**	**5 Years**
CUIEX	$1133.70	$1382.96	$1818.98
S&P 500	$1252.94	$1730.46	$2257.76
Total Return	**1 Year**	**3 Years***	**5 Years***
CUIEX	13.37%	11.41%	12.71%
S&P 500	25.29%	20.06%	17.69%

* - Total Return percentages for periods greater than 1 year are annualized.
Source: IDD Information Services

Top 10 Holdings
as of September 30, 1996

Banco Santander	Citic Pacific
Total Petroleum CI B	TDK
Astra CI B	V.A. Technologies
SGL Carbon	Canon
DDI	JUSCO

Key Statistics

Assets:	$2.89 bil.	Dividend Yield:	2.63%
Expense Ratio:	2.63%	Turnover Ratio:	39.24%
12b-1 Fee:	0.00%	Beta:	0.92

BALANCED

WARBURG PINCUS BALANCED

Managers: Team led by Dale Christensen and Anthony Orphanos

By now you have no doubt figured out that I harbor a lot of respect for Warburg Pincus and its talented fund managers. That's why it's no surprise to see its Balanced Fund on my list of All-Stars. While overall direction of this fund is the responsibility of Dale Christensen, head of the firm's fixed-income investing division, and Tony Orphanos, who formerly guided the Growth & Income Fund, several additional star Warburg Pincus managers contribute their best ideas to the portfolio as well.

Warburg Pincus Balanced spreads its assets among five different investment sectors, namely value stocks, small-company issues, mid-cap equities, international equities, and fixed-income obligations. Christensen and Orphanos are in charge of setting the precise allocations. They then let their top colleagues in each of these areas pick the specific investments. The overall team includes small-cap standouts Elizabeth Dater and Stephen Lurito, mid-cap gurus George Wyper and Susan Black, and international strategist Richard King (who also manages fellow All-Star Warburg Pincus International).

What you get with this fund is a professional team deciding which areas of the market your money should be in, along with access to Warburg Pincus' entire team of skilled portfolio managers, who work together to create value in each sector. Because of its extremely broad view, this is truly one of the only balanced funds available that gives you both domestic and foreign stock exposure in virtually all segments of the market. Although I normally don't recommend team-managed funds, this one is a clear exception. That's because I know precisely who's on the team, and they're all winners.

Fund Contact Information:

Warburg Pincus Funds
466 Lexington Avenue
New York, NY 10017-3147
800-927-2874

Warburg Pincus Balanced
Symbol: WAPBX

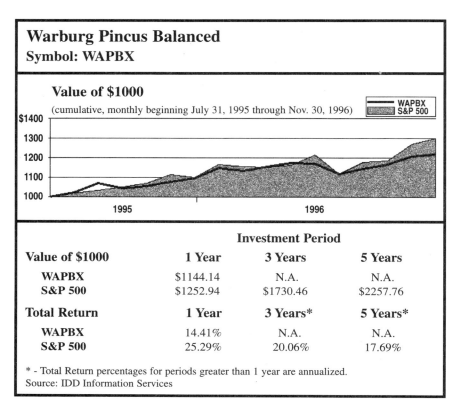

Value of $1000
(cumulative, monthly beginning July 31, 1995 through Nov. 30, 1996)

		Investment Period	
Value of $1000	**1 Year**	**3 Years**	**5 Years**
WAPBX	$1144.14	N.A.	N.A.
S&P 500	$1252.94	$1730.46	$2257.76
Total Return	**1 Year**	**3 Years***	**5 Years***
WAPBX	14.41%	N.A.	N.A.
S&P 500	25.29%	20.06%	17.69%

* - Total Return percentages for periods greater than 1 year are annualized.
Source: IDD Information Services

Top 10 Holdings
as of September 30, 1996

U.S. Treasury Note 8.5%	U.S. Treasury Note 6.5%
GNMA 7%	Texas Meridian Resources
NKK	Transaction SYS Architects A
Smith International	Wells Fargo
Healthcare Realty Trust	Newmont Mining

Key Statistics

Assets:	$32.7 mil.	Dividend Yield:	1.06%
Expense Ratio:	1.53%	Turnover Ratio:	107%
12b-1 Fee:	0.25%	Beta:	0.64

BALANCED

WESTWOOD BALANCED
Manager: Susan Byrne

Susan Byrne is a great asset allocator. While she generally keeps her Westwood Balanced portfolio equally divided between stocks and fixed-income obligations, the weightings change periodically based on the findings of her sophisticated top-down investment process. She begins by doing an analysis of the broad, long-term secular trends in the economy. Next, she makes an assessment as to where we are in the business cycle to develop a capital market outlook and thus identify sectors that should benefit from that environment. Finally, individual securities likely to perform well under this scenario are selected for the portfolio.

The fund seeks both capital appreciation and current income. It pays out a quarterly dividend. Byrne has the flexibility to adjust her allocation between stocks, bonds, and cash as she feels appropriate in light of present economic and business conditions. She will generally have 60 to 70 percent of the portfolio in securities issued by seasoned companies with market capitalizations in excess of $500 million and proven records of above-average historical earnings growth. Smaller companies that offer the potential for impressive capital appreciation may also occasionally find their way inside. The rest of the assets are placed in corporate and government fixed-income securities.

Byrne founded Westwood Management Corporation, the fund's sub-adviser, in 1983. She has since entered into a joint venture with superstar money manager Mario Gabelli to handle the distribution of this and her other four funds. That's why they'll probably answer the phone "Gabelli" when you call for more information.

Fund Contact Information:
Westwood Funds
One Corporate Center
Rye, NY 10580-1434
800-422-3554

Westwood Balanced
Symbol: WEBAX

Value of $1000 over 5 Years
(cumulative, monthly through Nov. 30, 1996)

			Investment Period	
Value of $1000	**1 Year**	**3 Years**	**5 Years**	
WEBAX	$1206.10	$1581.91	$2009.99	
S&P 500	$1252.94	$1730.46	$2257.76	
Total Return	**1 Year**	**3 Years***	**5 Years***	
WEBAX	20.61%	16.52%	14.98%	
S&P 500	25.29%	20.06%	17.69%	

* - Total Return percentages for periods greater than 1 year are annualized.
Source: IDD Information Services

Top 10 Holdings
as of March 31, 1996

U.S. Treasury Note 5%	U.S. Treasury Note 6.25%
U.S. Treasury Note 5.875%	U.S. Treasury Note 5.875%
U.S. Treasury Bill	U.S. Treasury Note 5.625%
U.S. Treasury Note 7.375%	U.S. Treasury Bond 7.625%
U.S. Treasury Note 7.125%	Sterling Software

Key Statistics

Assets:	$25.1 mil.	Dividend Yield:	2.12%
Expense Ratio:	1.35%	Turnover Ratio:	133%
12b-1 Fee:	0.25%	Beta:	0.68

FLEXIBLE PORTFOLIO

CRABBE HUSON ASSET ALLOCATION
Managers: Richard Huson and Team

I like Dick Huson. He's not afraid to do the exact opposite of everyone else on Wall Street. Over time, his contrarian instincts have made those wise enough to entrust their money to him a lot richer. In the short-term, however, things haven't been quite as rosy. Through most of the 1990s, investors have been fixated on playing the earnings momentum game, chasing those companies with rising earnings and share prices that the rest of the herd is in love with. What I respect about Huson is that even though his performance has suffered by not joining the crowd, he hasn't wavered from his entrenched belief that an asset is more attractive when it is falling in price than when it is rising.

He's convinced that the majority of investors are correct most of the time. Otherwise, it wouldn't be possible for both up and down market trends to develop. However, he contends that fear and greed get in the way of sound investment decisions, especially at the top and bottom of market cycles. It is the opportunities that are created by these emotions that Huson and his team seek to capitalize on.

This strategy may not create chart-topping performance, but it does tend to cushion any downward falls. The reason in simple. Many of the securities Huson buys have already been hit, as investors are expecting the worst from them. When the worst materializes, not much happens, since it's no surprise. On the other hand, when good things take place, the issues can substantially rise. With its mix of stocks, bonds, and cash, this fund will position a portion of your portfolio to go against the traditional tide in the marketplace.

Fund Contact Information:

Crabbe Huson Funds
121 S.W. Morrison, Suite 1400
Portland, OR 97204
800-541-2732

Crabbe Huson Asset Allocation
Symbol: CHAAX

Value of $1000
(cumulative, monthly beginning Apr. 30, 1992 through Nov. 30, 1996)

Value of $1000	1 Year	3 Years	5 Years
CHAAX	$1076.74	$1292.02	N.A.
S&P 500	$1252.94	$1730.46	$2257.76

Total Return	1 Year	3 Years*	5 Years*
CHAAX	7.67%	8.92%	N.A.
S&P 500	25.29%	20.06%	17.69%

* - Total Return percentages for periods greater than 1 year are annualized.
Source: IDD Information Services

Top 10 Holdings
as of March 31, 1996

U.S. Treasury Note 5.125%
U.S. Treasury Note 5.625%
USG
Occidental Petroleum
Lousiana Pacific

U.S. Treasury Note 6%
U.S. Treasury Note 6.125%
Burlington Resources
Consolidated Freightways
Equitable

Key Statistics

Assets:	$124.5 mil.	Dividend Yield:	2.26%
Expense Ratio:	1.48%	Turnover Ratio:	256%
12b-1 Fee:	0.25%	Beta:	0.64

FLEXIBLE PORTFOLIO

MONTGOMERY ASSET ALLOCATION

Managers: Roger Honour and Bill Stevens

The managers of Montgomery Asset Allocation can put their money in stocks, bonds, or cash, depending on their outlook for the market. The fund's objective is to produce a high total return while reducing risk by actively making asset allocation changes and keeping a close eye on what's inside the portfolio. It can keep from 20 to 80 percent of total assets in stocks, 20 to 80 percent in debt instruments of any maturity, and 0 to 50 percent in cash equivalents.

This unique fund is managed by Roger Honour and Bill Stevens. Honour is the equity pro and also oversees Montgomery's Growth and Micro Cap funds, while Stevens is the firm's fixed-income expert. Although they are the human minds who pick the actual holdings, they rely on a quantitative risk model and computer optimization program to tell them how exactly to allocate the assets.

Montgomery Asset Allocation is appropriate for those of you wanting to spread your bets over many asset classes, but unwilling to do the work on your own. What makes this different from a balanced or growth and income fund is that the management team can buy any stocks it wants (regardless of whether they pay a dividend) and doesn't have to maintain an equal weighting to "balance" out the portfolio. As a matter of fact, this fund has historically had a stock bias with very little cash, and not just in big blue chip names. There are plenty of small technology firms in the portfolio as well. That's why its returns have rivaled even aggressive growth funds. In addition, the fund doesn't throw off a monthly or quarterly dividend, since all earnings are reinvested. That may make it inappropriate for those seeking monthly income.

Fund Contact Information:

Montgomery Funds
101 California Street
San Francisco, CA 94111
800-572-3863

Montgomery Asset Allocation
Symbol: MNAAX

Value of $1000

(cumulative, monthly beginning Feb. 28, 1995 through Nov. 30, 1996)

MNAAX
S&P 500

1995   1996

Value of $1000	Investment Period		
	1 Year	3 Years	5 Years
MNAAX	$1172.34	N.A.	N.A.
S&P 500	$1252.94	$1730.46	$2257.76
Total Return	**1 Year**	**3 Years***	**5 Years***
MNAAX	17.23%	N.A.	N.A.
S&P 500	25.29%	20.06%	17.69%

* - Total Return percentages for periods greater than 1 year are annualized.
Source: IDD Information Services

Top 10 Holdings
as of June 30, 1996

FHLMC CMO PAC 7%   U.S. Treasury Note 6%
U.S. Treasury Note 6.875%   U.S. Treasury Note 6.875%
Octel Communications   International Paper
Dayton Hudson   Masco
U.S. Treasury Bond 6.25%

Key Statistics

Assets:	$141.3 mil.	Dividend Yield:	1.27%
Expense Ratio:	1.31%	Turnover Ratio:	95.75%
12b-1 Fee:	0.00%	Beta:	N/A

LONG-TERM GENERAL CORPORATE

JANUS FLEXIBLE INCOME
Managers: Ronald Speaker and Sandy Rufenacht

Janus Flexible Income's mission is to produce the maximum possible total return, while also seeking to preserve capital. It does this primarily by investing in income-producing securities, such as corporate bonds and notes, government securities, preferred stocks, income-producing common stocks, and debt securities. As you'll notice, managers Ronald Speaker and Sandy Rufenacht can buy stocks, but this is primarily a bond fund. In the latest annual report, only 2 percent was in common stock, with 37 percent in investment-grade corporates and 45 percent in high-yield/high-risk bonds. The fund's weighted average maturity was 9.2 years, which is shorter than its norm. By charter, however, it can purchase securities of any maturity and quality. (That's why it's called *Flexible Income*.)

Speaker and Rufenacht are also allowed to invest as much as they want in foreign securities and high-yielding "junk" bonds. In turn, it is riskier than your average long-term bond fund, but also more interesting. This element helps to add a little punch to overall returns, while bringing up the yield. In return, the exposure to interest rate risk is amplified.

Several studies have shown that you achieve the best risk/reward ratio in bonds when you stick with maturities of 10 to 15 years. That's why I generally recommend intermediate-term funds. Janus Flexible Income fits that bill, although Speaker and Rufenacht are free to adjust their portfolio's average maturity and credit rating quality to whatever figure they feel offers the most upside potential, given the present outlook for such variables as the direction of interest rates and the economy.

Fund Contact Information:

Janus Group
100 Fillmore Street, Suite 300
Denver, CO 80206-4923
800-525-8983

Janus Flexible Income
Symbol: JAFIX

Value of $1000 over 5 Years
(cumulative, monthly through Nov. 30, 1996)

Value of $1000	Investment Period		
	1 Year	**3 Years**	**5 Years**
JAFIX	$1087.44	$1252.66	$1651.55
S&P 500	$1252.94	$1730.46	$2257.76
Total Return	**1 Year**	**3 Years***	**5 Years***
JAFIX	8.74%	7.80%	10.56%
S&P 500	25.29%	20.06%	17.69%

* - Total Return percentages for periods greater than 1 year are annualized.
Source: IDD Information Services

Top 10 Holdings
as of September 30, 1996

U.S. Treasury Note 7%
Chase Manhattan 6.75%
Courtyard/Marriott 144A 10.75%
Delphi Financial Group 8%
Wireless One 13%

Ford Motor Credit 7.75%
Time Warner 8.11%
Levcadia National 10.375%
First Nationwide 144A 10.625%
Selmer 11%

Key Statistics

Assets:	$600.4 mil.	Dividend Yield:	N/A
Expense Ratio:	0.96%	Turnover Ratio:	250%
12b-1 Fee:	0.00%	Beta:	0.97

HIGH-QUALITY CORPORATE

STRONG CORPORATE BOND

Managers: Jeffrey Koch and John Bender

If you need to create a high level of current income and are willing to accept a moderate amount of share-price fluctuation, you should consider the Strong Corporate Bond Fund. It is geared toward long-term investors who want higher returns than short-term securities provide, as well as the added level of volatility inherent with this pursuit.

While there are no stated restrictions, most of the securities in the portfolio have maturities ranging from 7 to 12 years. Under normal market conditions, at least 65 percent of the fund's total assets will be invested in corporate bonds, with the rest in various types of fixed-income securities, including U.S. government and mortgage-backed issues.

Fund managers Jeffrey Koch and John Bender buy mostly high- or medium-quality instruments, namely those rated BBB or better by S&P. They sometimes put as much as a quarter of the portfolio in high-yielding, and therefore higher-risk, issues like those rated C or better.

Koch and Bender believe credit research and issue selection are paramount to their continued success. They do their homework, using intense analysis to find bonds that are either ignored, dismissed, or under-appreciated by other investors.

This fund will fluctuate less than Janus Flexible Income or Strong High Yield, but more than Montgomery Short Government Bond. That puts it near the middle of the risk spectrum. It's a good fund for long-term investors who want some bond representation without being overly exposed to fluctuations in interest rates, which eat away at your principal as they rise.

Fund Contact Information:

Strong Funds
PO Box 2936
Milwaukee, WI 53201-2936
800-368-1030

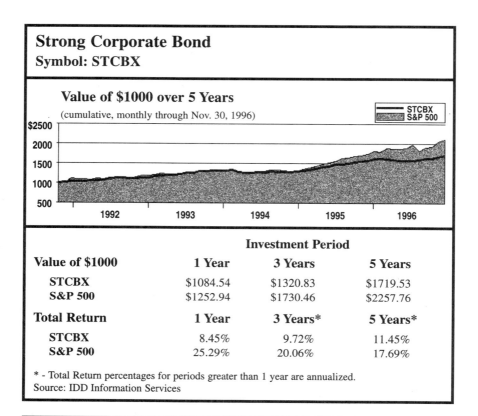

Strong Corporate Bond
Symbol: STCBX

Value of $1000 over 5 Years
(cumulative, monthly through Nov. 30, 1996)

	Investment Period		
Value of $1000	**1 Year**	**3 Years**	**5 Years**
STCBX	$1084.54	$1320.83	$1719.53
S&P 500	$1252.94	$1730.46	$2257.76
Total Return	**1 Year**	**3 Years***	**5 Years***
STCBX	8.45%	9.72%	11.45%
S&P 500	25.29%	20.06%	17.69%

* - Total Return percentages for periods greater than 1 year are annualized.
Source: IDD Information Services

Top 10 Holdings
as of March 31, 1996

Parker & Parsley Petro. 8.25%
Freeport-McMoRan Res. 7%
USAir 144A 8.93%
Viacom 6.75%
360 Communications 7.125%

U.S. Treasury Bond 6.875%
Principal Mutual Insurance 144A 8%
Lehman Brothers Holdings 8.8%
Coastal 10.75%
ARA Services 10.625%

Key Statistics

Assets:	$297.6 mil.	Dividend Yield:	7.33%
Expense Ratio:	1.00%	Turnover Ratio:	603%
12b-1 Fee:	0.00%	Beta:	1.21

HIGH YIELD CORPORATE

STRONG HIGH YIELD BOND

Manager: Jeffrey Koch

I realize that some of you need to receive a monthly check from your investments and are looking for funds with high yields to produce this income. That's why I've added the Strong High Yield Bond-Fund to my list of All-Stars. This is a relatively new offering without much of a track record. However, it is run by Jeffrey Koch, who has done an outstanding job with other fixed-income funds at Strong. As I mentioned earlier, I choose my funds based in large part on the people running them. I have a lot of respect for Koch (even though I'm not a big fan of bond funds) and selected this fund because of his great past performance.

Don't forget, though, that higher yields come with a greater degree of risk. While this fund will give you an impressive level of current income and the potential for growth, it does that through buying medium- and lower-quality debt obligations with an average maturity of 5 to 10 years. Medium-quality obligations are those rated BBB or comparable by S&P, which, although considered investment grade, have speculative character-istics. Lower-quality obligations, also referred to as "junk" bonds, are those rated as low as C by S&P. Furthermore, the fund is allowed to invest a small portion in debt obligations that are in default. As an added feature, the fund can have up to 20 percent of its entire portfolio invested in com-mon stocks and warrants.

High-yield bonds tend to be affected more by the economy than inter-est rates. Therefore, this is not a fund to buy if you think we're headed for a recession, since companies with lower-rated securities are usually the first to go out of business.

Fund Contact Information:

Strong Funds
PO Box 2936
Milwaukee, WI 53201-2936
800-368-1030

Strong High Yield Bond
Symbol: STHYX

Value of $1000

(cumulative, monthly beginning Mar. 29, 1996 through Nov. 30, 1996)

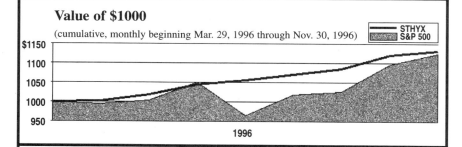

1996

Value of $1000	Investment Period		
	1 Year	3 Years	5 Years
STHYX	N.A.	N.A.	N.A.
S&P 500	$1252.94	$1730.46	$2257.76
Total Return	**1 Year**	**3 Years***	**5 Years***
STHYX	N.A.	N.A.	N.A.
S&P 500	25.29%	20.06%	17.69%

* - Total Return percentages for periods greater than 1 year are annualized.
Source: IDD Information Services

Top 10 Holdings
as of April 30, 1996

Cantor Fitzgerald & Co. 5.34%   Stratosphere Corporation 14.25%
Clark Oil & Refining 11%   Triton Energy Corporation 0%
Owens-Illinois 11%   KCS Energy 11%
Showboat Marina Casino 13.5%   First Nationwide 12.5%
Doane Products 10.625%   Benton Oil & Gas 11.625%

Key Statistics

Assets:	$217 mil.	Dividend Yield:	10.25%
Expense Ratio:	0.63%	Turnover Ratio:	N/A
12b-1 Fee:	0.00%	Beta:	N/A

SHORT/INTERMEDIATE-TERM GOVERNMENT BOND

MONTGOMERY SHORT GOVERNMENT BOND

Manager: Bill Stevens

If you're looking to preserve your capital, while earning a little more than you could from a money market fund, you might want to consider Montgomery Short Government Bond, which is an All-Star performer in the short-term bond category. Just keep in mind that, unlike money market funds that try to maintain a steady $1 net asset value, your share price will fluctuate. If interest rates go up, the value of your investment will fall, and vice versa. In return, you are usually offered a higher yield than you could expect from a money market fund, but not by much.

This particular fund invests primarily in U.S. Treasury bills, notes, bonds, and other obligations that are issued and/or guaranteed by the U.S. Government. To manage that inherent interest rate risk, manager Bill Stevens maintains an average portfolio effective duration (how sensitive the portfolio should be to changes in interest rates) similar to that of three-year U.S. Treasury notes. His objective is to achieve the maximum possible total return, while preserving principal. Total return includes the interest and dividends paid from the underlying securities, plus capital appreciation.

This fund allows you to earn higher yields than a money market fund with less fluctuation in share price than you would find in a longer term bond investment. It also gives you exposure to the bond market, allowing you to participate when bonds go up, though you'll suffer like everyone else when they fall. The point is, the impact won't be that dramatic in either direction because of the short-term nature of the fund's investments. Still, if you seek absolute protection of your principal, you're better off in a money market fund.

Fund Contact Information:

Montgomery Funds
101 California Street
San Francisco, CA 94111
800-572-3863

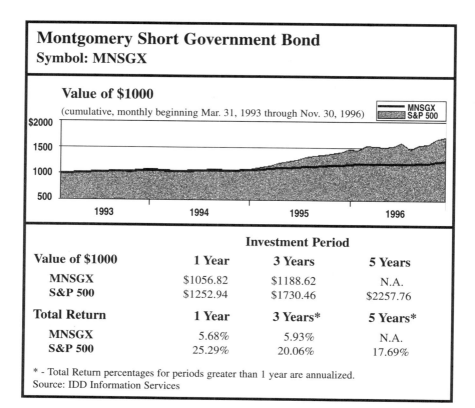

Montgomery Short Government Bond
Symbol: MNSGX

Value of $1000

(cumulative, monthly beginning Mar. 31, 1993 through Nov. 30, 1996)

MNSGX / S&P 500

Value of $1000	Investment Period		
	1 Year	**3 Years**	**5 Years**
MNSGX	$1056.82	$1188.62	N.A.
S&P 500	$1252.94	$1730.46	$2257.76
Total Return	**1 Year**	**3 Years***	**5 Years***
MNSGX	5.68%	5.93%	N.A.
S&P 500	25.29%	20.06%	17.69%

* - Total Return percentages for periods greater than 1 year are annualized.
Source: IDD Information Services

Top 10 Holdings
as of September 30, 1996

U.S. Treasury Note 6.125%
FNMA Debenture FRN
FHLMC 5.5%
FHLMC CMO PAC 5.25%
FHLMC 8%

Federal Home Loan Bank FRN
FNMA TBA 7%
U.S. Treasury Note 6.875%
FNMA CMO PAC 4.5%
FHLMC CMO PAC 5%

Key Statistics

Assets:	$36.4 mil.	Dividend Yield:	5.87%
Expense Ratio:	0.47%	Turnover Ratio:	284.23%
12b-1 Fee:	0.00%	Beta:	0.40

MORTGAGE-BACKED GOVERNMENT BOND

LEXINGTON GNMA INCOME

Manager: Denis Jamison

For high relative income and safety, you should consider investing with "Ginnie Mae." No, she's not some wise financial guru. Rather Ginnie Mae refers to the acronym GNMA, which stands for Government National Mortgage Association. GNMA is a U.S. Government corporation within the U.S. Department of Housing and Urban Development. It issues what are known as GNMA certificates. These mortgage-backed securities represent part ownership in a pool of mortgage loans. Such loans are initially made by lenders like banks and savings and loans, and are backed by Uncle Sam.

GNMAs are lumped together and sold to investors through securities dealers. In essence, you're buying a batch of loans. Once approved by GNMA, the timely payment of interest and principal on these loans is guaranteed by the full faith and credit of the U.S. Government.

Historically, GNMA certificates have offered higher yields than other Treasury obligations. However, if mortgagors pay off their loans early, the principal returned to shareholders may be reinvested at more or less favorable rates. When rates fall, borrowers are more likely to refinance, driving the yields on GNMAs down. GNMAs also differ from bonds in that the principal is scheduled to be paid back over the entire length of the loan rather than in one lump sum at maturity.

Lexington GNMA Income has consistently been a standout performer in its category. Manager Denis Jamison, who has been at the helm since 1981, usually keeps 80 percent of his portfolio in GNMAs and the rest in other government obligations. This is a nice addition to the bond portion of your portfolio.

Fund Contact Information:

Lexington Group
PO Box 1515/Park 80 West Plaza Two
Saddle Brook, NJ 07663
800-526-0056

Lexington GNMA Income
Symbol: LEXNX

Value of $1000 over 5 Years

(cumulative, monthly through Nov. 30, 1996)

Legend
LEXNX
S&P 500

	Investment Period		
Value of $1000	**1 Year**	**3 Years**	**5 Years**
LEXNX	$1067.98	$1210.52	$1404.95
S&P 500	$1252.94	$1730.46	$2257.76
Total Return	**1 Year**	**3 Years***	**5 Years***
LEXNX	6.80%	6.58%	7.04%
S&P 500	25.29%	20.06%	17.69%

* - Total Return percentages for periods greater than 1 year are annualized.
Source: IDD Information Services

Top 10 Holdings
as of June 30, 1996

GNMA 8.15%	GNMA Project Loan 9.25%
GNMA 8.25%	GNMA Project Loan 8.625%
GNMA Project Loan 8.2%	U.S. Treasury Bond 6.25%
GNMA Project Loan 9.75%	GNMA Project Loan 8%
GNMA Project Loan 7.65%	GNMA Project Loan 9.75%

Key Statistics

Assets:	$127.2 mil.	Dividend Yield:	7.01%
Expense Ratio:	1.01%	Turnover Ratio:	31%
12b-1 Fee:	0.00%	Beta:	0.68

INTERNATIONAL/GLOBAL BOND

WARBURG PINCUS GLOBAL FIXED INCOME

Managers: Dale Christensen and Laxmi Bhandari

First of all, let me say that while this fund is an All-Star for its category, I don't recommend it unless your portfolio is almost entirely composed of bonds. That's because, despite its juicy yield, you get much more bang for your buck at about the same level of risk by investing overseas through stock funds.

The Warburg Pincus Global Fixed Income fund tries to achieve a maximum rate of return through a combination of interest income, currency gains, and capital appreciation. This is done through purchasing a wide range of investment-grade, income-producing securities of governmental and corporate issuers around the world, denominated in various currencies. Its charter calls for always being in at least three different countries and, except for the United States, it can't have more than 40 percent of total assets in any one place.

To protect against currency fluctuations, the fund's managers sometimes hedge the portfolio by using instruments such as options or futures. This either helps or hampers returns, depending on whether their bets are placed in the right direction.

The securities in this portfolio will usually have maturities ranging from three to ten years. Managers Dale Christensen and Laxmi Bhandari look for investments that offer the greatest value based on their expectations for a given country's economy, movements in the general level of interest rates, political developments, and variations in the supply of capital available for investment in the world bond market. While the fund tends to stick with high-quality issues, Christensen and Bhandari are allowed to keep up to 35 percent of all assets in lower-grade securities.

Fund Contact Information:

Warburg Pincus Funds
466 Lexington Avenue
New York, NY 10017-3147
800-927-2874

Warburg Pincus Global Fixed Income
Symbol: CGFIX

Value of $1000 over 5 Years
(cumulative, monthly through Nov. 30, 1996))

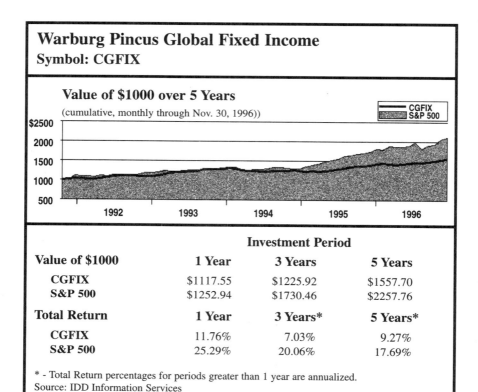

Value of $1000	Investment Period		
	1 Year	3 Years	5 Years
CGFIX	$1117.55	$1225.92	$1557.70
S&P 500	$1252.94	$1730.46	$2257.76
Total Return	**1 Year**	**3 Years***	**5 Years***
CGFIX	11.76%	7.03%	9.27%
S&P 500	25.29%	20.06%	17.69%

* - Total Return percentages for periods greater than 1 year are annualized.
Source: IDD Information Services

Top 10 Holdings
as of September 30, 1996

Kingdom of Denmark 8%   U.S. Treasury Note 9%
Treuhandanstalt 7.5%   Republic of Germany 6.5%
Lloyds TSB Group 8.5%   Govt. of Netherlands 6%
Republic of Ireland 9.75%   Landesbank Rheinland Finance 7.25%
Govt. of Canada 6.5%   Landesbank Schleswig-Hol 6.5%

Key Statistics

Assets:	$131.5 mil.	Dividend Yield:	10.30%
Expense Ratio:	0.95%	Turnover Ratio:	128.70%
12b-1 Fee:	0.00%	Beta:	0.68

LONG-TERM MUNICIPALS

JANUS FEDERAL TAX EXEMPT

Manager: Darrell Watters

If you're not in a high federal income tax bracket, don't even bother reading this profile. The yields on municipal investments are often less than 85 percent of what you would find on comparable taxable securities. Therefore, if Uncle Sam isn't stealing the maximum amount from your pocket each April, municipals won't make sense for you. I recommend them only for high wage earners in need of monthly income that is protected from federal (and sometimes state) taxation.

Janus Federal Tax Exempt concentrates its investments in municipal obligations of any length of maturity as long as they pay interest exempt from federal income taxes. Capital appreciation is not an important consideration. The portion of interest earned from obligations purchased in your home state may be exempt from taxes on your state return as well. However, and this is an important point, any capital gain you realize upon selling your shares is fully taxable. Once again, the earned interest is tax-free, yet any gains are treated the same way as they are in any other mutual fund.

One cloud hanging over the municipal bond market is the possibility of a flat tax, which would make all investment interest and dividends tax-free. Each time this issue comes up, it cripples the municipal market, since such a law would destroy the attractiveness of these bonds and force issuers to pay higher interest rates. This is a minor concern, but it's something you should be aware of before plunging into this or any other municipal fund. Janus Federal Tax Exempt's recent weighted average maturity was 15.8 years. Although manager Darrell Watters is a relative newcomer, he's off to an impressive start and has made this among the top offerings in the category.

Fund Contact Information:

Janus Group
100 Fillmore Street, Suite 300
Denver, CO 80206-4923
800-525-8983

Janus Federal Tax Exempt
Symbol: JATEX

Value of $1000 over 5 Years
(cumulative, monthly beginning June 30, 1993 through Nov. 30, 1996))

Value of $1000	Investment Period		
	1 Year	3 Years	5 Years
JATEX	$1058.11	$1141.15	N.A.
S&P 500	$1252.94	$1730.46	$2257.76
Total Return	**1 Year**	**3 Years***	**5 Years***
JATEX	5.81%	4.50%	N.A.
S&P 500	25.29%	20.06%	17.69%

* - Total Return percentages for periods greater than 1 year are annualized.
Source: IDD Information Services

Top 10 Holdings
as of June 30, 1996

CO Denver Airport SYS 5.5%
FL Jacksonville Elec St. John Rvr
MT Brd Invest Payroll Tax
OK Grand River Dam 6.25%
NM Gallup Poll Cntrl Plains Elec.

OH Tpk Comm 5.5%
CO San Miguel GO Mtn Vlg
CO GO Meridian Metro Dist. 7.5%
IL Metro Pier/Expo McCormick Pl
IL Chicago Motor Fuel Tax 6.125%

Key Statistics

Assets:	$44.5 mil.	Dividend Yield:	N/A
Expense Ratio:	0.65%	Turnover Ratio:	164%
12b-1 Fee:	0.00%	Beta:	1.02

5

BUILDING YOUR WINNING PORTFOLIO

By now, you not only know that no-load, NTF funds are the way to go, you also have a great shopping list of the best funds available through America's leading discount brokers. In this chapter, we'll put all of the information you've learned thus far together to help you construct a market-beating portfolio, depending on your goals and objectives.

Your first step, of course, is to open an account with your favorite discount broker. I have given you enough information to make a wise decision as to which firm offers the greatest number services and features to meet your specific needs. Needless to say, if you haven't already ordered a new application kit from each broker you are interested in, do so right now. Then, once you've decided who to go with, either send in a check for your opening deposit if you're just starting out, or make arrangements to transfer your account holdings over from your full-service broker or the funds directly. (For more on this and the tax implications, see Chapter 3.)

Take Stock of Your Assets

Once your account is open, and even before, you need to begin the process of determining your desired asset allocation. In other words, you must figure out which basic asset classes you want your investment money in, be it stocks, bonds, cash, or even precious metals. (While I'm not a fan of precious metals to begin with, if you're determined to buy them, I highly recommend that you do so through a mutual fund as opposed to purchasing the metal itself. Your chances of appreciation are greater, and it makes your investment much more liquid.) Furthermore, keep in mind that investment money is the amount above and beyond what you need to live on. Before you put any money into mutual funds, you should consider setting aside three to six months of living expenses in a money market fund or similar cash-equivalent vehicle to give you a cushion against unexpected events, such as a job loss or medical emergency.

Stocks for the Long Run

While age in itself isn't the end-all consideration for determining your asset allocation structure, it does play a role. If you are under 40 with several decades to grow your money before retirement, you will likely want to be aggressive with your investments, putting most, if not all, of it in the stock market. As you get older, you'll want to reduce your risk somewhat, since you won't have as much time to make up any short-term losses, especially if you'll need this money to live off of in the near future.

Stocks have historically always provided the highest rates of return of any asset class. During the 20-year period from 1965 to 1995, U.S. Treasury Bills produced an average annualized return of 6.94 percent, compared to 8.17 percent for long-term government bonds and 10.56 percent for the S&P 500. Both stocks and bonds did considerably better from 1985 to 1995, a period in which the S&P returned an average of 18.76 percent per year, compared to a return of 12.09 percent for bonds. In many respects, these high returns are an aberration, given that they were earned during one of the greatest bull markets in history.

Clearly, if the past is any indication of the future, the stock market is where you're going to build the most wealth over time. That's why, even if you're older, you should still consider keeping a substantial portion of your portfolio in equities. If you don't believe me, listen to my friend Philip Carret. He is 100 years old. Carret started one of the first mutual funds in the nation and lived through the crash of 1929. Warren Buffet claims he has "the best long-term investment record of anyone in America." Carret tells me that, even at his mature age, he keeps 75 percent of his portfolio in stocks, since he knows that's the only place it's going to significantly grow.

Whether you're investing in a regular or retirement account, asset allocation is still the driving factor in figuring out which funds to buy.

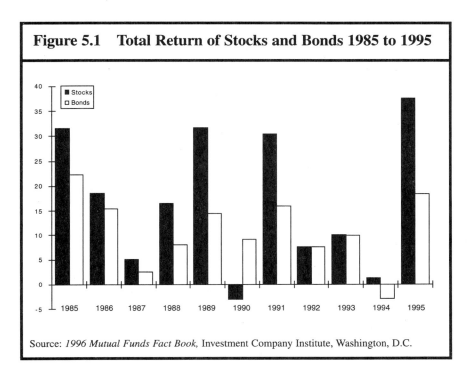

Figure 5.1   Total Return of Stocks and Bonds 1985 to 1995

Source: *1996 Mutual Funds Fact Book,* Investment Company Institute, Washington, D.C.

Some brokerage firms have asset allocation "personality tests" to determine the proper mix for you. They ask a lot of questions such as:

- How much income do you expect to earn in the coming years?
- When do you plan to start withdrawing your money?
- How are you likely to respond if your investments suffer a loss in value?
- How much of a deductible do you carry on your car insurance?

They then take these answers and run them through a computer model, which spits out a recommended allocation based on your responses. Sure, it's an interesting exercise, but I'm not certain this is the most effective way to make such an important decision about your financial future.

Instead, I suggest that you sit down with yourself and realistically figure out the following: What are your objectives (e.g., long-term growth, income), and how much volatility can you truly stomach? Does the thought of losing 5, 10, 20, or even 50 percent of your portfolio make you lose sleep at night? If so, you might be better off staying away from the stock market.

A Perfect Plan for Retirement

Equities are especially appropriate for those of you with 401(k) plans at work. That's because these tax-deferred accounts enable you to take advantage of the power of dollar-cost-averaging. Simply put, this is the practice of investing an equal amount of money on a regular basis, regardless of where the market is at. This allows you to take advantage of fluctuations in price and can reduce your average per share cost, since you'll buy more shares when the market is down, fewer when it is up, lowering overall volatility in the process. If your employer offers a 401(k) plan at work, you're lucky. If you've signed up for it and are contributing the maximum possible amount you can afford, congratulations. If not, do so immediately. If your company doesn't offer a 401(k) plan, pressure management to start one. Many of the discount brokers will allow employers to set up a low-cost 401(k) program, enabling workers to invest their money through the many NTF funds found in this book. It's the best of all worlds! If you're a small business owner, ask the discount brokers for information on starting a 401(k) plan. If you only have a few or no employees, you're better off looking into an SEP-IRA or Keogh account. With a small minimum balance, the brokers will set these accounts up for you and your employees with no annual fees whatsoever. (It goes without saying that you should also establish a regular IRA account and contribute the maximum $2,000 a year, if you can afford it, whether it's deductible or not. That's because any distributions earned in IRAs are tax-deferred until retirement. You can then make adjustments to your portfolio without worrying about any short-term capital gains implications.)

Kirk Kazanjian's All-Star Model Portfolios

I have set up four model portfolios for you to consider, along with the specific funds I would select and what percentage of the total pie they would comprise in the overall scheme of things for various situations and goals. Below each portfolio is a brief description of how it is structured and what type of investor it is most appropriate for.

Change with the Times

Before I give you the specific funds and breakdowns for each model portfolio, I want you to know that these are my recommended funds and weightings as of the time I am writing this book. I am continually reevaluating my portfolio allocations in light of what's going on with the economy and overall market. In other words, even though I believe that those following the Aggressive Wealth Builder portfolio should remain 100 percent invested in the stock market at most times, I might put more of this money into value funds if I was convinced those types of issues were going to outperform in the immediate future. Should I feel the market was about to get hit hard, it's possible I would even suggest a portion of the money be put into cash. (This is something that is very rare for me. I don't believe in short-term market timing—it's a fool's game. However, if my indicators show a sustained bear market is developing, I would recommend increasing the amount of cash with the intention of buying back into the market at lower levels in the future.) The point is, even though I always stay true to the portfolio's overall objective, the exact funds I recommend at any given point in time are always subject to change, since I am constantly looking to be in areas that are going to make me the most money.

In addition, my list of All-Star funds is continually being revised. As established managers take on new funds, I bring more names on board. Conversely, when current All-Stars lose their manager or get too big for their britches, they are subject to being taken off the list and replaced by better options.

The point is this: the following portfolios are full of great funds that I'm confident will make you wealthy over time. However, my choices are always subject to change, and I recommend that you keep up with what's happening with these and all of the other funds. The best way to do this is by subscribing to my monthly newsletter, *Fund Connection*. Each month, I will update these model portfolios, bring you exclusive one-on-one interviews with top fund managers, tell you about promising new funds before the general public ever hears about them, and let you know what's happening with the market. (For subscription information, please see the special offer at the back of this book.) Even if you choose to go it alone, I highly recommend that you stay up-to-date on what's happening with your funds. If one of your current managers leaves, find out why, and learn who is taking over. If you don't like the replacement, consider switching into another alternative. Remember, buy *managers* not funds.

It's Quality, Not Quantity That Counts

You'll notice that not all of my 30 All-Star funds are represented in these portfolios. The reason is you don't need to own 30 different funds to have a diversified portfolio. Besides, many of the funds within their respective categories own the exact same stocks. Therefore, the names in these portfolios are somewhat interchangeable, depending on your preferences. Here's what I mean: The Long-Term Steady Performer portfolio recommends a 20 percent weighting in Strong Growth. That fund is one of the aggressive growth All-Stars that seeks fast-growing stocks with rapidly growing earnings. If you are more intrigued by the Bonnel Growth Fund, which is another All-Star in the category that follows the same strategy, you can certainly use that fund instead. It achieves the exact same purpose, which is exposing 10 percent of your portfolio to aggressive growth stocks. On the other hand, in the Long-Term, Steady Performer portfolio, I deliberately chose the Warburg Pincus Small Company Value fund, since it is the most conservative fund in the small company growth category, and I'm seeking to reduce risk here. So if you do change around, make sure you're dealing with apples and apples, in terms of the fund's overall investment style.

One thing is for sure: once you determine your proper asset allocation and which model portfolio is right for you, stick with your investment plan and contribute to it regularly. Patience and time are two virtues that make investors rich. In the short run, the markets may not be kind to you. But over time, they will reward you with the power of compounding.

Aggressive Growth Wealth Builder

This portfolio is invested 100 percent in the stock markets of the world and is heavily weighted in small-capitalization, fast-growing issues. It is the most volatile of the four portfolios and, therefore, will likely go up higher in good markets and down further in bad ones. This portfolio is appropriate for anyone under 40, who has plenty of time to let their money grow and isn't afraid of short-term fluctuations in the value of their investments.

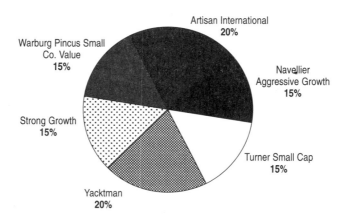

Long-Term, Steady Performer

This globally diversified portfolio is also designed for long-term growth, though it gets there with a less-volatile mix of stock funds and 20 percent in bonds. It is perfect for people of all ages, especially those under 50, who want to see their capital grow, but are willing to sacrifice some potential gains in return for greater capital protection.

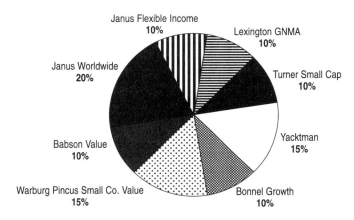

Preretirement, Conservative Grower

If you're just a few years from retirement or a younger investor in search of moderate growth without a lot of risk, this portfolio is for you. It holds a mix of 60 percent stocks and 40 percent bonds. The stocks are internationally diversified, and emphasize value and quality, along with the potential for capital appreciation. The intermediate-term bond funds generate steady income, while moderating price fluctuations.

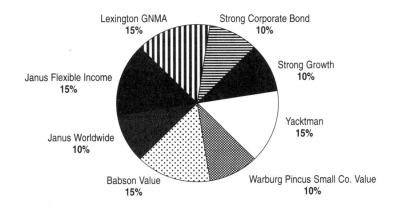

Stock-Free Income Producer

Let me preface this by once again saying that I believe every investor, regardless of age, should have some exposure to the stock market. However, I know not everyone can handle the volatility, and others need to generate income from their investments. Therefore, if you are in your retirement years, don't need to grow your capital, and only want to receive income, this all-bond portfolio is for you. It contains a broad mix of both high- and lower-quality issues of various maturities, including some foreign obligations, to provide regular interest without taking a lot of market risk.

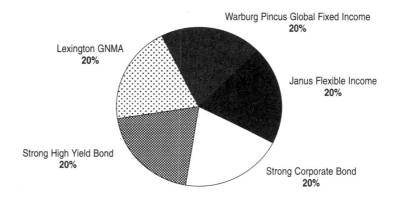

6

THE 50 MOST FREQUENTLY ASKED QUESTIONS
about Mutual Fund Investing

By now you should be an expert on the subject of mutual fund investing, especially as it relates to the various no-load, NTF programs. But just to make sure, on the following pages you will find answers to 50 of the most commonly asked questions about funds. Although we've covered these topics in the preceding pages, this section will bring all of the most important concepts together.

1. Does it ever make sense to buy mutual funds that charge a sales load?

In my opinion, the answer is no. There are just too many good no-load funds out there that you can purchase through the leading discount brokers without paying a penny in commissions. Remember, a sales load usually comes right off the top and reduces the amount of your investment. It does nothing more than go into the pocket of the person who sells you the fund. Despite what some salespeople might tell you, the ongoing expense ratio for load funds is not less than what is charged by their no-load counterparts. In terms of performance, most studies show there is little overall difference in the returns generated by load and no-load funds, though there is an obvious advantage to no-loads, given that you are able to invest more money right from the start.

2. How important of a factor should a fund's annual expense ratio be when deciding whether or not to buy a fund?

The expense ratio is a number found in the prospectus that you should always pay attention to. In terms of bond and money market funds, you generally want to stick with those offering the lowest fees. That's because your overall return is bound to be small to begin with, so there's no use weighing yourself down further with hefty expenses. You will find that bond and money market funds with the lowest expense ratios are almost always the top performers, since everyone is basically buying the same securities. However, when it comes to stock funds, that's an entirely different story. In this case, you are never wise to make a decision on whether or not to invest solely on the basis of a fund's expense ratio. Instead, it's best to focus on the real bottom line: *performance*. The difference in return achieved by equity funds can be dramatic. If one stock fund has a 1 percent annual expense ratio and has posted gains of 12 percent annually over the past five years, while another has a 2.5 percent fee structure but has generated an 18 percent return over that same period, the higher priced fund is obviously a better buy. Of course, you want to see stock fund expense ratios as low as possible, since these costs directly impact your returns. Therefore, if your fund asks you to vote on whether or not to increase management fees, you are advised to always vote a resounding "no." Nevertheless, in terms of stock funds, it makes more sense to concentrate more on overall performance than expenses.

3. How long should you hold on to a poor-performing fund before moving on?

First of all, you need to look at how a fund is performing compared to the overall market and its peers. For example, if you have a stock fund that has declined 10 percent over the past two years, while the overall market and its peers have dropped 20 percent, your fund is technically a standout performer and is doing well. On the other hand, if your fund is down 10 percent while the market is up 20 percent, it's clearly a dog. This is my general rule: If a fund you like spearheaded by a manager you believe in underperforms badly for one year, it should be put under close scrutiny. If it continues to underperform for another six months, it should be sold. There are simply too many good funds available for you to hold on to any losers.

4. What are the major advantages to buying mutual funds through a discount broker?

There are so many, it's hard to know where to begin. In addition to eliminating tons of paperwork, you are able to consolidate all of your holdings on one statement. Furthermore, when your account is held at a discount broker, you can buy and sell funds when you want with a simple phone call, exchange between fund families with ease, and even monitor all of your holdings on your computer. When tax time rolls around, your broker will give you one form 1099-DIV, along with a year-end activity statement, so filling out your 1040 will be a breeze. The amazing thing is that all of these features are available absolutely free. The truth is, it's hard to come up with any reason why you wouldn't want to buy your funds through a discount broker.

5. Well, what are the major disadvantages to buying through a broker?

There are only three that immediately come to mind. First, when your fund shares are held by a broker, you must call the broker whenever you have questions about your account. When you do, you need to remember the person you are talking with probably doesn't know much about your particular fund because they represent so many different offerings. (Of course, you can still call the fund directly with any technical questions, such as what its top holdings are and any new developments.) Also, some fund families, most notably Neuberger & Berman, offer separate classes of their funds through the supermarkets that charge slightly higher expense ratios to cover the cost of participating in these programs. In my opinion, this is ridiculous, and the discount brokers should refuse to accept such funds. Nevertheless, given the convenience the supermarkets offer, it is still better to buy from the brokers than through the funds direct. The final downfall is that when you own your funds through a broker, the fund families often don't even know your name. Instead, your account is set up under the broker's name. The broker then keeps track of how many shares you own. Therefore, you won't receive some of the promotional mailings from the fund announcing such things as new funds in the works and portfolio manager profiles. However, you will still receive annual reports, updated prospectuses, and proxies, though they will come from the broker (or a third-party administrator) instead of the fund.

6.   When it comes to choosing mutual funds, is it best to simply go out and pick last year's top performers?

Absolutely not. That's the worst thing you can do. Hot performers often cool off considerably in the following year. Not only do they hold stocks that have greatly appreciated and are likely ripe for profit-taking, but since the general public traditionally follows performance, they also grow bloated rather quickly, and that almost always hampers future returns. This isn't to say you should never buy a top-performing fund. Just don't buy it solely for that reason. Rather, you should base your decision to buy a fund on its long-term track record and/or the quality of the manager. To further support this notion, *Worth* magazine conducted a survey in its March 1996 issue and found that if you had bought the top ten no-load diversified stock funds over the previous ten years, held them for a full 12 months, and then repeated the whole process, your returns would have been less than you would have earned by simply sticking with a fund that mirrored the S&P 500 Index.

7.   I'm a young investor with a long time horizon. Is it OK to put all of my money into aggressive growth mutual funds?

If you're willing to accept a great deal of volatility, on both the up and down side, it's perfectly all right to keep the majority of your money in aggressive growth funds. In fact, even older investors should have representation in this area. Aggressive growth funds typically hold the stocks of smaller, emerging companies, and therefore offer the greatest potential for rapid appreciation.

8.   How many funds do you need to own to have a diversified portfolio?

Technically, you could own one fund and still have a highly diversified portfolio, since mutual funds by definition are diversified investments. But the real answer is five to eight funds should be sufficient, regardless of how much money you have to invest. Once you've determined how to allocate your assets and which areas of the market you want representation in, you can go out and find the best funds for the job.

9.   Should I buy gold sector funds as an inflation hedge?

This is a personal decision. Some people feel like they must own a little gold to sleep well at night. I, on the other hand, would rather buy a diversified mutual fund and let the manager decide whether or not to own any gold stocks in the portfolio. Gold has been an abysmal performer in recent years, and given the low inflation environment we now live in, I don't expect that to change anytime soon.

10. What about sector funds in general? Should I own any in my portfolio?

Again, if you happen to fall in love with a certain sector, like health care or technology, I have no problem with putting a small portion (5 to 10 percent) of your money in a sector fund. But I generally avoid sector funds altogether. It's hard to consistently be in the right sector at the right time. That's why diversification is so important. Also, many sector funds charge sales loads and are run by relatively inexperienced managers. Fidelity, for example, gives its analysts their first shot at portfolio management by putting them in charge of a sector fund. Those are two more reasons I think you are better off sticking with a broadly based fund instead of placing all your bets in one area.

11. Do you recommend dollar-cost-averaging and, if so, how does it work?

Yes. Dollar-cost-averaging refers to the practice of contributing money to your favorite mutual funds each month on a regular basis over the course of your life. It allows you to use the market's volatility to your advantage. When the market is down, you will purchase more shares. When it is higher, you'll buy fewer shares. Over time, this technique will allow you to build a substantial portfolio, while benefiting from the power of compounding.

12. I'm ready to retire and will need a monthly income check to live on. However, I would like to keep most of my money in growth stock mutual funds, which don't pay any dividends. What can I do?

You are wise to want to keep most of your money in the stock market. After all, that is where people have consistently earned the most money over time. Here's how you can stay in growth stocks and still get a monthly check: Have your discount broker set up what's called a *systematic withdrawal program*. You specify exactly how much you need to live on, and your broker will redeem enough shares each month to produce this amount of income. It's really dollar-cost-averaging in reverse. You can either receive a regular check or have the funds deposited into your brokerage cash account. Not only will you continue to enjoy the compounded growth of your stock holdings, you will also come out ahead with Uncle Sam because you'll be paying out capital gains taxes over an extended period of time instead of all at once.

13. Does investing in a diversified stock fund eliminate all market risk?

Of course not. When you buy a stock fund, you are effectively purchasing the market, or at least a segment of it. The stock market is inherently risky. It moves up and down each day. When the market falls, so will the value of your fund. When the market rises, your fund will, too. The degree to which it goes up or down depends on the stocks your fund owns. Just keep in mind that the market has always had an upward bias, so market risk will usually work in your favor, assuming you're in for the long haul and consistently stick with your investment program.

14. What is the best measure of a fund's overall performance?

Total return. This is a measure that encompasses all aspects affecting a fund's performance, including dividends, capital gains distributions, and changes in NAV over a given period of time. Simply looking at a fund's yield gives you a very distorted view of how well it has performed. Also, you should always compare a fund's return to its peers and benchmark index. Just because your fund tumbles in a given period doesn't necessarily mean your manager is doing a bad job. It could be that everyone is having a hard time because of the choppy market environment.

15. Can a mutual fund ever go bankrupt?

Technically, the answer is no. However, the mutual fund company itself can. But even in such an extreme case as this, your overall investment would still be protected, since the fund is a completely separate entity. A mutual fund is comprised of a wide assortment of securities. The only way you would ever be impacted by a bankruptcy is if a company in your portfolio filed for Chapter 11 and/or went out of business. In this case, the value of that holding would drop to zero. Nevertheless, since each fund owns so many different stocks, such an event would essentially be meaningless.

16. What are 12b-1 fees?

12b-1 fees are so named for a SEC rule that enabled funds to assess a fee (usually around 0.25 percent of assets) to help pay for marketing and distribution costs. Not all funds charge this fee, which can reduce share-holder returns over time.

17. How is a fund's net asset value (NAV) determined?

At the close of each business day, the fund adds up the value of every security in the portfolio (including stocks, bonds, and cash), subtracts any fees and other liabilities, and divides that figure by the number of out-standing shares. The result is the NAV.

18. What's the difference between a money market fund and a mutual fund?

A money market fund is a mutual fund that invests in ultrashort-term income-producing securities. One reason people get this concept confused is that, unlike other types of mutual funds, money markets seek to maintain a stable $1 per share price and pay monthly dividends, like bank savings accounts. (While there are no assurances, the safety record of money market funds is excellent.) The net asset value of stock and bond funds, on the other hand, fluctuates daily and distributions are generally paid either quarterly or annually.

19. How important is it when a mutual fund splits?

It's really a nonevent. Though such a move allows you to buy more shares and may make the fund seem to be a more attractive value, the truth is it does nothing to affect the overall return and usually serves to confuse current shareholders more than anything else. The net impact is that if you own 100 shares of a fund selling for $20 per share prior to the split, you'll own 200 shares at $10 immediately after.

20. If no-load funds are sold without any commissions, how do the fund families make any money?

The exact same way load fund families do: by charging an annual management fee, known as the expense ratio. This is generally less than 1 percent for bond funds and under 2 percent for stock funds. The average expense ratio for load and no-load funds is virtually the same, despite what some stockbrokers might tell you. The *load* you pay is a commission that essentially goes into the pocket of the person who sells you the fund. It doesn't go to the fund company or contribute in any way to operating expenses.

21. I'm convinced that it makes much more sense to open an account with a discount broker rather than dealing with the fund families direct. But how do I figure out which discount broker is best for me?

First off, read through Chapter 3 so you can see which features are offered by each of the brokers. Then, figure out which one provides all of the services you're after. For example, if you're looking for a broker with branch offices around the country and 24-hour customer service, you'll want to go with either Schwab or Fidelity. If you prefer to do most of your trading online without ever talking to a broker, you might want to check out Accutrade. If you want a cash management account that lets you withdraw cash from an ATM without a transaction fee, stick with Waterhouse Securities. Or, if you prefer to deal with a broker that allows you to sell funds short, Jack White is your man. Without doubt, all of the major brokers have a lot to offer. You really can't go wrong with any of them. What's more, there's no law preventing you from doing business with more than one. That's what I do. I have my IRA at one broker and my regular account with another. I suggest you write down all of the services and benefits most important to you and match those up with the appropriate broker. (It might also be helpful to map out a list of the funds you own and/or plan to buy. That way you can check to see which broker offers the funds on your list.)

22. My broker just asked whether I wanted to reinvest my dividends or have the proceeds deposited in my cash account. What should I do?

Unless you need the income to live on, I recommend that you always reinvest your dividends to take advantage of the power of compounding, which can be amazing over time. Money compounding at 10 percent doubles every seven years, triples in about 12 years, and quadruples in less than 15 years. You'll only delay the process by cashing in your dividends. Just keep in mind that you'll have to pay taxes on any dividends, regardless of whether you reinvest them or not.

23. What's the difference between an open-end and a closed-end fund?

All no-load, NTF funds are open-ended. This simply means they can issue an unlimited number of shares as demand dictates and are available for direct purchase either through the fund or a participating discount broker.

Open-end funds are priced each day at their actual NAV. Closed-end funds, on the other hand, issue a fixed number of shares and are traded on one of the major stock exchanges. As a result, you must pay a commission to buy shares through a broker. The value of such funds is determined by supply and demand, and they may sell at or below NAV.

24. What are the tax consequences for owning mutual funds?

If your fund shares are in an IRA account, there are no tax consequences, at least until you retire and start making withdrawals. Otherwise, unless you own a municipal bond fund, you will be responsible for paying taxes on any dividends and capital gains reported by your fund. By law, funds must distribute 90 percent of all taxable income to shareholders at the end of each year. Dividends and short-term capital gains are taxed as ordinary income, while long-term capital gains are currently capped at 28 percent. You will also have to pay taxes for any gain in the value of your fund shares since the time of purchase. If the shares were held more than one year, it's considered a long-term gain. Otherwise, you'll have to report such an increase as ordinary income. If your fund shares are worth less when you sell out, you can claim a capital loss, which will offset any other gains you might have. Your discount broker will keep track of all losses and gains for you and send you a year-end tax statement to make filling out your form 1040 a breeze.

25. I've got a great idea. I own a fund that's currently trading at a loss. Can I sell it and buy it back the next day, thus deducting the loss from this year's taxes?

Great idea, but your Uncle Sam outfoxed you on this one by establishing the "wash sale" rule. This states that you can only write off losses if you wait at least 30 days before buying back the same security. There is one way around this: Let's say the fund showing a loss invests in aggressive growth stocks. You can sell the fund and buy a similar but different one right away. That will pass the test.

26. How can I most effectively evaluate a fund's long-term performance record?

There's an old saying that past performance is no guarantee of future results. I agree. However, the past is the only indication we have of what the future might hold in the world of mutual funds. Therefore, I believe that what a fund manager has done in the past is a good predictor of what he or she will do going forward. That's why past performance figures should be one of the factors used in determining which funds to add to your portfolio. While I like to see what a fund has done in the previous one, three, and five years, I think the one- and three-year numbers are most relevant. Also, make sure these returns were earned by the same manager who is currently in place. Otherwise, they are meaningless. Once the numbers have been crunched, I always like to stick with funds that are consistently in the top 20 percent of their peer group. Once they fall behind for any extended period of time (18 months or longer), I move on to a more attractive candidate. (While one- and three-year numbers are about the best for you to work with, I monitor performance daily for all of the funds in my monthly newsletter *Fund Connection*, which enables me to keep closer tabs on not only existing funds, but also any promising new-comers being run by seasoned professionals. This helps me to spot diamonds in the rough before the rest of the world finds out about them. It also lets me see which managers are making the most money right now.)

27. How much money does it take to get started in a mutual fund?

The figure varies from broker to broker, and fund to fund. Fidelity Brokerage's minimum initial investment is $2,500, regardless of what the individual fund says. Schwab, Waterhouse, Siebert, and Accutrade have their minimums set in tandem with the funds, which is usually from $1,000 to $2,000, even less for IRAs.

28. Are stock and bond mutual funds purchased from my local bank insured by the FDIC?

Absolutely not. In an effort to stem the flow of money from low-paying CDs, banks have gone into the mutual fund business in recent years, with dismal results overall. Bank funds, most of which carry front- and/or back-end sales loads, are some of the nation's worst performers. Even though banks were never allowed to tell customers their funds were FDIC insured, many clueless investors assumed they were. After being lured to stock and high-yielding bond funds, thinking they had nothing to lose, you can imagine what happened when these folks saw their share prices start to fall. A flurry of complaints forced the SEC to crack down and require that fund salespeople have their offices off of the bank's main floor, to give the appearance that they are a separate entity. Also, you'll find that bank fund brochures now feature a prominent logo with a slash line through the letters FDIC. Unfortunately, many people who buy their funds through banks are first-time stock and bond investors who think their fund is somehow safer since it comes from a bank. Don't believe it! When your bank calls to sell you today's hot fund, say "no thanks," since you are smart enough to buy your mutual funds for free.

29. What are the main risks involved with mutual fund investing?

In terms of stock funds, my feeling is the biggest risk is not investing at all, since equities have consistently outperformed all other investments over time. Aside from that, you obviously endure the inherent risk of the market, which constantly fluctuates, so your original investment may be worth more or less when it is redeemed. You should not invest in stock funds unless you are willing to live with this risk. In terms of bond funds, the biggest threat to your overall returns is interest rates. When rates rise, the value of your shares will fall. When rates fall, your fund's price will go up.

30. What's the difference between yield and total return?

Yield refers to the amount paid out in the form of dividends and is expressed as a percentage of the fund's total NAV. Simply put, if you have a fund selling for $10 that pays a $1 annual dividend, its yield is 10 percent. This says nothing about how well the fund has performed overall. That information comes from looking at its total return. This is a measure, taken over a given period of time, that encompasses all aspects affecting return, including dividends, capital gains distributions, and other changes in NAV. If you're simply looking for a monthly income check, the yield is an important number to you. Otherwise, it is virtually meaningless. Instead, you should focus on a fund's total return, since it is a clearer picture of how well the manager is doing.

31. Is it easy to get my hands on money held in a mutual fund?

If your fund shares are held with a discount broker, the answer is a resounding "yes." With a simple phone call, or by punching a few keys on your computer, you can access cash or make an exchange from one fund to another in a matter of seconds. You are able to redeem shares in a no-load mutual fund on demand, making them one of the most liquid investments in the country today.

32. Does it make sense to invest in brand new mutual funds that don't have any kind of long-term performance record?

Sometimes. In my newsletter, *Fund Connection,* I keep close tabs on all of the new funds coming to market. A brand new offering from an experienced manager can be an explosive performer. That's because it's usually easier to make money with a small portfolio. Also, fund families often give their best ideas to their newest offerings. The key is to get in on the ground floor. There are dozens of new funds opening up each month. The sad truth is, most of them aren't worth a dime. I spend a lot of time evaluating each one and only recommend those I believe hold the most promise.

33. Several of the discount brokers charge a commission for selling NTF funds held less than three months. How can they get away with this?

Even though the funds are technically available transaction-free, some brokers, including Schwab and Jack White, do charge a commission for selling shares held less than 90 days. This is really designed to prevent rampant short-term trading, which can be a big problem since these programs make it so easy to trade in and out. It costs the broker money each time you place a trade, and this short-term trading penalty is a way of keeping expenses to a minimum. I don't recommend short-term trading. However, if you think you'll be jumping in and out a lot, you can always go with Muriel Siebert, Waterhouse, or Fidelity, all of which have much more liberal short-term trading policies.

34. What's the best source to monitor fund performance?

The easiest way, of course, is to subscribe to *Fund Connection,* since I monitor the top funds offered by all of the no-load, NTF supermarkets every month. Aside from that, daily prices are reported in all major newspapers, and both *Barron's* and *The Wall Street Journal* publish special sections on funds each quarter.

35. What is a prospectus and should I read it?

A prospectus is the document provided by a fund that describes its investment objectives, services, fees, and past performance history. It also tells you about the portfolio manager's background and experience. Yes, you should read through the prospectus to make sure you thoroughly understand what you're getting into. Granted, prospectuses are written by lawyers and can be confusing. To help out, turn back to Chapter 1, where you'll find several examples to help you decipher some of this financial jargon.

36. How about the annual report? Is it important to look over?

Absolutely. An annual report not only provides you with the fund manager's perspective as to where the fund has been and where it may be going, but also outlines the exact holdings contained in the portfolio. In addition to learning which companies you own stock in (assuming we're talking about an equity fund), you can make sure the fund is buying the kind of securities it's supposed to. In other words, if you're in a small-cap fund and see the top holdings are McDonald's and Coca-Cola, you'll know the fund isn't sticking to its charter and may want to move on.

37. I ordered a prospectus and annual report, but both were almost eight months old. Why do the funds distribute such outdated material?

Unfortunately, the SEC only requires funds to publish and distribute prospectuses and annual reports once a year. Yes, they are outdated by the time they reach you, but the numbers in the prospectus should still be valid. As for the portfolio holdings in the annual report, that's another question entirely. They may have dramatically changed, but you'll still get a good feel for what kind of companies your manager is buying. One thing you can do to get the latest information is ask the fund to also send you the "Statement of Additional Information," which is a supplement to the prospectus and contains more complete and updated details about the fund.

38. Is there ever a point when mutual funds become too large to be attractive?

In terms of bond, money market, and large company growth stock funds, the answer is not really. The truth is, bigger funds tend to have lower expense ratios, since they can spread operating costs over a wider asset base (although greed prevents some fund companies from passing on these savings). They can also afford to hire the most sought after managers in the industry. However, all other things being equal, when dealing with micro- and small-cap stock funds, the tinier the better. That's because smaller funds can more easily navigate through these relatively illiquid markets. They can also hold fewer names, which usually helps to bolster overall returns. As a result, these funds tend to be top performers early on, before they attract a lot of money. When small-cap funds get too big, they are forced to seek out new ideas in the large-cap arena, since they have so much money to put to work. Having said this, I want to make it clear that just because a small-cap fund is big doesn't mean it can't continue to post impressive returns. There are many tiny funds (in terms of assets) that are real losers. So don't go out and buy a fund based solely on the amount of assets it contains. Nevertheless, if you're in a leading small-cap fund that suddenly gets bloated in size, this may be a good reason to put it under careful review for possible sale should returns begin to suffer.

39. What are the main advantages to mutual fund investing?

There are four: low cost, professional management, ease of investing, and diversification. For a small fee, far less than what you would pay in stock commissions alone, you can hire some of Wall Street's leading minds to pick investments on your behalf. Plus, when you open an account with your favorite discount broker, you can place trades with ease and avoid paying any transaction costs. Most importantly, even with a small amount of money, mutual funds enable you to buy a highly diversified basket of stocks, an essential ingredient to achieving strong returns in the market.

40. Since roughly 80 percent of all fund managers have historically underperformed the market averages, should I just buy an index fund?

This is certainly an option. I often recommend index funds for investors who say, "I want to participate in the stock market, but don't want to follow my investments. Instead, I prefer to buy and hold forever." In that case, index funds make sense because you are assured of always doing what the market does, not better or worse. However, as a professional money manager, my goal is to beat the market, and I believe it can be done. That's why I prefer actively managed funds over those that simply track an index. If you are willing to do even a small amount of homework and keep up with which fund managers have their eye on the ball, I believe that over time you will make more money in actively managed funds as opposed to putting your money into an index. That doesn't mean index funds can't be part of an overall portfolio. I just think there are so many brilliant managers out there, you're hurting yourself by not allowing them to work for you.

41. You recommend that part of the equity portion of my portfolio be placed in international funds. Does overseas investing entail greater risk than sticking with funds that concentrate on companies in the United States?

Sure, but it also provides an added element of diversification. International investing comes with the risk of political uncertainty, currency fluctuations, and differences in financial reporting standards. But much of the world's major growth these days comes from outside the United States, making the potential rewards worth this added volatility. In addition, foreign markets don't always move in tandem with the United States, meaning they may go up when the United States goes down, and vice versa. As a result, international holdings provide an extra cushion in your portfolio. Many overseas markets are also more reasonably priced than the United States right now, making them a bargain hunter's delight.

42. Is it possible to lose money in a U.S. Treasury bond fund?

Yes, especially in long-term funds. That's because as interest rates rise, the NAV of your shares will fall. While Treasury bonds purchased directly from the government are guaranteed if held to maturity, this is not true of bond funds, which fluctuate daily.

43. The All-Star listings in this book include each fund's **beta factor. What does beta stand for, and how should I use this information in evaluating funds?**

Beta is a measure of a fund's volatility relative to the overall market. The S&P 500 Index has a beta of 1. A fund with a beta below 1 is less volatile than the S&P, while one with a beta above 1 is bound to jump around even more. The higher the beta, the more risk the fund takes in its pursuit of profits. This means you can expect swings on both the upside and downside to be more dramatic than the market as a whole. This information is helpful in determining which funds are right for you, in that if you are seeking a more conservative fund and can't handle a lot of volatility, you'll want to stick with low beta funds. On the other hand, if you are trying to achieve maximum gains, have a long time horizon, and don't mind seeing your investment value fluctuate significantly, you might want to concentrate on those funds sporting higher betas.

44. In reading through various prospectuses, I found one fund that claims to be diversified and another that's nondiversified. What's that all about?

Most mutual funds are established as "diversified" investment companies. That means that the fund can keep no more than 5 percent of its assets in any one stock. Conversely, a *nondiversified* fund portfolio can invest up to 25 percent in any one stock. Neither type of fund is allowed to own more than 10 percent of the total outstanding shares of any single company. As you might imagine, nondiversified funds tend to be more risky, since their assets are more concentrated. However, the potential for price appreciation is greater, assuming the manager picks the right stocks.

45. Can I set up a no-load, NTF IRA, Keogh, or 401(k) plan for my business through one of the discount brokers?

Not only is this possible, I highly recommend it. All of the brokers allow you to establish an IRA, SEP-IRA, or Keogh account, but only Schwab, Fidelity, and Jack White are equipped for 401(k)s. The annual fees for these accounts is low and usually zero, as long as you meet certain minimum balance requirements.

46. I just retired from my job and have a large 401(k) account I would like to transfer over to my discount broker and manage through no-load mutual funds. Can this be done while still protecting my tax-deferred status?

Sure, as long as you roll it into an IRA account. Just set up an IRA with your favorite discount broker and arrange to have the proceeds transferred from your current 401(k) plan into the new account. You can then put together a portfolio of no-load, NTF funds, while preserving your favorable tax status.

47. I've decided to include some bonds in my portfolio and want to know whether it makes sense to include municipal funds in that mix.

The answer depends on your tax bracket and whether you think Congress is going to pass a flat tax. If you're not in a very high tax bracket, municipals are rarely a wise choice, since the interest they pay is almost always considerably less than taxable bonds. In terms of the flat tax, if such a law were to include a provision for not taxing interest and dividends, which has been proposed in the past, municipal bonds would no longer be attractive investments and that could significantly drive down their prices. Please also remember that while interest earned from municipal bonds is free of federal (and sometimes state) taxes, any capital gains are fully taxable, just as they are for the rest of your mutual funds.

48. I'm thinking of opening my no-load, NTF account at a discount broker without any branch offices. This means I will have to conduct all of my transactions over the phone. Is this a good idea, or am I asking for trouble?

Some of the best discount brokers have made a conscious decision not to open branch offices around the country. That's an expensive proposition and, while convenient, adds to the overall bureaucracy of the firm, which some chief executives abhor. In my opinion, the fact that a broker doesn't have any branch offices is completely irrelevant, as long as that's not something you desire. In other words, if you prefer to conduct your business face-to-face, by all means go with a broker who has an office near you. Otherwise, sign up with the one that offers more of the features you are looking for, regardless of how many offices they have. (Personally, I have always conducted all of my business with discount brokers over the phone and through the mail, even though I am a client of a firm that has branch offices around the country. Quite frankly, it's a hassle for me to go to the branch in person when I can do everything right from the convenience of my own desk.)

49. Should the commissions charged for stock trades be a part of my decision in choosing a broker?

Not unless you plan to trade stocks. If you follow my advice and buy no-load, NTF funds, you won't have to worry about commissions of any kind. If, on the other hand, you plan to complement your fund portfolio with individual stocks, you should go with the broker offering the lowest trading commissions, based on the type of activity you expect to conduct.

50. What's the best way to stay on top of the funds in my portfolio and how often should I check them?

You can follow the daily price changes in your funds by reading through the daily mutual fund tables found in most major newspapers. More thorough publications, such as *The Wall Street Journal* and *Investor's Business Daily*, will even list total return figures for select time periods. In terms of no-load, NTF funds, you should also consider subscribing to my monthly newsletter *Fund Connection*. Not only do I monitor the performance of my most highly recommended mutual funds, I have four model portfolios for various investment objectives and will keep you up-to-date on my outlook for the market, which funds you should buy or sell, and which new funds are most likely to pump up your investment profits.

7

A COMPLETE DIRECTORY

of 500 No-Load, No-Transaction-Fee Funds

Now that you know how the no-load, NTF programs work and what services the various discount brokers offer, it's time to take a look at the entire universe of funds that are available. While more than 800 funds participate in at least one of the programs, I have elected to include only those that are available through at least two of the major brokers in the following directory. Even with that restriction, you will still be able to chose from among some 500 of the nation's leading funds in 30 different categories. (Once again, I want to point out that just because a fund is listed in this directory doesn't mean it's any good. The performance charts are structured to help you pick the jewels from the duds. I'll tell you more about that in just a moment.)

Why All Funds Are Not Available at All Brokers

There are many different reasons why all funds are not offered through every NTF program. For one thing, each brokerage firm has its own list of restrictions for accepting a fund. Some require a long operating history or minimum asset basis, while others simply make you ask to get in. Furthermore, not all funds want to be in these programs. The Vanguard Group claims its expense ratios are too low to participate. Conversely, Fidelity Investments has made a concerted effort to control distribution of its in-house funds by making them available only through its brokerage arm. (Incidentally, because Fidelity doesn't belong to any of the other NTF programs, its funds are not listed in this directory. That's really nothing to be concerned with, since Fidelity funds have been real laggards in recent years and rarely qualify for any of my buy lists. Among other things, Fidelity constantly plays musical chairs with its managers, and I like to know who is controlling my money. They also switch managers from one investment style to another. That doesn't mean you should stay away from Fidelity's FundsNetwork. It's a great program. Just concentrate on filling your portfolio with non-Fidelity funds.)

Understanding the Charts

The following directory is categorized by investment objective, with the available funds listed in alphabetical order. For each listing, you will find the name of the fund and who manages it, along with its date of inception, ticker symbol, operating expense ratio (including any 12b-1 fees), portfolio turnover rate, and current dividend yield. You will also find the fund's average annual returns over the past one-, three-, five-, and ten-years, as tracked by Lipper Analytical Services. (All performance figures are as of September 30, 1996, unless otherwise noted).

Remember, past performance is no guarantee of future results, but it is our only indication of what kind of numbers a given manager has produced in previous years.

After the performance results, you will discover which brokers offer each fund in their respective NTF programs. The symbols are as follows: A=Accutrade, F=Fidelity Brokerage, J=Jack White & Company, M=Muriel Siebert, S=Charles Schwab, and W=Waterhouse Securities.

I want to extend my special appreciation to the folks at Lipper Analytical Services for providing all of the data contained in these charts. They went out of their way to meet my requests and deadlines, for which I am extremely grateful. Lipper is a true leader in providing mutual fund performance data, and I am pleased to include their numbers on these pages.

Fund Categories and What They Mean

The funds in this book are listed by 30 different categories, which are defined as follows:

- **Aggressive Growth**—Aggressive growth funds seek maximum capital appreciation by investing in smaller companies, trading frequently, leveraging, purchasing unregistered securities, and buying options. These funds are highly volatility, but offer the highest potential returns.

- **Growth**—Growth funds normally invest in companies with proven track records and a history of long-term earnings that are expected to grow faster than the overall market.
- **Small Company**—Small company funds generally limit their investments to companies with market capitalizations falling below $1 billion. Smaller companies are often unproven and risky, though they can also be quite rewarding.
- **Growth and Income**—Growth and income funds look for both earnings growth, capital appreciation potential, and income by investing in both stocks and bonds. These funds are most appropriate for conservative investors in need of monthly income.
- **Equity Income**—Equity income funds seek high current income and growth by investing heavily in quality dividend paying stocks. They are different from growth and income funds in that they rarely hold bonds.
- **Index**—Index funds attempt to track the performance of a stated benchmark market index, like the S&P 500. By definition, these funds will never produce a return greater than the index, but rather should be expected to underperform it by the same percentage as its underlying expense ratio.
- **Global Stock**—Global stock funds invest in securities traded both in the United States and in international markets around the world. In a global fund, you're letting the manager decide where on the planet to invest your money.
- **International Equity**—International funds, by contrast, concentrate investments in companies whose main operations are in developed markets *outside* of the United States, including Western Europe, Japan, Australia, New Zealand, and Canada.
- **Emerging Markets**—Emerging markets funds, arguably the most volatile of all, seek growth by investing in equities of companies in developing nations outside of the United States, Canada, Japan, Australia, New Zealand, and Western Europe.
- **Country Specific**—Country specific funds concentrate investments in equities headquartered and/or traded in markets of a specific region or single country within a foreign region.

- **Balanced**—Balanced funds try to conserve principal while providing for growth by maintaining a balanced portfolio of both stocks and bonds.

- **Flexible Portfolio**—Flexible portfolio funds allow the manager to allocate investments across various asset classes at will, including domestic and foreign common stocks, bonds, and money market instruments, while focusing on total return.

- **Precious Metals/Gold**—Precious metals and gold funds invest a majority of all assets in the shares of gold mining companies, gold coins, bullion, or gold-oriented mining finance houses.

- **Sector**—Sector funds invest exclusively in the stocks of a specific industry, such as technology, health care, or financial services.

- **Short/Intermediate-Term General Corporates**—Short- and intermediate-term general corporate bond funds place assets in investment-grade corporate debt issues with dollar-weighted average maturities of ten years or less (five years or less for those with a short-term objective.)

- **Long-Term General Corporates**—Long-term general corporate bond funds keep the majority of assets in corporate and debt issues with maturities that can exceed ten years and generally do not have any quality restrictions.

- **High-Quality Corporates**—High-quality corporate bond funds invest at least 65 percent of total assets in investment-grade corporate and government debt issues.

- **High-Yield Corporates**—High-yield corporate bond funds invest for high current yields without regard to quality or maturity restrictions. In turn, these funds often hold lower grade debt issues.

- **Short/Intermediate-Term Government**—Short- and intermediate-term government bond funds invest a majority of assets in securities issued or guaranteed by the U.S. Government with dollar-weighted average maturities of less than five years (ten years for intermediate funds).

- **Long-Term General Government**—Long-term general government bond funds invest a majority of assets in securities issued by the U.S. Government of varying maturities, often extending out ten years or more.

- **Mortgage-Backed Government**—Mortgage-backed government funds invest in the assets of mortgage securities issued or guaranteed by the U.S. Government and certain federal agencies.
- **Short/Intermediate-Term U.S. Treasuries**—Short- and intermediate-term U.S. Treasury funds invest primarily in U.S. Treasury bills, notes and bonds with dollar weighted average maturities of five years or less (ten years or less for intermediate term funds).
- **Long-Term U.S. Treasuries**—Long-term U.S. Treasury funds invest in U.S. Treasury bills, notes and bonds, often with maturities extending out ten years or more.
- **International/Global Bond**—International and global bond funds invest in both U.S. and non-U.S. denominated debt instruments of various maturities and duration.
- **Short/Intermediate-Term Municipals**—Short- and intermediate-term municipal bond funds invest in the assets of top-rated municipal debt instruments with dollar-weighted average maturities of five years or less (ten years or less for intermediate term funds.)
- **Long-Term Municipals**—Long-term municipal bond funds invest in the assets of high quality municipal debt issues or various maturities that can exceed ten years or more.
- **High-Yield Municipals**—High-yield municipal bond funds focus on achieving a high current yield by investing at least half of all assets in lower-rated municipal debt issues.
- **California Municipals**—California municipal bond funds invest in securities of various maturities that are exempt from California state taxes.
- **New York Municipals**—New York municipal bond funds invest in securities of various maturities that are exempt from New York state taxes.
- **Other State Municipals**—Other state municipal bond funds invest in securities that are exempt from taxes in a specified state (double tax-exempt) or city and state (triple tax-exempt).

The Directory

Now that we have taken care of the formalities, you can begin perusing the directory of funds to see whether your current favorites are a part of any NTF program, while uncovering new names to add to your portfolio.

AGGRESSIVE GROWTH

Fund Name/ Start Date/ Manager	Symbol	Expense Ratio %	Portfolio Turnover %	Dividend Yield %	1-Year Annual Return	3-Year Annual Return	5-Year Annual Return	10-Year Annual Return	Broker Availability
American Heritage (1958) Heiko Theime	AHERX	6.25	606	N/A	−11.94	−22.49	−2.83	−2.38	FJM
	Objective: Seeks maximum capital growth through investing in equities, short-term trading, hedging, and leveraging.								
Bull & Bear Sp. Equities (1986) Brett Sneed	BBSEX	2.88	319	N/A	2.84	6.56	14.71	10.96	AFJMW
	Objective: Invests aggressively for maximum capital appreciation.								
Founders Special (1978) Charles Hooper	FRSPX	1.35	263	N/A	8.31	12.22	14.18	15.70	AFMSW
	Objective: Seeks capital appreciation by investing primarily in medium-sized U.S. and foreign companies.								
Invesco Dynamics (1967) T. Miller	FIDYX	1.14	196	N/A	21.68	16.42	18.98	17.01	AJSW
	Objective: Seeks capital appreciation through aggressively investing in common stocks of rapidly growing companies.								
Janus Enterprise (1992) James Goff	JAENX	1.26	194	N/A	21.95	19.19	N/A	N/A	FMS
	Objective: Seeks long-term growth of capital by emphasizing common stocks of companies with market capitalizations between $1 billion and $5 billion.								
Janus Mercury (1993) Warren Lammert	JAMRX	1.14	201	N/A	17.60	24.08	N/A	N/A	FMS
	Objective: Seeks long-term capital growth by investing in common stocks of all market capitalizations.								
Janus Olympus (1993) Scott Schoelzel	JAOLX	N/A	N/A	N/A	N/A	N/A	N/A	N/A	FMS
	Objective: Invests in issuers of all sizes, with an emphasis on small-capitalization issues poised for strong capital appreciation.								
Janus Twenty (1985) Thomas Marsico	JAVLX	1.00	147	N/A	21.53	14.28	13.74	16.13	FMS
	Objective: Concentrates its portfolio in 20 to 30 common stocks of companies that offer the potential for rapid growth.								
Montgomery Select 50 (1995) Team Managed	MNSFX	1.80	106	N/A	37.00	N/A	N/A	N/A	FJMSW
	Objective: Montgomery Funds managers put their 50 best ideas into this fund, which invests for long-term capital appreciation.								
Navellier Aggressive Growth (1995) Navellier/Alpers	NPFGX	N/A	N/A	N/A	N/A	N/A	N/A	N/A	FJMSW
	Objective: Seeks capital appreciation by concentrating investments in a broad range of under-valued securities with a mid-cap orientation.								
PBHG Growth (1985) Gary Pilgrim	PBHGX	1.48	45	N/A	29.57	24.62	31.76	23.36	FJMS
	Objective: Seeks capital appreciation by investing in companies with strong growth and earnings potential.								

AGGRESSIVE GROWTH

Fund Name/ Start Date/ Manager	Symbol	Expense Ratio %	Portfolio Turnover %	Dividend Yield %	1-Year Annual Return	3-Year Annual Return	5-Year Annual Return	10-Year Annual Return	Broker Availability
PBHG Select Equity* (1995) Pilgrim/McCall	PBHEX	1.50	206	N/A	45.20	N/A	N/A	N/A	FJMS
Objective: Invests in the securities of no more than 30 issuers showing strong growth and future earnings potential.									
Quantitative Disciplined Growth (1995) Dean Barr	USBOX	N/A	18	N/A	19.25	N/A	N/A	N/A	JW
Objective: Seeks long-term growth of capital by investing in common stocks of companies with market capitalizations less than $5 billion.									
Robertson Stephens Value + Gro. (1992) Ron Elijah	RSVPX	1.45	104	N/A	–9.34	24.80	N/A	N/A	FJMSW
Objective: Seeks capital appreciation by investing in small- and medium-sized companies with favorable growth prospects and attractive valuations based on earnings and assets.									
Royce Pennsylvania Mutual (1973) Charles Royce	PENNX	0.98	10	N/A	5.79	8.63	10.95	10.97	FJMSW
Objective: Seeks long-term growth of capital by investing in small- and medium-sized companies selected on a value basis.									
Royce Value (1982) Charles Royce	RYVFX	1.76	14	N/A	7.42	8.77	10.86	10.14	AFJMSW
Objective: Seeks long-term capital appreciation primarily through investing in common stocks and convertibles of small- and medium-sized companies selected on a value basis.									
Stein Roe Cap. Opps.* (1969) Santella/Maddix	SRFCX	1.05	60	N/A	49.55	28.12	24.47	16.33	FJMSW
Objective: Invests in selected companies, mostly with market capitalizations less than $1 billion, which the managers believe offer the opportunity for substantial capital appreciation.									
Strong Discovery (1987) Richard Strong	STDIX	1.40	516	N/A	0.26	11.05	12.04	N/A	FJMS
Objective: Maximum capital appreciation through investing a diversified portfolio of securities of smaller companies with favorable earnings growth prospects.									
Van Wagoner Emerg. Gro (1995) G. Van Wagoner	VWEGX	N/A	N/A	N/A	N/A	N/A	N/A	N/A	AFJMSW
Objective: Invests primarily in equity securities of companies of all sizes believed to have the potential for above-average long-term growth.									
Wasatch Mid Cap (1992) Stewart/Barker	WAMCX	1.75	46	N/A	–2.54	20.04	N/A	N/A	FJMSW
Objective: Pursues long-term growth of capital by investing in a diversified portfolio of common stocks believed by the manager to possess superior growth potential.									
Westwood Equity (1987) Susan Byrne	WESWX	1.61	107	N/A	26.88	20.34	16.88	N/A	FJMSW
Objective: Seeks capital appreciation.									

*=fund currently closed to new investors.

GROWTH

Fund Name/ Start Date/ Manager	Symbol	Expense Ratio %	Portfolio Turnover %	Dividend Yield %	1-Year Annual Return	3-Year Annual Return	5-Year Annual Return	10-Year Annual Return	Broker Availability
American Heritage Gro. (1994) Heiko Thieme	AHEGX	2.62	4263	N/A	3.56	N/A	N/A	N/A	FJM
Objective: Seeks long-term capital appreciation.									
Ariel Appreciation (1989) Eric McKissack	CAAPX	1.36	18	N/A	19.60	11.21	10.47	N/A	AFJMSW
Objective: Seeks long-term growth by investing in securities believed to be undervalued with market capitalizations between $200 million and $5 billion.									
Babson Growth (1960) Kirk/Gribbell	BABSX	0.85	33	N/A	17.71	14.86	13.63	11.93	FJMSW
Objective: Seeks long-term capital growth and income by investing in common stocks.									
Benham Equity Growth (1991) D. Zhang	BEQGX	0.71	126	N/A	22.22	15.62	15.32	N/A	JS
Objective: Invests in a portfolio of common stocks.									
Berger 100 (1974) Rodney Linafelter	BEONX	1.48	114	N/A	9.36	7.69	13.50	17.93	AFJMSW
Objective: Long-term capital appreciation, which it seeks to achieve by investing in common stocks of established companies.									
Berger New Generation (1996) William Keithler	BENGX	N/A	N/A	N/A	N/A	N/A	N/A	N/A	AFJMSW
Objective: Attempts to identify and invest in companies believed to have the potential to influence the way businesses or consumers conduct their affairs.									
Bonnel Growth (1994) Art Bonnel	ACBGX	2.48	145	N/A	21.11	N/A	N/A	N/A	AFJSW
Objective: Seeks long-term growth by investing in common stocks with market capitalizations of approximately $1 billion with accelerating earnings.									
Bramwell Growth (1994) Elizabeth Bramwell	BRGRX	1.75	118	N/A	9.71	N/A	N/A	N/A	FJMSW
Objective: Employs bottoms-up earnings analysis to find companies positioned to benefit from research, product development, and market expansion in the pursuit of capital growth.									
Cappiello-Rushmore Growth (1992) Frank Cappiello	CRGRX	1.50	75	N/A	3.28	15.13	N/A	N/A	FJMSW
Objective: Seeks capital appreciation by investing in larger, established companies with demonstrated consistent sales and earnings growth.									
Crabbe Huson Equity (1989) Huson/Maack/Anton	CHEVX	1.40	92	N/A	10.9	13.89	16.08	N/A	AFJMSW
Objective: Uses a contrarian investment style in the pursuit of long-term growth with an emphasis on capital preservation.									
Dreyfus Aggressive Value (1995) T. Ghriskey	DAGVX	N/A	N/A	N/A	69.58	N/A	N/A	N/A	FJMS
Objective: Seeks capital appreciation by investing in a portfolio of publicly traded equity securities of domestic and foreign issuers that would be characterized as value companies.									
Dreyfus Appreciation (1984) Fayez Sarofim	DGAGX	0.92	5	N/A	24.94	20.89	14.81	14.09	AFJMSW
Objective: Seeks long-term capital growth by investing primarily in common stocks of domestic and foreign issuers.									

GROWTH

Fund Name/ Start Date/ Manager	Symbol	Expense Ratio %	Portfolio Turnover %	Dividend Yield %	1-Year Annual Return	3-Year Annual Return	5-Year Annual Return	10-Year Annual Return	Broker Availability
Dreyfus Core Value Fund (1947) Guy Scott	DCVIX	0.88	54	N/A	17.62	N/A	N/A	N/A	AFJM

Objective: Seeks long-term growth of capital primarily by investing in equities, with current income as a secondary objective.

Dreyfus Growth Opportunity (1972) Timothy Ghriskey	DREQX	1.04	268	N/A	15.63	9.14	9.33	10.76	FJMS

Objective: Seeks long-term capital growth, with income as a secondary objective, by investing in undervalued stocks selected using fundamental analysis.

Dreyfus Large Company Growth (1993) Team Managed	N/A	0.85	87	N/A	22.76	N/A	N/A	N/A	AFJMS

Objective: Pursues capital appreciation by investing in a portfolio of publicly traded securities of growth companies.

Dreyfus Large Company Value (1993) Team Managed	DLCVX	0.83	144	N/A	31.34	N/A	N/A	N/A	AFJMS

Objective: Seeks capital appreciation by investing in a portfolio of publicly traded securities of growth companies selected on a value basis.

Dreyfus New Leaders (1984) Kandel/Woods	DNLDX	1.19	109	N/A	16.01	13.51	15.47	14.23	AJSW

Objective: Seeks maximum appreciation by investing in domestic and foreign companies believed to have significant growth potential primarily with market capitalizations less than $75 million.

Dreyfus Special Growth (1993) Guy Scott	DSGRX	1.15	69	N/A	6.68	0.90	N/A	N/A	AFJM

Objective: Seeks above-average capital growth without regard to income by investing primarily in securities thought to have significant growth potential.

Dreyfus Third Century (1972) Coffey/Sloan	DRTHX	1.11	92	N/A	22.57	14.77	11.87	13.11	FJMS

Objective: Invests in common stocks or convertible securities in pursuit of capital growth, with current income as a secondary objective.

Federated Growth Strategies A (1984) Team Managed	FGSAX	1.10	125	N/A	21.55	13.88	11.94	13.77	JS

Objective: Invests in companies the adviser feels have prospects for above-average growth in earnings or dividends.

Founders Growth (1963) Edward Keely	FRGRX	1.28	130	N/A	18.65	16.91	19.3	16.7	AFMSW

Objective: Seeks long-term capital growth by investing in common stocks of well-established, high quality growth companies.

Fremont Growth (1993) Team Managed	FEQFX	0.97	108	N/A	19.15	16.08	N/A	N/A	JS

Objective: Seeks to maximize total return and reduce risk by utilizing both value and growth styles when selecting stocks.

Gabelli Growth (1987) Howard F. Ward	GABGX	1.44	140	N/A	20.00	14.58	13.82	N/A	FJMSW

Objective: Seeks stocks undervalued in relation to prevailing market multiples with favorable earnings dynamics and prospects for significant price appreciation.

GROWTH

Fund Name/ Start Date/ Manager	Symbol	Expense Ratio %	Portfolio Turnover %	Dividend Yield %	1-Year Annual Return	3-Year Annual Return	5-Year Annual Return	10-Year Annual Return	Broker Availability
IAI Capital Appreciation (1996) Team Managed	IACAX	N/A	N/A	N/A	N/A	N/A	N/A	N/A	AFJMSW
Objective: Seeks long-term capital appreciation by investing primarily in equity securities of U.S. companies with above-average prospects for growth.									
IAI Growth (1993) Twele/Mc Donald	IAGRX	1.25	93	N/A	12.72	10.73	N/A	N/A	AFJMSW
Objective: Seeks long-term capital appreciation primarily by investing in equities of established companies that are expected to increase earnings at an above-average rate.									
IAI Midcap Growth (1992) Suzanne Zak	IAMCX	1.25	30	N/A	17.10	17.29	N/A	N/A	AFJMSW
Objective: Seeks long-term capital appreciation primarily by investing in equities of medium-sized U.S. companies with above-average growth prospects.									
IAI Regional (1980) Mark Hoonsbeen	IARGX	1.25	90	N/A	16.31	12.73	11.93	14.19	AFJMSW
Objective: Invests in stocks of companies headquartered in Minnesota, Wisconsin, Iowa, Illinois, Nebraska, Montana, North Dakota, and South Dakota.									
IAI Value (1983) Douglas Platt	IAAPX	1.25	73	N/A	8.08	9.08	11.47	12.11	AFJMSW
Objective: Seeks long-term capital appreciation by investing largely in equities believed by the manager to be undervalued and capable of future growth.									
Invesco Growth (1935) T. Miller	FLRFX	1.06	111	N/A	23.35	13	13.28	12.89	AJSW
Objective: Invests in common stocks of companies in business and industry.									
Janus Fund (1970) James P. Craig	JANSX	0.87	118	N/A	19.99	15.03	14.34	16.46	FMS
Objective: Seeks long-term growth of capital primarily by investing in a diversified portfolio of common stocks of all sizes.									
Loomis Sayles Growth (1991) J. Castellini	LSGRX	1.08	48	N/A	14.13	12.13	12.09	N/A	FJMSW
Objective: Seeks long-term capital appreciation by selecting stocks based on their growth potential.									
Managers Capital **Appreciation** (1992) Team Managed	MGCAX	1.36	134	N/A	11.50	13.80	14.38	14.4	JS
Objective: Seeks long-term capital appreciation by investing in common stocks, convertible securities, rights, and warrants.									
Merger* (1989) Green/Smith	MERFX	1.41	419	N/A	11.21	11.52	11.34	8.57	JMSW
Objective: Uses risk arbitrage, including the selective use of short sales and put and call options, in the pursuit of capital growth.									
Merriman Leveraged **Growth** (1992) Team Managed	MELGX	2.82	88	N/A	6.85	9.82	N/A	N/A	JSW
Objective: Seeks long-term growth through the use of leverage and other investment practices.									

*=fund currently closed to new investors.

GROWTH

Fund Name/ Start Date/ Manager	Symbol	Expense Ratio %	Portfolio Turnover %	Dividend Yield %	1-Year Annual Return	3-Year Annual Return	5-Year Annual Return	10-Year Annual Return	Broker Availability
Montag & Caldwell Growth (1994) R. Canakaris	MCGFX	1.30	34	N/A	32.38	N/A	N/A	N/A	JS
Objective: Seeks long-term capital appreciation by investing in established companies of various sizes with a history of growth.									
Montgomery Growth (1993) Roger Honour	MNGFX	1.35	118	N/A	18.74	27.27	N/A	N/A	FJMSW
Objective: Seeks capital appreciation by investing primarily in common stocks of domestic companies with market capitalizations more than $500 million.									
Neuberger & Berman Focus^ (1993) Marx/Simons	NBSSX	0.96	0	N/A	6.00	15.17	17.92	14.59	FMS
Objective: Seeks long-term capital appreciation by investing among 13 economic sectors believed by the manager to be undervalued.									
Neuberger & Berman Manhattan^ (1993) M. Goldstein	NMANX	1.06	0	N/A	0.23	9.62	13.02	12.8	FMS
Objective: Invests for capital appreciation, principally in securities that the manager believes show potential for increasing the fund's total net asset value.									
Neuberger & Berman Partners^ (1968) Kassen/Gendelman	NPRTX	0.92	0	N/A	17.49	15.39	16.65	13.88	FMS
Objective: Seeks capital growth by investing in stocks and, to a lesser-extent, bonds and debentures believed to have strong growth potential.									
Neuberger & Berman Socially Resp. (1994) J. Prindle	NBSRX	1.51	0	N/A	FS	19.71	N/A	N/A	N/A
Objective: Seeks long-term capital appreciation through investments in securities of companies that meet both financial and socially responsible criteria.									
Oakmark (1991) Robert Sanborn	OAKMX	1.17	18	N/A	15.54	18.00	27.98	N/A	SW
Objective: Seeks long-term appreciation by investing in securities selected at a market price representing a significant discount from the actual business value.									
PBHG Core Growth (1996) Jim McCall	PBCRX	N/A	N/A	N/A	N/A	N/A	N/A	N/A	FJMS
Objective: Seeks long-term capital appreciation by investing in a diversified portfolio of equity securities with various market capitalizations.									
PBHG Large Cap Growth (1995) Pilgrim/McCall	PBHLX	1.50	117	N/A	28.19	N/A	N/A	N/A	FJMS
Objective: Seeks long-term appreciation by investing primarily in companies with market capitalizations more than $1 billion that show strong earnings potential.									
Rainer Core Equity (1994) Margard/Veterane	RIMEX	1.29	138	N/A	21.64	N/A	N/A	N/A	AFJMS
Objective: Invests in equities of all sizes in the pursuit of long-term capital appreciation.									
Reich & Tang Equity (1985) Robert Hoerle	RCHTX	1.15	28	N/A	14.60	13.93	15.94	13.59	AJW
Objective: Seeks long-term capital growth by investing in a diversified portfolio of equities with no more than 35 percent in debt issues and preferred stocks.									

^=with some discount brokers, Neuberger & Berman funds are operated as Trust accounts. In essence, these are a separate share class of funds with the exact same name. Trust funds are different in that they charge slightly higher management fees and are offered exclusively through select brokers, including Fidelity.

GROWTH

Fund Name/ Start Date/ Manager	Symbol	Expense Ratio %	Portfolio Turnover %	Dividend Yield %	1-Year Annual Return	3-Year Annual Return	5-Year Annual Return	10-Year Annual Return	Broker Availability
Robertson Stephens Contrarian (1993) Paul Stephens	RSCOX	2.54	29	N/A	23.44	19.81	N/A	N/A	AFJMW
Objective: Unique fund that uses an aggressive style to take advantage of both rising and falling markets by looking for attractively priced, overlooked stocks worldwide and shorting select issues.									
Selected Special Shares (1939) Elizabeth Bramwell	SLSSX	1.48	127	N/A	9.33	12.38	13.20	12.08	AJSW
Objective: Equity fund that seeks capital appreciation by investing in a wide range of common stocks issued by small- to medium-size companies believed to have strong earnings potential.									
Skyline Special Equities II (1993) Kenneth Kailin	SPEQX	1.52	102	N/A	16.47	13.09	N/A	N/A	FJMSW
Objective: Invests for maximum capital growth in small- to mid-cap equities believed to be undervalued relative to earnings, book value, and earnings potential.									
Sound Shore (1985) Team Managed	SSHFX	1.15	53	N/A	25.48	18.05	17.13	14.1	JS
Objective: Invests in equities selected on the basis of fundamental value using factors such as price, earnings expectations, historical data, balance sheet characteristics, and management skills.									
Stein Roe Growth (1958) Gustafson/Hirschhorn	SRFSX	0.99	36	N/A	21.04	16.57	13.75	14.12	FJMSW
Objective: Invests in common stocks and other equity-type securities for long-term capital appreciation.									
Stein Roe Special (1958) Dunn/Peterson	SRSPX	1.02	41	N/A	17.89	11.29	13.85	15.53	FJMSW
Objective: Seeks capital appreciation by investing primarily in common stocks and convertibles.									
Stein Roe Young Investor (1994) Team Managed	SRYIX	0.99	55	N/A	35.55	N/A	N/A	N/A	FJMSW
Objective: Seeks long-term capital appreciation by investing in common stocks of companies that appeal to or affect the lives of children or teenagers.									
Strong Growth (1993) Ronald Ognar	SGROX	1.40	321	N/A	23.50	N/A	N/A	N/A	FJMSW
Objective: Pursues capital appreciation by investing primarily in equity securities with above-average growth prospects.									
Strong Opportunity (1985) Weiss/Carlson	SOPFX	1.30	93	N/A	13.11	13.53	16.38	13.92	FJMSW
Objective: Seeks capital appreciation by investing in a diversified portfolio of medium-sized companies believed to be under-researched and attractively priced.									
Strong Value (1995) L. Sloate	STVAX	N/A	N/A	N/A	N/A	N/A	N/A	N/A	FJMSW
Objective: Invests primarily in equity securities whose share price doesn't fully reflect the value of the company.									
Third Avenue Value (1990) Martin Whitman	TAVFX	1.25	15	N/A	12.41	13.05	16.35	N/A	JMSW
Objective: Provides long-term capital appreciation by investing in stocks acquired at a discount from the company's estimated value.									

GROWTH

Fund Name/ Start Date/ Manager	Symbol	Expense Ratio %	Portfolio Turnover %	Dividend Yield %	1-Year Annual Return	3-Year Annual Return	5-Year Annual Return	10-Year Annual Return	Broker Availability
Turner Growth Equity (1994) R. Turner	TRGEX	1.03	178	N/A	22.91	12.98	N/A	N/A	JS
Objective: Seeks capital appreciation by buying common stocks with various market capitalizations.									
UAM C&B Equity (1990) P. Thompson	CBEQX	0.79	42	N/A	18.91	15.85	12.4	N/A	JS
Objective: Seeks maximum long-term returns by investing in common stocks of companies with strong financial positions and consistency in earnings growth.									
UAM Chicago Asset Value/Contr. (1994) W. Zimmer	N/A	0.95	4	N/A	13.7	N/A	N/A	N/A	JS
Objective: Seeks to outperform the market by identifying attractive stocks.									
UAM Sirach Growth (1993) Team Managed	SGRWX	0.86	119	N/A	20.93	N/A	N/A	N/A	JS
Objective: Attempts to provide long-term growth consistent with reasonable risk to principal by investing in stocks of companies offering long-term growth potential.									
Van Wagoner Mid-Cap (1995) Garrett Van Wagoner	VWMDX	N/A	N/A	N/A	N/A	N/A	N/A	N/A	AFJMS
Objective: Invests in equity securities of companies whose market capitalizations are between $500 million and $5 billion.									
Warburg Pincus Post Vent. Cap. (1995) Dater/Lurito	WPVCX	N/A	N/A	N/A	65.33	N/A	N/A	N/A	FJMSW
Objective: Invests in the stocks of companies that have received venture capital in the past ten years in the pursuit of capital appreciation.									
Wasatch Growth (1986) Stewart/Cardon	WGROX	1.50	88	N/A	12.39	17.74	14.21	N/A	FJMSW
Objective: Seeks high quality small- and mid-cap growth stocks with such characteristics as superior earnings growth, quality management, and high insider ownership.									
Westwood Equity Ret. (1987) Susan Byrne	WESWX	1.61	107	N/A	26.88	20.34	16.88	N/A	FJMSW
Objective: Seeks to provide investors with capital appreciation and secondary income.									
William Blair Growth (1946) Team Managed	WBGSX	0.65	32	N/A	18.30	18.93	17.73	16.27	JS
Objective: Seeks to provide long-term capital appreciation by investing in well-managed companies in growing industries.									
Yacktman Fund (1992) Donald Yacktman	YACKX	0.99	55	N/A	18.96	20.15	N/A	N/A	AFJMSW
Objective: Seeks long-term capital growth, with income as a secondary objective, by investing primarily in common stocks and other equity securities.									

SMALL COMPANY

Fund Name/ Start Date/ Manager	Symbol	Expense Ratio %	Portfolio Turnover %	Dividend Yield %	1-Year Annual Return	3-Year Annual Return	5-Year Annual Return	10-Year Annual Return	Broker Availability
Ariel Growth (1986) John W. Rogers	ARGFX	1.37	16	N/A	16.28	10.50	10.35	13.30	FJMSW
Objective: Seeks long-term appreciation primarily by investing in undervalued securities with market capitalizations less than $1 billion.									
Artisan Small Cap.* (1995) Carlene Murphy-Ziegler	ARTSX	1.52	105	N/A	11.94	N/A	N/A	N/A	FJMS
Objective: Seeks long-term capital growth by investing primarily in undervalued common stocks of companies with market capitalization of less than $1 billion.									
Babson Enterprise* (1983) Peter Schliemann	BABEX	1.09	13	N/A	14.33	11.69	15.52	13.30	JW
Objective: Invests primarily in the common stocks of small, fast-growing companies.									
Babson Enterprise II (1991) Schliemann/James	BAETX	1.45	15	N/A	23.64	12.39	14.44	N/A	FJMSW
Objective: Seeks long-term growth by investing in the stocks of a diversified portfolio of small, fast-growing companies that are considered to be undervalued at the time of purchase.									
Babson Shadow Stock (1987) Schliemann/Whitridge	SHSTX	1.14	25	N/A	10.92	10.03	12.98	N/A	FJMSW
Objective: Takes an index-like approach to investing in small company stocks.									
Baron Asset (1987) Ronald Baron	BARAX	1.40	35	N/A	21.30	20.12	21.02	N/A	AFJMSW
Objective: Pursues capital appreciation through investing in securities of small- and medium-sized companies, with undervalued assets and/or favorable growth prospects.									
Berger Small Co. Growth (1993) William Keithler	BESCX	1.89	109	N/A	31.30	N/A	N/A	N/A	AFJMSW
Objective: Seeks capital appreciation by investing in equities of small growth companies with market capitalizations less than $1 billion at the time of initial purchase.									
Blanchard Capital Growth (1994) Chase Manhattan	N/A	5.72	0	N/A	9.55	N/A	N/A	N/A	AFJMW
Objective: Seeks to provide long-term capital growth through a portfolio of common stocks the adviser believes are likely to benefit from economic, demographic, and legislative changes.									
Cappiello-Rushmore Emer. Gro. (1992) F. Cappiello	CREGX	1.50	121	N/A	–3.60	11.01	N/A	N/A	FJMSW
Objective: Pursues capital appreciation by investing in small, emerging growth companies with market capitalizations between $50 million and $750 million.									
Crabbe Huson Special (1987) Crabbe/Johnson	CHSPX	1.40	123	N/A	–3.79	11.16	15.29	N/A	AFJMSW
Objective: Seeks long-term capital appreciation and preservation of purchasing power through a flexible policy of investing in common stocks. Can also short positions believed to be overvalued.									
Dreyfus Disciplined Mid Cap Stock (1993) J. O'Toole	DDMRX	1.10	71	N/A	23.80	N/A	N/A	N/A	FJM
Objective: Seeks investment returns, including capital appreciation and income, that consistently outperform the Standard & Poor's 400 Mid-Cap Index.									

*=fund currently closed to new investors.

SMALL COMPANY

Fund Name/ Start Date/ Manager	Symbol	Expense Ratio %	Portfolio Turnover %	Dividend Yield %	1-Year Annual Return	3-Year Annual Return	5-Year Annual Return	10-Year Annual Return	Broker Availability
Dreyfus Emerging Leaders (1995) Kandel/Woods	DRELX	N/A	N/A	N/A	57.75	N/A	N/A	N/A	FJMS
Objective: Invests for capital growth by buying publicly traded equities with market caps of $750 million or less.									
Dreyfus Small Co. Value (1993) Team Managed	DSCVX	0.91	161	N/A	30.09	N/A	N/A	N/A	FJMS
Objective: Seeks capital appreciation by investing principally in a portfolio of foreign and domestic securities selected on a value basis.									
Founders Discovery (1989) David Kern	FDISX	1.63	118	N/A	20.10	13.65	16.13	N/A	AFMSW
Objective: Invests primarily in common stocks of small, rapidly growing U.S. companies.									
Founders Frontier (1987) Michael Haines	FOUNX	1.57	92	N/A	18.63	15.28	15.65	N/A	AFMSW
Objective: Invests primarily in common stocks of small- and medium-sized U.S. and foreign companies.									
Fremont U.S. Micro-Cap (1994) R. Kern	FUSMX	2.04	144	N/A	44.41	N/A	N/A	N/A	JS
Objective: Ordinarily invests at least 65 percent of its assets in common stocks and convertible securities of companies that fall in the smallest 10 percent in terms of market capitalization.									
Gateway Small Cap Index Fund (1993) Team Managed	GSCIX	1.68	20	N/A	11.62	8.31	N/A	N/A	JS
Objective: Seeks long-term capital growth by investing in smaller cap stocks of the Wilshire 250 Index, though it can buy put options to reduce risk or call options to increase potential gains.									
Heartland Small Cap Contrarian (1995) W. Nasgovitz	HRSMX	1.44	45	N/A	20.80	N/A	N/A	N/A	AFJMSW
Objective: Seeks maximum long-term growth through aggressive, yet flexible, investing in micro-cap stocks. Takes a value approach and can also short positions as the manager feels appropriate.									
Heartland Value* (1984) Nasgovitz/Denison	HRTVX	1.29	31	N/A	12.88	15.82	22.56	14.87	FJMSW
Objective: Seeks long-term growth by investing in micro-cap stocks selected on a value basis.									
Hotchkis & Wiley Small Cap (1985) Hitchman/Miles	HWSCX	1.00	119	N/A	10.70	10.41	13.45	11.6	FJMSW
Objective: Pursues capital appreciation by applying a value approach to investing in companies with market capitalizations of $500 million or less.									
IAI Emerging Growth* (1991) Rick Leggott	IAEGX	1.24	63	N/A	30.75	22.94	24.75	N/A	AFJMSW
Objective: Seeks long-term appreciation with little or no current income by investing in small- and medium-sized proven companies in the early stages of their life cycles.									
Invesco Emerging Growth (1991) Team Managed	FIEGX	1.48	221	N/A	31.08	15.52	N/A	N/A	JS
Objective: Invests principally in equity securities of emerging growth companies.									

*=fund currently closed to new investors.

SMALL COMPANY

Fund Name/ Start Date/ Manager	Symbol	Expense Ratio %	Portfolio Turnover %	Dividend Yield %	1-Year Annual Return	3-Year Annual Return	5-Year Annual Return	10-Year Annual Return	Broker Availability
Janus Venture* (1985) Lammert/Goff	JAVTX	0.92	113	N/A	8.37	15.04	13.92	16.18	FMS

Objective: Seeks long-term appreciation by investing in small capitalization companies in a manner consistent with the preservation of capital.

| **Kaufmann Fund** (1986) Utsch/Auriana | KAUFX | 2.17 | 60 | N/A | 24.32 | 23.85 | 23.01 | 19.84 | AFJMW |

Objective: Seeks capital appreciation by investing is small growth companies, primarily those beyond the venture stage, although the fund can also purchase initial public offerings.

| **Lexington Small Cap Value** (1996) Team Managed | N/A | N/A | N/A | N/A | N/A | N/A | N/A | N/A | FJMS |

Objective: Seeks long-term capital appreciation through investments in U.S.-based companies with market capitalizations of less than $1 billion.

| **Loomis Sayles Small Cap** (1991) Team Managed | LSSCX | 1.25 | 155 | N/A | 22.84 | 13.50 | 18.22 | N/A | FJMSW |

Objective: Invests in both undervalued stocks and those of companies with significant growth opportunity.

| **Managers Special Equity** (1984) Team Managed | MGSEX | 1.44 | 65 | N/A | 28.61 | 18.31 | 18.90 | 17.6 | JS |

Objective: Diversified portfolio seeking capital appreciation through investing in securities of companies expected to have superior growth potential.

| **Montgomery Micro Cap*** (1994) Team Managed | MNMCX | 1.75 | 89 | N/A | 16.90 | N/A | N/A | N/A | FJMSW |

Objective: Pursues capital appreciation through investing in common stocks whose total market caps are less than $300 million.

| **Montgomery Small Cap Opportunities** (1996) Team Managed | MNSOX | 1.50 | 81 | N/A | N/A | N/A | N/A | N/A | FJMSW |

Objective: Seeks long-term capital appreciation by investing in small-cap companies using strict valuation parameters.

| **Neuberger & Berman Genesis^** (1988) Judith Vale | NBGEX | 1.42 | N/A | N/A | 23.21 | 16.14 | 15.52 | N/A | FMS |

Objective: Pursues capital appreciation through investing in common stocks with small market capitalizations.

| **Oakmark Small Cap** (1995) S. Reid | OAKSX | N/A | N/A | N/A | N/A | N/A | N/A | N/A | SW |

Objective: Seeks long-term capital appreciation by investing in undervalued small companies.

| **Oberweis Emerging Growth*** (1987) James Oberweis | OBEGX | 1.73 | 79 | N/A | 22.90 | 18.25 | 18.72 | N/A | AFJM |

Objective: Seeks to maximize capital appreciation by investing in companies with average market caps of $500 million and showing the potential for above-average growth based on eight factors called the Oberweis Octagon.

*=fund currently closed to new investors.

^=with some discount brokers, Neuberger & Berman funds are operated as Trust accounts. In essence, these are a separate share class of funds with the exact same name. Trust funds are different in that they charge slightly higher management fees and are offered exclusively through select brokers, including Fidelity.

SMALL COMPANY

Fund Name/ Start Date/ Manager	Symbol	Expense Ratio %	Portfolio Turnover %	Dividend Yield %	1-Year Annual Return	3-Year Annual Return	5-Year Annual Return	10-Year Annual Return	Broker Availability
PBHG Emerging Growth (1993) Pilgrim/Baxter	PBEGX	1.47	97	N/A	32.58	33.35	N/A	N/A	FJMS

Objective: Seeks long-term growth by investing in micro-cap stocks with proven earnings potential.

Fund Name/ Start Date/ Manager	Symbol	Expense Ratio %	Portfolio Turnover %	Dividend Yield %	1-Year Annual Return	3-Year Annual Return	5-Year Annual Return	10-Year Annual Return	Broker Availability
Rainier Small/Mid Cap Eq. (1994) Margard/Veterane	RIMSX	1.48	151	N/A	22.78	N/A	N/A	N/A	AFJMS

Objective: Seeks to maximum long-term appreciation by investing in small- and mid-cap stocks.

Fund Name/ Start Date/ Manager	Symbol	Expense Ratio %	Portfolio Turnover %	Dividend Yield %	1-Year Annual Return	3-Year Annual Return	5-Year Annual Return	10-Year Annual Return	Broker Availability
Robertson Stephens Em. Gro. (1987) James Callinan	RSEGX	1.64	147	N/A	17.74	17.87	12.91	N/A	AFJMSW

Objective: Seeks capital appreciation by investing in a diversified portfolio of emerging growth companies.

Fund Name/ Start Date/ Manager	Symbol	Expense Ratio %	Portfolio Turnover %	Dividend Yield %	1-Year Annual Return	3-Year Annual Return	5-Year Annual Return	10-Year Annual Return	Broker Availability
Robertson Stephens Partners (1995) Andrew Pilara	RSPFX	2.41	71	N/A	38.08	N/A	N/A	N/A	AFJMSW

Objective: Pursues long-term capital appreciation by investing in equity securities of domestic small companies.

Fund Name/ Start Date/ Manager	Symbol	Expense Ratio %	Portfolio Turnover %	Dividend Yield %	1-Year Annual Return	3-Year Annual Return	5-Year Annual Return	10-Year Annual Return	Broker Availability
Royce Low-Priced Stock (1993) Charles Royce	RYLPX	1.97	114	N/A	13.47	N/A	N/A	N/A	AFJMSW

Objective: Seeks long-term capital appreciation by investing primarily in common stocks and convertible securities trading less than $15 per share selected on a value basis.

Fund Name/ Start Date/ Manager	Symbol	Expense Ratio %	Portfolio Turnover %	Dividend Yield %	1-Year Annual Return	3-Year Annual Return	5-Year Annual Return	10-Year Annual Return	Broker Availability
Royce Micro-Cap Fund (1991) Charles Royce	RYOTX	1.94	25	N/A	7.38	11.40	N/A	N/A	AFJMSW

Objective: Seeks long-term growth by investing in small companies primarily traded in the over-the-counter market with capitalizations less than $500 million selected on a value basis.

Fund Name/ Start Date/ Manager	Symbol	Expense Ratio %	Portfolio Turnover %	Dividend Yield %	1-Year Annual Return	3-Year Annual Return	5-Year Annual Return	10-Year Annual Return	Broker Availability
Royce Premier (1991) Charles Royce	RYPRX	1.50	70	N/A	9.89	12.63	N/A	N/A	AFJMSW

Objective: Pursues long-term growth, with income as a secondary consideration, by investing in small companies selected on a value basis.

Fund Name/ Start Date/ Manager	Symbol	Expense Ratio %	Portfolio Turnover %	Dividend Yield %	1-Year Annual Return	3-Year Annual Return	5-Year Annual Return	10-Year Annual Return	Broker Availability
Sit Small Cap Growth (1994) E. Sit	SSMGX	1.50	70	N/A	22.92	N/A	N/A	N/A	FJMS

Objective: Seeks to maximize long-term capital appreciation by investing primarily in common stocks of companies with market capitalizations less than $500 million.

Fund Name/ Start Date/ Manager	Symbol	Expense Ratio %	Portfolio Turnover %	Dividend Yield %	1-Year Annual Return	3-Year Annual Return	5-Year Annual Return	10-Year Annual Return	Broker Availability
Skyline Special Equities (1987) W. Dutton	SKSEX	1.51	71	N/A	19.97	12.97	20.29	N/A	FJMS

Objective: Invests primarily in small companies for aggressive growth.

Fund Name/ Start Date/ Manager	Symbol	Expense Ratio %	Portfolio Turnover %	Dividend Yield %	1-Year Annual Return	3-Year Annual Return	5-Year Annual Return	10-Year Annual Return	Broker Availability
Stein Roe Special Venture (1994) Dunn/Peterson	SRSVX	1.25	84	N/A	31.81	N/A	N/A	N/A	FJMSW

Objective: Pursues long-term capital appreciation by investing in a diversified portfolio of financially strong small companies based on management appraisal and stock valuation.

Fund Name/ Start Date/ Manager	Symbol	Expense Ratio %	Portfolio Turnover %	Dividend Yield %	1-Year Annual Return	3-Year Annual Return	5-Year Annual Return	10-Year Annual Return	Broker Availability
Strong Small Cap (1995) C. Daquele	SCAPX	N/A	N/A	N/A	N/A	N/A	N/A	N/A	FJMSW

Objective: Seeks capital growth primarily by investing in equity securities of companies with small market capitalizations.

SMALL COMPANY

Fund Name/ Start Date/ Manager	Symbol	Expense Ratio %	Portfolio Turnover %	Dividend Yield %	1-Year Annual Return	3-Year Annual Return	5-Year Annual Return	10-Year Annual Return	Broker Availability
Turner Small Cap Equity (1994) W. Chenoweth	TSCEX	1.25	183	N/A	52.43	N/A	N/A	N/A	JS
Objective: Seeks capital appreciation by investing in a diversified portfolio of common stocks with market capitalizations less than $1 billion that are reasonably valued and offer strong earnings potential.									
UAM Sirach Special Equity (1989) Team Managed	SSEPX	0.85	137	N/A	28.51	15.24	17.64	N/A	JS
Objective: To provide maximum long-term growth with reasonable risk by investing in small- to medium-capitalized companies with attractive financial characteristics.									
Value Line Small-Cap Grth (1993) Team Managed	N/A	2.15	57	N/A	7.51	14.46	N/A	N/A	AJW
Objective: Invests primarily in stocks with market capitalizations less than $1 billion to provide long-term growth of capital.									
Van Wagoner Micro-Cap (1995) G. Van Wagoner	VWMCX	N/A	N/A	N/A	N/A	N/A	N/A	N/A	AFJMSW
Objective: Invests primarily in companies with market capitalizations of less than $350 million.									
Warburg Pincus Cap. Apprec. (1987) Black/Wyper	CUCAX	1.12	146	N/A	24.00	16.33	16.45	N/A	FJMSW
Objective: Seeks long-term capital appreciation by investing in domestic equity securities.									
Warburg Pincus Emerging Growth (1988) Dater/Lurio	CUEGX	1.26	85	N/A	14.11	15.89	19.67	N/A	FJMSW
Objective: The fund is designed to generate maximum capital appreciation by investing in a diversified portfolio of small, emerging growth stocks.									
Warburg Pincus Small Co. Value (1995) Wyper/Frey	WPSVX	N/A	N/A	N/A	N/A	N/A	N/A	N/A	FJMSW
Objective: Seeks long-term capital appreciation by investing in a portfolio of equity securities of small capitalization companies.									
Wasatch Aggressive Equity* (1986) Samuel Stewart	WAAEX	1.47	29	N/A	−1.09	12.63	13.64	N/A	FJMSW
Objective: Seeks long-term growth of capital.									
Wasatch Microcap (1995) Stewart/Gardiner	WMICX	2.50	N/A	N/A	15.81	N/A	N/A	N/A	FJMSW
Objective: Seeks long-term growth of capital by investing primarily in common stocks of companies with market capitalizations of less than $150 million at the time of purchase.									
Wright Junior Blue Chip Equ. (1985) Team Managed	WJBEX	1.17	40	N/A	8.74	9.48	9.24	8.60	AFJMSW
Objective: Seeks long-term total return consisting of price appreciation plus income.									

*=fund currently closed to new investors.

GROWTH AND INCOME

Fund Name/ Start Date/ Manager	Symbol	Expense Ratio %	Portfolio Turnover %	Dividend Yield %	1-Year Annual Return	3-Year Annual Return	5-Year Annual Return	10-Year Annual Return	Broker Availability
American AAdvantage Gro. & Inc. (1994) Team	N/A	0.99	26	N/A	17.29	N/A	N/A	N/A	AFJMW

Objective: To realize long-term capital appreciation and current income through investing in a diversified portfolio of domestic equities.

Babson Value (1984) Nick Whitridge	BVALX	0.98	6	N/A	17.18	17.94	17.82	14.16	FJMSW

Objective: Invests in common stocks considered to be undervalued in relation to earnings, dividends, and/or assets.

Baron Growth and Income (1995) Ronald Baron	BGINX	2.00	41	N/A	25.76	N/A	N/A	N/A	AFJMSW

Objective: Seeks capital appreciation with income as a secondary objective through investing in securities of undervalued small- and medium-sized companies.

Benham Income & Growth (1990) S. Colton	BIGRX	0.67	70	N/A	20.66	15.49	15.57	N/A	JS

Objective: Seeks to provide dividend growth, current income, and capital appreciation by investing in a portfolio of common stocks.

Berger Growth & Income (1974) Rodney Linafelter	BEOOX	1.63	85	N/A	10.66	9.11	12.14	11.36	AFJMSW

Objective: The fund is designed to provide for capital appreciation, while throwing off a moderate level of current income.

Blanchard Growth & Income (1984) Chase Man. Bk.	BGIFX	3.81	N/A	N/A	14.73	N/A	N/A	N/A	AFJMW

Objective: Seeks to provide long-term capital appreciation and dividend income by investing in a broad portfolio of stocks (including foreign equities) of all market capitalizations.

Brinson U.S. Equity (1994) G. Brinson	BPEQX	0.80	36	N/A	23.22	N/A	N/A	N/A	JS

Objective: Seeks to maximize total return, consisting of capital appreciation and current income, while controlling risk.

Bull & Bear US & Overseas Fund (1993) Bassett Winmill	BBOGX	3.55	214	N/A	0.03	6.85	8.11	N/A	AJMW

Objective: Seeks growth of capital, with income as a secondary objective, by investing in common stocks of large, quality companies.

Dreyfus Disciplined Stock (1994) Bert Mullilns	DDSFX	0.90	60	N/A	20.85	16.47	15.42	N/A	AFJM

Objective: Tries to produce a total return in excess of the S&P 500 by investing in a diversified portfolio of equities selected through quantative research with an emphasis on risk control.

Dreyfus Fund (1951) Ernest Wiggins	DREVX	0.74	269	N/A	16.26	11.25	10.22	10.68	FJM

Objective: Seeks capital growth and secondarily current income by investing primarily in common stocks.

Dreyfus Growth & Income (1991) Richard Hoey	DGRIX	1.06	132	N/A	16.38	11.16	N/A	N/A	FJMS

Objective: Pursues long-term capital growth, current income, and growth of income by investing in equities and debt securities of domestic and foreign issuers.

GROWTH AND INCOME

Fund Name/ Start Date/ Manager	Symbol	Expense Ratio %	Portfolio Turnover %	Dividend Yield %	1-Year Annual Return	3-Year Annual Return	5-Year Annual Return	10-Year Annual Return	Broker Availability
Dreyfus Midcap Value (1995) P. Higgins	N/A	N/A	N/A	N/A	32.42	N/A	N/A	N/A	FJMS

Objective: Attempts to provide investment results that exceed the total return performance of companies represented by a recognized index of mid-cap stocks.

Dreyfus Special Growth (1993) Guy Scott	DSGRX	1.15	69	N/A	6.68	0.90	N/A	N/A	AFJM

Objective: Seeks above-average capital growth without regard to income by investing primarily in securities thought to have significant growth potential.

FAM Value (1986) Putnam/Van Buren	FAMVX	1.25	10	N/A	6.45	10.02	11.96	N/A	FJMS

Objective: Tries to maximize total return on capital by selecting stocks using a value approach.

Federated Stock Trust (1982) Fred Plautz	FSTKX	1.01	42	N/A	17.53	15.18	15.62	12.14	FJS

Objective: Seeks growth of income and capital primarily through investing in a diversified portfolio of common stocks of high-quality companies.

Founders Blue Chip (1958) Patrick Adams	FRMUX	1.22	235	N/A	20.99	15.92	13.76	13.58	AFMSW

Objective: Seeks long-term capital growth and income by investing primarily in common stocks of large, mature, well-established companies of strong financial strength.

Gateway Index Plus (1977) Team Managed	GATEX	1.19	5	N/A	9.51	8.69	8.13	10.11	JS

Objective: Seeks a high total return with reduced risk by investing in securities of the S&P 500, but also buying puts and calls.

Heartland Value & Income (1993) William Nasgovitz	HRVIX	1.54	150	N/A	19.79	N/A	N/A	N/A	AFJMSW

Objective: Seeks to generate an attractive current yield and substantial capital growth by investing in stocks and bonds selected on a valuation basis.

IAI Growth & Income (1971) Todd McCallister	IASKX	1.25	89	N/A	15.43	11.50	11.44	12.22	AFJMSW

Objective: Seeks capital appreciation and income by investing in a diversified portfolio of common stocks.

Invesco Value Equity (1986) M. Marhai	FSEQX	0.97	34	N/A	18.69	17.21	14.13	N/A	SW

Objective: Invests in common stocks and, to a lesser extent, convertible securities that pay regular dividends.

Janus Growth and Income (1991) Thomas Marsico	JAGIX	1.19	195	N/A	23.22	15.60	14.90	N/A	FMS

Objective: Pursues growth and the generation of current income by investing up to 75 percent of assets in common stock and the rest in income-producing securities.

Lexington Corporate Leaders (1935) Team Managed	LEXCX	0.58	N/A	N/A	21.51	15.69	16.08	14.79	FJMSW

Objective: Seeks long-term capital appreciation by investing in the common stocks of large, well-managed, and financially secure companies. Income is a secondary objective.

GROWTH AND INCOME

Fund Name/ Start Date/ Manager	Symbol	Expense Ratio %	Portfolio Turnover %	Dividend Yield %	1-Year Annual Return	3-Year Annual Return	5-Year Annual Return	10-Year Annual Return	Broker Availability
Lexington Growth & Income (1959) Alan Wapnick	LEXRX	1.09	160	N/A	26.27	14.10	13.98	11.34	AFJMSW
Objective: To provide long-term capital appreciation through investing in the common stocks of large, well-managed and financially sound companies.									
Loomis Sayles Gro. & Inc. (1991) Jeffrey Wardlow	LSGIX	1.20	60	N/A	15.58	15.75	14.69	N/A	FJMW
Objective: To achieve long-term growth of capital and current income by investing in undervalued common stocks or their equivalents.									
Merriman Growth & Income (1988) Paul Merriman	MTBCX	1.76	79	N/A	12.18	9.21	7.18	N/A	JSW
Objective: Seeks long-term growth of capital, income, and preservation of capital by investing in common stocks, bonds, and convertible securities of foreign and domestic issuers.									
Neuberger & Berman Guardian^ (1958) Simons/Marx	NGUAX	0.90	N/A	N/A	7.06	14.50	16.16	14.63	FMS
Objective: Seeks capital appreciation, and to a lesser extent current income, by investing primarily in common stocks.									
Robertson Steph. Gro. & Income (1995) J. Wallace	RSGIX	1.94	97	N/A	23.98	N/A	N/A	N/A	AFJMSW
Objective: Tries to maximum long-term total return by investing primarily in small- and mid-cap equities, along with convertible bonds and preferred stock.									
Selected American Shares (1993) Shelby Davis	SLASX	1.09	27	N/A	19.55	14.85	13.88	13.95	AJMSW
Objective: Invests principally in domestic common stocks with an emphasis on blue chip companies for both capital growth and income.									
Sit Growth & Income (1982) Team Managed	SNIGX	1.00	50	N/A	19.53	17.31	14.35	13.28	FJMS
Objective: Invests in dividend-paying stocks and convertibles, along with corporate and government bonds.									
Stein Roe Growth & Income (1987) Cantor/Christensen	SRPEX	0.96	70	N/A	22.67	15.62	15.76	N/A	FJMSW
Objective: Pursues growth of capital by investing primarily in large, well-established companies.									
Strong Growth & Income (1995) R. Milatis	SGRIX	N/A	N/A	N/A	N/A	N/A	N/A	N/A	FJMSW
Objective: A conservative equity fund seeking high total return by investing for capital growth and income.									
Strong Schafer Value Fund (1985) David Schafer	SCHVIX	1.28	33	N/A	12.99	14.14	17.84	15.59	FJMSW
Objective: Seeks long-term growth of capital by investing in large and medium capitalization stocks that have price-earnings ratios below that of the S&P 500.									

^=with some discount brokers, Neuberger & Berman funds are operated as Trust accounts. In essence, these are a separate share class of funds with the exact same name. Trust funds are different in that they charge slightly higher management fees and are offered exclusively through select brokers, including Fidelity.

GROWTH AND INCOME

Fund Name/ Start Date/ Manager	Symbol	Expense Ratio %	Portfolio Turnover %	Dividend Yield %	1-Year Annual Return	3-Year Annual Return	5-Year Annual Return	10-Year Annual Return	Broker Availability
Strong Total Return (1981) Ognar/Rogers	STRFX	1.10	299	N/A	12.74	11.57	13.11	10.56	FJMSW

Objective: Seeks a combination of income and capital appreciation while assuming reasonable risk by investing primarily in large companies with steady or growing dividends.

Fund Name/ Start Date/ Manager	Symbol	Expense Ratio %	Portfolio Turnover %	Dividend Yield %	1-Year Annual Return	3-Year Annual Return	5-Year Annual Return	10-Year Annual Return	Broker Availability
Vontobel U.S. Value (1990) Ed Walczak	VUSVX	1.65	96	N/A	21.58	17.28	15.07	N/A	FJMSW

Objective: Seeks to achieve capital appreciation by investing primarily in equities of companies listed on one of the major exchanges or with an established over-the-counter market.

Fund Name/ Start Date/ Manager	Symbol	Expense Ratio %	Portfolio Turnover %	Dividend Yield %	1-Year Annual Return	3-Year Annual Return	5-Year Annual Return	10-Year Annual Return	Broker Availability
Warburg Pincus Gro. & Income (1988) A. Orphanos	RBEGX	1.22	109	N/A	−3.60	9.62	13.64	N/A	FJMSW

Objective: Seeks long-term growth and a reasonable current return by investing in dividend-paying common stocks, convertibles, and readily marketable securities.

Fund Name/ Start Date/ Manager	Symbol	Expense Ratio %	Portfolio Turnover %	Dividend Yield %	1-Year Annual Return	3-Year Annual Return	5-Year Annual Return	10-Year Annual Return	Broker Availability
Wright Quality Core Equities (1995) Team Managed	WQCEX	1.07	83	N/A	16.05	13.84	11.20	12.23	AFJMSW

Objective: Seeks long-term total return consisting of price appreciation plus income.

Fund Name/ Start Date/ Manager	Symbol	Expense Ratio %	Portfolio Turnover %	Dividend Yield %	1-Year Annual Return	3-Year Annual Return	5-Year Annual Return	10-Year Annual Return	Broker Availability
Wright Selected Blue Chip Equities (1983) Team Managed	WSBEX	1.04	44	N/A	16.32	12.95	10.80	11.65	AFJMSW

Objective: Seeks long-term total return consisting of price appreciation plus income.

EQUITY INCOME

Fund Name/ Start Date/ Manager	Symbol	Expense Ratio %	Portfolio Turnover %	Dividend Yield %	1-Year Annual Return	3-Year Annual Return	5-Year Annual Return	10-Year Annual Return	Broker Availability
Dreyfus Equity Income (1994) Bert Mullins	DEIRX	0.90	38	N/A	19.31	N/A	N/A	N/A	FJM

Objective: Seeks an above-average level of income, along with moderate long-term growth of principal, by investing in a diversified list of securities.

FAM Equity Income (1996) Putnam/Van Buren	N/A	N/A	N/A	N/A	N/A	N/A	N/A	N/A	FJMS

Objective: Seeks income and growth by investing primarily in equity securities using a value approach.

Hotchkis & Wiley Equity Income (1987) Wiley/Bardin	HWEQX	0.98	24	N/A	12.93	13.88	13.83	N/A	FJMSW

Objective: The fund seeks to provide current income and capital growth by purchasing the securities of companies that are attractively priced, have significant current earnings, and a high dividend yield.

Invesco Industrial Income (1960) Team Managed	FIIIX	0.93	63	N/A	14.57	11.30	11.52	14.18	AJSW

Objective: Seeks high-yield and stable return by investing in common stocks, along with convertible bonds and preferred stocks.

Lexington Convertible Securities (1988) R. Russell	CNCVX	2.52	11	N/A	12.81	N/A	11.31	N/A	AFJMSW

Objective: Seeks total return, capital appreciation, current income, and preservation of capital by using convertible securities, which can be exchanged into common stock of the underlying companies.

Managers Income Equity (1984) Team Managed	MGIEX	1.45	36	N/A	16.45	14.33	13.86	12.13	JS

Objective: Seeks a high level of current income through investment primarily in income-producing equity securities.

Montgomery Equity Income (1994) John Brown	MNEIX	0.85	90	N/A	19.21	N/A	N/A	N/A	FJMSW

Objective: Seeks steady growth of capital and moderate current income by investing in quality dividend paying stocks.

Royce Equity Income (1990) Charles Royce	RYEQX	1.24	29	N/A	9.02	8.15	11.5	N/A	AFJMSW

Objective: Seeks reasonable income by investing primarily in dividend-paying common stocks and convertible securities of small companies.

Stein Roe Balanced (1949) Harry Hirschhorn	SRFBX	0.87	45	3.29	14.83	N/A	10.93	10.58	FJMSW

Objective: Pursues current income and capital appreciation through investing in a combination of equity, convertible, and fixed-income securities.

Strong Equity Income (1995) R. Milaitis	SEQIX	N/A	N/A	N/A	N/A	N/A	N/A	N/A	FJMSW

Objective: A conservative equity fund seeking high total return by investing for capital growth and income.

United Services Income (1983) R. Aldis	USINX	2.08	51	N/A	9.23	N/A	8.83	8.80	FJMSW

Objective: Invests in U.S. government securities, common stock, bonds, and senior convertible securities.

INDEX

Fund Name/ Start Date/ Manager	Symbol	Expense Ratio %	Portfolio Turnover %	Dividend Yield %	1-Year Annual Return	3-Year Annual Return	5-Year Annual Return	10-Year Annual Return	Broker Availability
ASM Fund (1991) Steven Adler	ASMUX	3.01	340	N/A	21.19	15.87	13.35	N/A	JW

Objective: To generate a total return through a combination of capital appreciation and current income by constructing a portfolio of the 30 stocks that comprise the Dow Jones Industrial Average.

Benham Global Gold Fund (1988) W. Martin	BGEIX	0.61	28	0.07	–3.22	N/A	9.73	N/A	JS

Objective: Invests in an index consisting of North American gold company securities.

Benham Glo. Nat Resources Index (1994) W. Martin	BGRIX	0.76	39	1.27	12.91	N/A	N/A	N/A	JS

Objective: Seeks to provide total return consistent with investments in energy and non-chemical components of the Dow World Stock Index.

Dreyfus MidCap Index Fund (1991) Team Managed	PESPX	0.50	20	N/A	13.34	12.82	14.79	N/A	JS

Objective: Invests in a composite of 400 small- to moderate-size companies.

Dreyfus S&P 500 Index Fund (1990) G. Hom	PEOPX	0.55	4	N/A	19.59	16.69	14.72	N/A	JS

Objective: Seeks to provide investment results corresponding to stocks in the S&P 500 Index.

Federated Index Trust Mid-Cap (1992) F. Plautz	FMDCX	0.60	26	N/A	12.47	12.01	N/A	N/A	JS

Objective: Attempts to match the investment results of the S&P 400 Mid-Cap Index.

Federated Index Trust Mini-Cap (1992) F. Plautz	FMCPX	0.75	42	N/A	11.65	11.38	N/A	N/A	JS

Objective: Seeks investment results that correspond to the performance of the Russell 2000 Index.

GLOBAL STOCK

Fund Name/ Start Date/ Manager	Symbol	Expense Ratio %	Portfolio Turnover %	Dividend Yield %	1-Year Annual Return	3-Year Annual Return	5-Year Annual Return	10-Year Annual Return	Broker Availability
Brinson Global Equity (1994) G. Brinson	BPGEX	1.00	74	N/A	18.17	N/A	N/A	N/A	JS
Objective: Allocates assets around the world using a value style.									
Bull & Bear US & Overseas (1987) Brett Sneed	BBOSX	3.55	214	N/A	0.03	6.85	8.11	N/A	FJMW
Objective: Seeks the highest possible total return consisting of income and capital growth by investing in a diversified portfolio of equities of U.S. and non-U.S. companies.									
Founders Worldwide Growth (1989) Michael Gerding	FWWGX	1.65	54	N/A	9.94	14.1	13.27	N/A	AFMSW
Objective: Pursues long-term growth of capital by investing in stocks of both emerging and established companies throughout the world.									
Gabelli Glo. Convert. Securities (1994) H. Woodson	GABCX	2.41	152	N/A	7.02	N/A	N/A	N/A	FJMSW
Objective: Seeks a high level of total return through a combination of current income and capital appreciation by investing primarily in convertible securities.									
Gabelli Glo. Interact. Couch Potato (1994) Mario Gabelli	GICPX	2.47	33	N/A	10.81	N/A	N/A	N/A	FJMSW
Objective: Invests in companies around the world involved in communications, creativity, and copyright, along with those engaged in emerging technologies and interactive services.									
Invesco Worldwide Cap. Goods (1994) A. Grossi	ISWGX	2.11	247	N/A	10.98	N/A	N/A	N/A	AJSW
Objective: Invests in companies that design, develop, and distribute capital goods and/or raw materials.									
Janus Worldwide (1991) Helen Young Hayes	JAWWX	1.24	142	N/A	27.48	20.03	18.69	N/A	FMS
Objective: Seeks long-term growth of capital by investing in a diversified portfolio of common stocks from foreign and domestic issuers of all sizes, usually from at least five different countries.									
Lexington Global (1987) Wapnick/Saler	LXGLX	1.67	167	N/A	17.07	10.55	10.57	N/A	FJMSW
Objective: Pursues long-term capital growth primarily by investing in common stocks of companies domiciled in foreign countries and the United States.									
Montgomery Global Comms. (1993) Castro/Boich	MNGCX	1.90	104	N/A	4.44	7.51	N/A	N/A	FJMSW
Objective: Seeks capital appreciation by investing in equity securities of communication companies throughout the world with solid fundamental values and the potential for long-term growth.									
Montgomery Global Opps. (1993) Castro/Boich	MNGOX	1.90	164	N/A	20.83	14.17	N/A	N/A	FJMSW
Objective: Pursues capital appreciation by investing in equities of companies around the world with market capitalizations more than $1 billion that are reasonably priced and have growth potential.									
Rob. Steph. Glo. Low Pr. Stock (1994) M. Sullivan	RSLPX	N/A	N/A	N/A	N/A	N/A	N/A	N/A	AFJMSW
Objective: Seeks to invest in equities of low priced securities of issuers around the world.									
Royce Global Services (1994) Charles Royce	N/A	1.97	106	N/A	8.70	N/A	N/A	N/A	AFJM
Objective: Seeks long-term capital appreciation by investing primarily in common stocks and convertibles of domestic and foreign companies engaged in service industries.									

INTERNATIONAL EQUITY

Fund Name/ Start Date/ Manager	Symbol	Expense Ratio %	Portfolio Turnover %	Dividend Yield %	1-Year Annual Return	3-Year Annual Return	5-Year Annual Return	10-Year Annual Return	Broker Availability
American AAdvantage International (1994) Team	N/A	1.33	21	N/A	13.70	N/A	N/A	N/A	FJMW

Objective: Invests primarily in a diversified portfolio of equity securities from issuers based outside the United States with the goal of long-term appreciation.

Artisan International (1995) Mark Yockey	ARTIX	2.50	57	N/A	N/A	N/A	N/A	N/A	AFJMS

Objective: Seeks long-term capital appreciation by investing in an internationally diversified portfolio of common stocks.

Babson-Stewart Ivory Intl. (1987) John Wright	BAINX	1.26	33	N/A	10.84	10.57	10.81	N/A	FJMSW

Objective: Tries to achieve a favorable total return by investing in a globally diverse portfolio composed primarily of common stocks.

Brinson Non-U.S. Equity (1993) G. Brinson	BNUEX	1.00	20	N/A	13.72	7.65	N/A	N/A	JS

Objective: Invests for maximum total return in a diversified portfolio of primarily non-U.S. equities.

Dreyfus International Equity (1993) M&G Investment	DITFX	1.50	65	N/A	13.02	N/A	N/A	N/A	FJM

Objective: Seeks capital growth by investing primarily in the equity securities of foreign issuers.

Dreyfus International Value (1994) S. Cseh	DIVLX	N/A	N/A	N/A	8.93	N/A	N/A	N/A	FJMS

Objective: Seeks long-term capital growth by investing in a portfolio of publicly traded foreign equities that are viewed as value companies.

Founders International Equity (1995) Michael Gerding	FOIEX	N/A	N/A	N/A	N/A	N/A	N/A	N/A	AFMSW

Objective: Pursues long-term appreciation by investing primarily in common stocks of foreign-based companies.

Founders Passport (1993) Michael Gerding	FPSSX	1.84	37	N/A	16.21	N/A	N/A	N/A	AFMSW

Objective: Invests primarily in common stocks of small, rapidly growing companies headquartered outside the United States in both established and emerging economies around the world.

Fremont International Growth (1994) Team Managed	FIGFX	1.50	32	N/A	7.80	N/A	N/A	N/A	JS

Objective: Seeks long-term capital growth by investing in international stocks.

Fremont International Small Cap (1994) G. Bergstrom	FIGFX	2.06	96	N/A	8.33	N/A	N/A	N/A	JS

Objective: Seeks to achieve long-term capital appreciation by investing in equity securities of issuers domiciled outside of the United States.

Gabelli International (1995) Caesar Bryan	GIGRX	2.75	30	N/A	18.54	N/A	N/A	N/A	FJMSW

Objective: Seeks capital appreciation by investing in a diversified portfolio of foreign-based equities.

Hotchkis & Wiley Intl. (1990)/Bouwer/Ketterer	HWINX	1.00	12	N/A	13.29	13.50	13.78	N/A	FJMSW

Objective: Seeks current and long-term income and growth of capital by investing in undervalued, dividend-paying common stocks of companies domiciled outside of the United States.

INTERNATIONAL EQUITY

Fund Name/ Start Date/ Manager	Symbol	Expense Ratio %	Portfolio Turnover %	Dividend Yield %	1-Year Annual Return	3-Year Annual Return	5-Year Annual Return	10-Year Annual Return	Broker Availability
IAI International (1987) Roy Gillson	IAINX	1.66	39	N/A	7.06	8.24	9.12	N/A	AFJMSW

Objective: Pursues capital appreciation by investing 95 percent of its portfolio in equity securities of non-U.S. issuers believed to have the potential for above-average capital appreciation.

Janus Overseas (1994) Helen Young Hayes	JAOSX	1.76	188	N/A	26.57	N/A	N/A	N/A	FMS

Objective: Seeks long-term growth of capital by investing primarily in common stocks of foreign issuers of all sizes.

Lexington International (1993) Richard Saler	LEXIX	2.46	138	N/A	14.62	N/A	N/A	N/A	AFJMSW

Objective: Seeks long-term capital growth through investment in common stocks of firms domiciled in overseas countries.

Loomis Sayles Intl. Equity (1991) Frank Jedlicka	LSIEX	1.45	133	N/A	7.82	9.50	8.99	N/A	FJMSW

Objective: Seeks high total return through a combination of capital appreciation and current income by investing in equities of companies organized or headquartered outside the United States.

Managers International Equity (1986) Team Managed	LSIEX	1.58	73	N/A	8.75	11.82	13.44	11.35	JS

Objective: Seeks long-term capital appreciation as its primary objective and secondarily income through investments in non-U.S. equity securities.

Montgomery Intl. Growth (1995) Castro/Boich	MNIGX	1.65	239	N/A	22.08	N/A	N/A	N/A	FJMSW

Objective: Pursues capital appreciation by investing primarily in common stocks of foreign-based issuers.

Montgomery Intl. Small Cap (1993) Castro/Boich	MNISX	1.90	177	N/A	15.55	7.50	N/A	N/A	FJMSW

Objective: Seeks capital appreciation by investing primarily in reasonably priced equity securities of non-U.S. based companies with market capitalizations of less than $1 billion.

Neuberger & Berman Intl.^ (1994) Felix Rovelli	NBISX	1.70	N/A	N/A	12.30	N/A	N/A	N/A	FMS

Objective: Pursues long-term capital appreciation by investing primarily in a diversified portfolio of foreign equity securities.

Oakmark International (1992) David Herro	OAKIX	1.40	27	N/A	18.31	11.08	N/A	N/A	SW

Objective: Invests in a diversified portfolio of international securities that are selling at a discount to actual market value.

PBHG International (1994) Murray Johnstone	PBHIX	2.25	140	N/A	11.75	N/A	N/A	N/A	FJMS

Objective: Seeks long-term growth of capital by investing primarily in a diversified portfolio of non-U.S. issued securities with large and intermediate market capitalizations.

^=with some discount brokers, Neuberger & Berman funds are operated as Trust accounts. In essence, these are a separate share class of funds with the exact same name. Trust funds are different in that they charge slightly higher management fees and are offered exclusively through select brokers, including Fidelity.

INTERNATIONAL EQUITY

Fund Name/ Start Date/ Manager	Symbol	Expense Ratio %	Portfolio Turnover %	Dividend Yield %	1-Year Annual Return	3-Year Annual Return	5-Year Annual Return	10-Year Annual Return	Broker Availability
Sit International Growth (1991) Team Managed	SNGRX	1.50	39	N/A	4.99	9.91	N/A	N/A	FJMS

Objective: Normally invests at least 90 percent of its assets in equity securities of issuers domiciled outside of the United States.

Stein Roe International (1994) Bertocci/Harris	STISX	1.59	59	N/A	8.23	N/A	N/A	N/A	FJMSW

Objective: Seeks capital appreciation by investing primarily in equities of foreign-based issuers.

UAM Acadian Intl Equity (1993) B. Wolahan	N/A	2.54	76	N/A	11.15	6.08	N/A	N/A	JS

Objective: Seeks maximum long-term total return by investing in a diversified portfolio of equity securities of primarily non-U.S. issuers.

UAM MJI International Equity (1994) R. Scullion	N/A	1.00	81	N/A	7.19	N/A	N/A	N/A	JS

Objective: Seeks to maximize total return by investing primarily in the common stocks of companies based outside the United States.

Vontobel EuroPacific (1985) Fabrizio Pierallini	VNEPX	1.63	68	N/A	15.33	9.65	10.09	7.63	FJMSW

Objective: Holds a diversified portfolio of equities designed to take advantage of opportunities in markets around the world.

Warburg Pincus Intl. Equity (1989) Richard King	CUIEX	1.39	39	N/A	9.25	11.37	11.39	N/A	FJMSW

Objective: Seeks long-term capital appreciation by investing in a diversified portfolio of foreign equities.

William Blair International Gro. (1992) Team Managed	WBIGX	1.48	77	N/A	8.70	7.59	N/A	N/A	JS

Objective: Invests primarily in common stocks issued by companies domiciled outside of the United States in an effort to generate long-term capital appreciation.

Wright Intl. Blue Chip (1989) Team Managed	WIBCX	1.29	12	N/A	14.28	11.69	10.26	N/A	AFJMSW

Objective: Attempts to provide long-term capital growth and reasonable current income by investing in a portfolio of equities composed of high-quality non-U.S. companies.

EMERGING MARKETS

Fund Name/ Start Date/ Manager	Symbol	Expense Ratio %	Portfolio Turnover %	Dividend Yield %	1-Year Annual Return	3-Year Annual Return	5-Year Annual Return	10-Year Annual Return	Broker Availability
IAI Developing Countries (1995) Roy Gillson	IADCX	2.15	42	N/A	3.57	N/A	N/A	N/A	AFJMSW

Objective: Seeks to achieve long-term capital appreciation by investing primarily in equities of companies domiciled or having substantial operations in developing countries.

Lexington World. Emerg. Mkts. (1969) Richard Saler	LEXGX	1.88	93	N/A	6.91	5.60	9.37	N/A	FJMSW

Objective: Pursues long-term capital growth by investing in equity securities of companies headquarted or doing business in the emerging markets countries.

Montgomery Emerg. Mkts. (1992) Jimenez/Sudweeks	MNEMX	1.72	110	N/A	7.47	6.46	N/A	N/A	FJMSW

Objective: Seeks capital appreciation by investing in securities of companies doing business in markets generally considered to be emerging or developing by the World Bank or United Nations.

Oakmark International Emerging Value (1995) Team	OAKEX	1.40	27	N/A	N/A	N/A	N/A	N/A	SW

Objective: Pursues long-term capital appreciation by investing in equity securities of non-U.S. issuers with small market capitalizations or that are located in the emerging markets.

Quantitative Foreign Frontier (1994) Lyle Davis	N/A	2.54	11	N/A	8.86	N/A	N/A	N/A	JW

Objective: To provide long-term capital growth through investment in securities of foreign issuers located in the emerging markets.

Rob. Steph. Develop. Countries (1994) M. Hoffman	RSDCX	1.83	103	N/A	6.60	N/A	N/A	N/A	AFJMS

Objective: Seeks long-term capital appreciation by investing in securities of companies domiciled in one of the emerging markets.

Sit Developing Markets Growth (1995) A. Kim	SDMGX	2.00	46	N/A	17.03	N/A	N/A	N/A	FJMS

Objective: Seeks to maximize long-term capital appreciation by investing at least 65 percent of total assets in companies domiciled in the emerging markets.

UAM Acadian Emerging Markets (1993) B. Wolahan	AEMGX	1.78	21	N/A	4.82	4.73	N/A	N/A	JS

Objective: Seeks long-term capital appreciation by investing primarily in common stocks of emerging country issuers.

Warburg Pin. Emerging Mkts. (1994) King/Horsley	WPEMX	1.00	69	N/A	7.90	N/A	N/A	N/A	FJMSW

Objective: Seeks long-term capital appreciation by investing in a diversified portfolio of foreign equities.

COUNTRY SPECIFIC

Fund Name/ Start Date/ Manager	Symbol	Expense Ratio %	Portfolio Turnover %	Dividend Yield %	1-Year Annual Return	3-Year Annual Return	5-Year Annual Return	10-Year Annual Return	Broker Availability
Guinness Flt. Asia Blue Chip (1996) Team Managed	GFABX	N/A	N/A	N/A	N/A	N/A	N/A	N/A	FJMSW

Objective: Seeks long-term capital appreciation by investing in the stocks of companies in Hong Kong, Singapore, Malaysia, Thailand, Korea, Taiwan, Indonesia, and the Philippines.

Guinness Flt. China & H.K. (1994) Lynda Johnstone	GFCHX	2.00	11	N/A	22.23	N/A	N/A	N/A	FJMSW

Objective: Seeks to provide investors with long-term capital of growth by investing in securities listed in the markets of China and Hong Kong.

Invesco Asian Growth (1996) W. Barron	IVAGX	2.19	2	N/A	N/A	N/A	N/A	N/A	ASW

Objective: Seeks to achieve capital appreciation by investing at least 65 percent of total assets in stocks of companies with primary operations in Asia and the Pacific Rim, excluding Japan.

Invesco European Small Co. (1994) Team Managed	IVECX	1.68	141	N/A	25.66	N/A	N/A	N/A	AJSW

Objective: Seeks to achieve capital appreciation by investing at least 65 percent of total assets in equity securities of European companies with market capitalizations of less than $1 billion.

Invesco Latin America Growth (1995) F. Bertoni	IVSLX	2.14	29	N/A	18.66	N/A	N/A	N/A	ASW

Objective: Seeks capital appreciation by investing at least 65 percent of all assets in equity securities of issuers from Mexico, Central America, and Spanish-speaking islands of the Carribean.

Invesco Pacific Basin (1984) Team Managed	FPBSX	1.52	56	N/A	5.32	6.17	6.23	7.29	SW

Objective: Invests primarily in companies listed on stock exchanges in Far Eastern or Western Pacific countries.

Lexington Cros. Small Cap Asia (1994) Lam/Webber	N/A	1.75	40	N/A	6.99	N/A	N/A	N/A	FJMSW

Objective: Pursues capital appreciation by investing in equities with market capitalizations of less than $1 billion and domiciled in the Asia Region.

Matthews Asian Conv. Securities (1994) G. Matthews	N/A	2.26	122	N/A	10.47	N/A	N/A	N/A	JS

Objective: Invests for growth and income in the Asian convertible securities markets.

Matthews Korea (1994) G. Matthews	MAXOX	0.24	42	N/A	–24.75	N/A	N/A	N/A	JS

Objective: Invests for growth in the Korean equity market using a bottom-up research technique.

Strong Asia Pacific (1993) Anthony L.T. Cragg	SASPX	2.00	104	N/A	4.51	N/A	N/A	N/A	FJMSW

Objective: Seeks maximum capital appreciation by investing in equities of issuers located in Asia or the Pacific Basin.

Vontobel Eastern European (1996) Team Managed	VEEEX	N/A	N/A	N/A	N/A	N/A	N/A	N/A	JSW

Objective: Invests in international equities to take advantage of opportunities in the newly reorganized capital and securities markets of Central and Eastern Europe.

COUNTRY SPECIFIC

Fund Name/ Start Date/ Manager	Symbol	Expense Ratio %	Portfolio Turnover %	Dividend Yield %	1-Year Annual Return	3-Year Annual Return	5-Year Annual Return	10-Year Annual Return	Broker Availability
Warburg Pincus Japan Growth (1995) N. Edwards	N/A	N/A	N/A	N/A	N/A	N/A	N/A	N/A	FJMSW
	Objective: Seeks long-term growth of capital by investing in equity securities of Japanese issuers that present attractive opportunities for growth.								
Warburg Pincus Japan OTC (1994) King/Abe	WPJPX	1.41	83	N/A	2.72	N/A	N/A	N/A	FJMSW
	Objective: Pursues long-term capital appreciation by investing at least 65 percent of total assets in securities registered on JASDAQ (Japan's OTC Market).								
Wright EquiFund Belgium/Luxembourg (1994) Team Managed	WEBEX	1.76	38	N/A	18.97	N/A	N/A	N/A	AFJMSW
	Objective: Seeks to provide capital appreciation by investing in equity securities of companies domiciled in Belgium and Luxembourg.								
Wright EquiFund Britain (1994) Steve Loban	WFGBX	1.56	42	N/A	10.84	N/A	N/A	N/A	AFJMSW
	Objective: Seeks to provide capital appreciation by investing in equity securities of companies domiciled in Britain.								
Wright EquiFund Germany (1994) Steve Loban	WEDEX	1.59	18	N/A	–0.24	N/A	N/A	N/A	AFJMSW
	Objective: Seeks to provide capital appreciation by investing in equity securities of companies domiciled in Germany.								
Wright EquiFund Hong Kong (1990) Team Managed	WEHKX	1.59	100	N/A	11.63	1.03	9.93	N/A	AFJMSW
	Objective: Seeks to provide capital appreciation by investing in equity securities of companies domiciled in Hong Kong.								
Wright EquiFund Japan (1994) Team Managed	WEJPX	1.81	112	N/A	1.05	N/A	N/A	N/A	AFJMSW
	Objective: Seeks to provide capital appreciation by investing in equity securities of companies domiciled in Japan.								
Wright EquiFund Mexico (1994) Team Managed	WEMEX	1.72	110	N/A	11.75	N/A	N/A	N/A	AFJMSW
	Objective: Seeks to provide capital appreciation by investing in equity securities of companies domiciled in Mexico.								
Wright EquiFund Netherlands (1990) Team Managed	WENLX	2.26	87	N/A	26.44	20.75	13.76	N/A	AFJMSW
	Objective: Seeks to provide capital appreciation by investing in equity securities of companies domiciled in the Netherlands.								
Wright EquiFund Nordic (1994) Team Managed	WENOX	2.24	94	N/A	20.74	N/A	N/A	N/A	AFJMSW
	Objective: Seeks to provide capital appreciation by investing in equity securities of companies domiciled in the Nordic region.								
Wright EquiFund Switzerland (1994) Team Managed	WECHX	2.26	95	N/A	1.90	N/A	N/A	N/A	AFJMSW
	Objective: Seeks to provide capital appreciation by investing in equity securities of companies domiciled in Switzerland.								

BALANCED

Fund Name/ Start Date/ Manager	Symbol	Expense Ratio %	Portfolio Turnover %	Dividend Yield %	1-Year Annual Return	3-Year Annual Return	5-Year Annual Return	10-Year Annual Return	Broker Availability
American AAdvantage: Balanced (1994) Team	N/A	0.99	73	N/A	12.10	N/A	12.10	N/A	AFJMW

Objective: To realize both income and capital appreciation by investing all assets in the AMR Trust Balanced Portfolio which, in turn, invests primarily in equity and debt securities.

Brinson U.S. Balanced (1994) Team Managed	BPBLX	0.80	240	N/A	11.00	N/A	N/A	N/A	JS

Objective: U.S. balanced fund that seeks to maximize total return while controlling risk.

Dreyfus Balanced (1992) Ernest Wiggins	DRBAX	1.04	72	N/A	6.79	11.67	N/A	N/A	FJMS

Objective: Seeks long-term capital growth and current income, consistent with taking a reasonable amount of investment risk.

Federated Stock & Bond A (1934) Team Managed	FSTBX	1.07	68	N/A	11.86	9.83	10.29	9.25	JS

Objective: Seeks safety of capital with possible long-term growth of principal and income.

Founders Balanced (1963) Patrick Adams	FRINX	1.23	286	N/A	20.37	14.24	14.53	12.35	AFMSW

Objective: Seeks a combination of income and capital appreciation by investing primarily in a balanced portfolio of dividend-paying common stocks, along with a variety of foreign and domestic fixed-income securities.

Hotchkis & Wiley Balanced Income (1985) Team	HWBAX	1.00	92	N/A	10.17	10.52	11.21	11.24	FJMSW

Objective: Seeks to preserve capital while producing a high total return by allocating assets between dividend-paying common stocks and investment-grade fixed-income securities.

IAI Balanced (1992) Hill/Twele/Simenstad	IABLX	1.25	194	N/A	8.22	6.94	N/A	N/A	AFJMSW

Objective: Seeks to maximize total return by investing in a broadly diversified portfolio of stocks, bonds, and short-term instruments.

Invesco Balanced (1993) J. Paul	IMABX	1.25	255	2.51	17.27	N/A	N/A	N/A	AJSW

Objective: Normally invests 50 percent to 70 percent of total assets in common stocks, with the remainder in fixed-income securities.

Janus Balanced (1992) Blaine Rollins	JABAX	1.35	185	N/A	19.21	13.59	N/A	N/A	FMS

Objective: Pursues long-term capital appreciation and current income by investing in a blend of equities and fixed-income securities.

Merriman Asset Alloc. (1989) Merriman/Notaro	MTASX	1.76	288	N/A	7.41	6.24	7.66	N/A	JSW

Objective: To provide high total return with reasonable risk by allocating assets, either directly or through other mutual funds, among equities, fixed-income, foreign, and gold securities.

Montag & Caldwell Balanced (1994) R. Canakaris	MOBAX	1.25	27	N/A	21	N/A	N/A	N/A	JS

Objective: Seeks long-term total return by investing in equities, fixed-income and short-term securities.

BALANCED

Fund Name/ Start Date/ Manager	Symbol	Expense Ratio %	Portfolio Turnover %	Dividend Yield %	1-Year Annual Return	3-Year Annual Return	5-Year Annual Return	10-Year Annual Return	Broker Availability
Oakmark Balanced (1995) C. McGregor	OAKBX	N/A	N/A	N/A	N/A	N/A	N/A	N/A	SW

Objective: Seeks high current income and growth of capital by investing in a diversified portfolio of equity and fixed-income securities.

Fund Name/ Start Date/ Manager	Symbol	Expense Ratio %	Portfolio Turnover %	Dividend Yield %	1-Year Annual Return	3-Year Annual Return	5-Year Annual Return	10-Year Annual Return	Broker Availability
Rainier Balanced (1994) Frost/Margard	RIMBX	1.19	115	N/A	14.18	N/A	N/A	N/A	AFJMS

Objective: Seeks to provide a balance of long-term capital appreciation and current income.

Fund Name/ Start Date/ Manager	Symbol	Expense Ratio %	Portfolio Turnover %	Dividend Yield %	1-Year Annual Return	3-Year Annual Return	5-Year Annual Return	10-Year Annual Return	Broker Availability
Sit Balanced (1993) Team Managed	N/A	1.00	101	N/A	14.13	N/A	N/A	N/A	FJMS

Objective: Seeks long-term growth of capital consistent with the preservation of principal.

Fund Name/ Start Date/ Manager	Symbol	Expense Ratio %	Portfolio Turnover %	Dividend Yield %	1-Year Annual Return	3-Year Annual Return	5-Year Annual Return	10-Year Annual Return	Broker Availability
Stein Roe Balanced (1949) H. Hirschhorn	SRFBX	0.87	45	N/A	14.84	9.68	10.93	10.58	FJMSW

Objective: Strives for maximum total return consistent with reasonable risk by investing in a combination of stocks, bonds, and convertible securities.

Fund Name/ Start Date/ Manager	Symbol	Expense Ratio %	Portfolio Turnover %	Dividend Yield %	1-Year Annual Return	3-Year Annual Return	5-Year Annual Return	10-Year Annual Return	Broker Availability
UAM C&B Balanced (1989) P. Thompson	CBBAX	1.00	22	N/A	12.57	10.50	9.91	N/A	JS

Objective: Seeks maximum long-term total return with minimal risk to principal by investing in a combined portfolio of common stocks and fixed-income securities.

Fund Name/ Start Date/ Manager	Symbol	Expense Ratio %	Portfolio Turnover %	Dividend Yield %	1-Year Annual Return	3-Year Annual Return	5-Year Annual Return	10-Year Annual Return	Broker Availability
UAM Sirach Strat. Balanced (1993) Team Managed	SSBAX	0.87	158	N/A	13.19	N/A	N/A	N/A	JS

Objective: Seeks long-term capital growth by investing 60 percent of assets in common stock and the remaining 40 percent in fixed-income securities, though those percentages may vary with market conditions.

Fund Name/ Start Date/ Manager	Symbol	Expense Ratio %	Portfolio Turnover %	Dividend Yield %	1-Year Annual Return	3-Year Annual Return	5-Year Annual Return	10-Year Annual Return	Broker Availability
Warburg Pincus Balanced (1988) Team Managed	WAPBX	1.53	107	N/A	12.02	13.81	12.74	N/A	FJMSW

Objective: Uses strategic asset allocation techniques to divide assets over a geographically diverse portfolio of equities and fixed-income securities.

Fund Name/ Start Date/ Manager	Symbol	Expense Ratio %	Portfolio Turnover %	Dividend Yield %	1-Year Annual Return	3-Year Annual Return	5-Year Annual Return	10-Year Annual Return	Broker Availability
Westwood Balanced (1991) Byrne/Fraze	WEBAX	1.35	133	N/A	19.11	15.22	N/A	N/A	AFJMS

Objective: Designed to generate both capital appreciation and current income by using a balanced investment approach.

FLEXIBLE PORTFOLIO

Fund Name/ Start Date/ Manager	Symbol	Expense Ratio %	Portfolio Turnover %	Dividend Yield %	1-Year Annual Return	3-Year Annual Return	5-Year Annual Return	10-Year Annual Return	Broker Availability
Benham Capital Manager (1994) J. Tyler	BCMFX	1.01	100	N/A	11.15	N/A	N/A	N/A	JS

Objective: Seeks to maximize total return by allocating assets among U.S. and foreign equities, along with fixed-income securities, money market funds, and gold-related instruments.

Fund Name/ Start Date/ Manager	Symbol	Expense Ratio %	Portfolio Turnover %	Dividend Yield %	1-Year Annual Return	3-Year Annual Return	5-Year Annual Return	10-Year Annual Return	Broker Availability
Blanchard Global Growth (1986) Team Managed	BGGFX	2.54	91	N/A	13.13	7.87	8.30	8.42	FJSW

Objective: Seeks to provide long-term growth by allocating assets among six globally diverse sectors, depending on prevailing market conditions.

Fund Name/ Start Date/ Manager	Symbol	Expense Ratio %	Portfolio Turnover %	Dividend Yield %	1-Year Annual Return	3-Year Annual Return	5-Year Annual Return	10-Year Annual Return	Broker Availability
Brinson Global (1992) G. Brinson	BPGLX	1.04	142	N/A	14.25	10.05	N/A	N/A	JS

Objective: Invests at least 65 percent of assets in securities of at least three different countries, one of which may be the United States.

Fund Name/ Start Date/ Manager	Symbol	Expense Ratio %	Portfolio Turnover %	Dividend Yield %	1-Year Annual Return	3-Year Annual Return	5-Year Annual Return	10-Year Annual Return	Broker Availability
Crabbe Huson Asset Allocation (1989) Huson/Maack	CHAAX	1.48	226	N/A	6.75	9.00	11.34	N/A	AFJMSW

Objective: Pursues a high total return in every type of market while emphasizing capital preservation in down markets.

Fund Name/ Start Date/ Manager	Symbol	Expense Ratio %	Portfolio Turnover %	Dividend Yield %	1-Year Annual Return	3-Year Annual Return	5-Year Annual Return	10-Year Annual Return	Broker Availability
Federated Managed Aggressive Gro. (1994) C. Ritter	FMGGX	1.00	139	N/A	11.03	N/A	N/A	N/A	FJS

Objective: Seeks capital appreciation by investing in both stocks and bonds.

Fund Name/ Start Date/ Manager	Symbol	Expense Ratio %	Portfolio Turnover %	Dividend Yield %	1-Year Annual Return	3-Year Annual Return	5-Year Annual Return	10-Year Annual Return	Broker Availability
Federated Managed Growth (1994) Charles Ritter	FMGFX	1.00	106	N/A	9.87	N/A	N/A	N/A	FJS

Objective: Seeks capital appreciation by investing in both stocks and bonds.

Fund Name/ Start Date/ Manager	Symbol	Expense Ratio %	Portfolio Turnover %	Dividend Yield %	1-Year Annual Return	3-Year Annual Return	5-Year Annual Return	10-Year Annual Return	Broker Availability
Federated Managed Gro. & Income (1994) C. Ritter	FMRIX	1.00	157	N/A	6.63	N/A	N/A	N/A	FJS

Objective: Seeks current income and capital appreciation by investing in both stocks and bonds.

Fund Name/ Start Date/ Manager	Symbol	Expense Ratio %	Portfolio Turnover %	Dividend Yield %	1-Year Annual Return	3-Year Annual Return	5-Year Annual Return	10-Year Annual Return	Broker Availability
Federated Managed Income (1994) Team Managed	FMIFX	0.75	165	6.08	6.04	N/A	N/A	N/A	FJS

Objective: Seeks to provide current income by normally investing 70 percent to 90 percent of assets in bonds and 10 percent to 30 percent in equities.

Fund Name/ Start Date/ Manager	Symbol	Expense Ratio %	Portfolio Turnover %	Dividend Yield %	1-Year Annual Return	3-Year Annual Return	5-Year Annual Return	10-Year Annual Return	Broker Availability
Fremont Global (1988) Team Managed	FMAFX	0.88	83	N/A	13.43	9.95	10.63	N/A	JS

Objective: Allocates assets across a broadly diversified array of investment categories, including U.S. and international stocks and bonds, real estate, and money market instruments.

Fund Name/ Start Date/ Manager	Symbol	Expense Ratio %	Portfolio Turnover %	Dividend Yield %	1-Year Annual Return	3-Year Annual Return	5-Year Annual Return	10-Year Annual Return	Broker Availability
Invesco Multi-Asset Allocation (1993) R. Slotpole	IMAAX	1.62	92	N/A	14.25	N/A	N/A	N/A	JSW

Objective: Invests in six different asset classes: large-cap stocks, small-cap stocks, fixed-income securities, real estate investment trusts, international stocks, and money market instruments.

Fund Name/ Start Date/ Manager	Symbol	Expense Ratio %	Portfolio Turnover %	Dividend Yield %	1-Year Annual Return	3-Year Annual Return	5-Year Annual Return	10-Year Annual Return	Broker Availability
Invesco Total Return (1987) E. Mitchell	FSLFX	0.95	30	N/A	12.33	13.55	13.20	N/A	SW

Objective: Invests in common stocks, convertible securities, and fixed-income instruments, seeking reasonable total returns over a variety of market cycles.

FLEXIBLE PORTFOLIO

Fund Name/ Start Date/ Manager	Symbol	Expense Ratio %	Portfolio Turnover %	Dividend Yield %	1-Year Annual Return	3-Year Annual Return	5-Year Annual Return	10-Year Annual Return	Broker Availability
Montgomery Asset Allocation (1994) Stevens/Honour	MNAAX	1.30	226	N/A	18.10	N/A	N/A	N/A	FJMSW

Objective: Pursues capital appreciation, but strives to minimize risk through an active asset allocation strategy using cash, domestic stocks, and fixed-income securities.

Fund Name/ Start Date/ Manager	Symbol	Expense Ratio %	Portfolio Turnover %	Dividend Yield %	1-Year Annual Return	3-Year Annual Return	5-Year Annual Return	10-Year Annual Return	Broker Availability
Strong Asset Allocation (1981) Team Managed	STAAX	1.20	327	N/A	9.35	8.73	10.04	8.55	FJMSW

Objective: Seeks a combination of income and capital appreciation by taking a reasonable amount of risk and investing assets among a globally diverse portfolio of equities, bonds, and fixed-income instruments.

Fund Name/ Start Date/ Manager	Symbol	Expense Ratio %	Portfolio Turnover %	Dividend Yield %	1-Year Annual Return	3-Year Annual Return	5-Year Annual Return	10-Year Annual Return	Broker Availability
Value Line Asset Allocation (1993) Team Managed	VLAAX	1.39	244	N/A	29.26	20.27	N/A	N/A	AJW

Objective: Seeks to achieve high total investment return consistent with reasonable risk by periodically shifting assets among equities, debt securities, and money market instruments.

PRECIOUS METALS/GOLD

Fund Name/ Start Date/ Manager	Symbol	Expense Ratio %	Portfolio Turnover %	Dividend Yield %	1-Year Annual Return	3-Year Annual Return	5-Year Annual Return	10-Year Annual Return	Broker Availability
Blanchard Precious Metals (1988) Peter Cavelti	BLPMX	2.36	176	N/A	19.30	10.99	13.29	N/A	FJMW
Objective: Seeks long-term capital appreciation and preservation of purchasing power by investing in precious metals and securities of companies involved with precious metals.									
Bull & Bear Gold Investors (1958) Kjeld Thygesen	BBGIX	2.93	158	N/A	19.88	6.80	9.45	4.83	AFJMW
Objective: Seeks capital appreciation by investing in securities with the potential to provide a hedge against inflation, while preserving the purchasing power of the dollar.									
Cappiello-Rushmore Gold (1994) Frank Cappiello	CRGDX	1.70	59	N/A	–10.14	N/A	N/A	N/A	FJMSW
Objective: Pursues capital appreciation by investing in securities engaged in the mining or processing of gold and other precious metals around the world.									
Gabelli Gold (1994) Caesar Bryan	GOLDX	2.25	38	N/A	9.70	N/A	N/A	N/A	AFJMSW
Objective: Seeks long-term capital appreciation by investing in a global portfolio of gold mining and related companies.									
Invesco Strategic Gold (1984) D. Leonard	FGLDX	1.32	72	N/A	44.91	16.37	15.65	5.15	SW
Objective: Invests principally in the common stocks and convertible securities of companies that mine, explore, process, or invest in gold.									
Lexington Goldfund (1979) Robert Radsch	LEXMX	1.70	40	N/A	11.72	10.73	9.42	6.18	FJMSW
Objective: Pursues capital appreciation and hedges against loss of buying power by investing in gold and equity securities of companies engaged in mining or the processing of gold around the world.									
Lexington Strat. Investments (1975) Team Managed	STIVX	1.77	84	N/A	–6.56	9.66	6.11	–3.66	FJMSW
Objective: Seeks capital appreciation through investment primarily in companies that explore, mine, process, fabricate, or distribute natural resources.									
Lexington Strategic Silver (1992) Robert Radsch	STSLX	1.73	44	N/A	3.24	11.73	7.76	0.18	FJMW
Objective: Seeks to maximize total return of both growth and income by investing in securities engaged in the mining, processing, fabrication, or distribution of silver.									
Midas Fund (1986) Kjeld Thygesen	EMGSX	2.26	48	N/A	22.27	22.06	23.53	11.98	AFJSW
Objective: Seeks capital appreciation and protection against inflation with current income as a secondary objective.									
United Services World Gold (1985) Victor Flores	UNWPX	1.51	26	N/A	28.69	16.07	18.85	7.49	FJMSW
Objective: Seeks long-term growth of capital and protection against inflation by investing in gold mining companies with low operating costs.									

SECTOR

Fund Name/ Start Date/ Manager	Symbol	Expense Ratio %	Portfolio Turnover %	Dividend Yield %	1-Year Annual Return	3-Year Annual Return	5-Year Annual Return	10-Year Annual Return	Broker Availability
Benham Utilities Income (1994) W. Martin	BULIX	0.75	68	N/A	5.11	3.54	N/A	N/A	JS

Objective: Seeks current income and long-term growth by investing in equity securities of utilities companies.

Cappiello-Rush. Utility Inc. (1992) Frank Cappiello	CRUTX	1.05	45	N/A	7.47	2.05	N/A	N/A	FJMSW

Objective: Seeks high dividend income, with capital growth as a secondary objective, by investing in high-quality utilities operating in growth areas under favorable regulatory climates.

Century Shares Trust (1928) Allan Fulkerson	CENSX	0.94	5	N/A	11.12	7.38	14.2	11.88	JSW

Objective: To achieve long-term growth of principal and income through investments in common stocks and convertible securities of insurance companies and banks.

Cohen & Steers Realty (1991) Cohen/Steers	CSRSX	1.14	23	N/A	19.68	9.07	16.22	N/A	FJMSW

Objective: Tries to achieve a maximum total return, in terms of both income and appreciation, by investing in publicly traded real estate securities.

Crabbe Huson Real Estate (1994) Richard Huson	CHREX	1.50	60	N/A	19.16	N/A	N/A	N/A	AFJMSW

Objective: Seeks capital appreciation and income by investing in a diversified portfolio consisting primarily of real estate investment trusts.

Gabelli Global Telecom. (1993) Mario Gabelli	GICPX	1.75	24	N/A	7.21	N/A	N/A	N/A	FJMSW

Objective: Under normal market conditions, the fund invests at least 65 percent of total assets in the telecommunications industry.

Invesco Strategic Energy (1984) T. Samuelson	FSTEX	1.53	300	0.66	33.87	N/A	5.58	7.55	SW

Objective: Invests at least 80 percent of assets in companies that explore, develop, produce, or distribute known and new sources of energy.

Invesco Strategic Financial Svcs. (1986) R. Sim	FSFSX	1.26	171	N/A	21.67	13.81	18.93	18.05	SW

Objective: Invests at least 80 percent of assets in common stocks and convertible securities of companies engaged in the financial services industry.

Invesco Strat. Health Sciences (1984) Team Managed	FHLSX	25.4	24.98	11.29	21.81	SW	1.19	107	N/A

Objective: Invests at least 80 percent of assets in companies that develop, produce, or distribute products and services related to the health sciences.

Invesco Strategic Leisure (1984) M. Greenberg	FLISX	1.29	119	N/A	9.26	7.39	17.9	17.45	SW

Objective: Invests at least 80 percent of assets in common stocks and convertible securities of companies in the leisure and entertainment fields.

Invesco Strategic Technology (1984) D. Leonard	FTCHX	1.12	191	N/A	24.65	22.52	23.85	21.92	SW

Objective: Invests in companies that derive at least 50 percent of all revenues from the development or application of products in the technology field.

SECTOR

Fund Name/ Start Date/ Manager	Symbol	Expense Ratio %	Portfolio Turnover %	Dividend Yield %	1-Year Annual Return	3-Year Annual Return	5-Year Annual Return	10-Year Annual Return	Broker Availability
Invesco Worldwide Communications (1994) Team Managed	ISWCX	1.66	157	N/A	15.14	N/A	N/A	N/A	JSW

Objective: Seeks to achieve a high total return by investing in companies that are engaged in the design, development, manufacture, distribution, or sale of communications services and equipment.

PBHG Technology & Communications (1995) Pilgrim	PBTCX	1.50	126	N/A	66.43	N/A	N/A	N/A	FJMS

Objective: Invests in the stocks of companies with strong earnings growth engaged in the field of technology and/or communications.

Rob. Steph. Glo. Natural Resources (1985) A. Pilara	N/A	N/A	N/A	N/A	N/A	N/A	N/A	N/A	AFJMSW

Objective: Seeks to achieve long-term capital appreciation by investing in companies engaged in the discovery, development, production, or distribution of natural resources.

Rob. Steph. Information Age (1995) Ron Elijah	RSIFX	N/A	N/A	N/A	N/A	N/A	N/A	N/A	AFJMSW

Objective: Seeks to achieve long-term capital appreciation by investing in companies in the information technology sector.

Rushmore American Gas Index (1989) Team	GASFX	0.85	10	N/A	20.64	6.88	11.33	N/A	FJSW

Objective: Seeks investment results that correlate with the index comprised of common stocks of natural gas distribution and members of the American Gas Association.

Strong American Utilities (1993) W.H. Reaves	SAMUX	1.20	56	N/A	10	8.77	N/A	N/A	FJMSW

Objective: Pursues current income and capital appreciation primarily by investing in the stocks of public utility companies headquartered in the United States.

United Svcs. Global Resources (1983) Ralph Aldis	PSPFX	2.57	117	N/A	21.81	7.58	6.79	5.40	FJMSW

Objective: Seeks to invest in equity securities of natural resource companies of any kind to provide long-term growth of capital, along with protection against inflation and monetary instability.

United Services Income (1983) Frank Holmes	USINX	2.08	51	N/A	9.23	3.84	8.83	8.80	FJMSW

Objective: Tries to preserve capital and produce current income by investing in common stocks and bonds of seasoned companies with a history of high dividends, usually in the utility sector.

United Services Real Estate (1987) Team Managed	UNREX	2.26	108	N/A	17.68	2.42	7.77	N/A	FJMSW

Objective: Seeks long-term capital appreciation primarily by investing in liquid real estate-related securities, such as real estate investment trusts and equities of home-building companies.

SHORT/INTERMEDIATE-TERM
GENERAL CORPORATES

Fund Name/ Start Date/ Manager	Symbol	Expense Ratio %	Portfolio Turnover %	Dividend Yield %	1-Year Annual Return	3-Year Annual Return	5-Year Annual Return	10-Year Annual Return	Broker Availability
Babson Bond Trust "S" (1988) Edward Martin	BBDSX	0.67	57	7.23	5.17	N/A	6.60	N/A	FJMSW

Objective: Seeks to provide maximum current income and reasonable price stability by investing in a diversified mix of fixed-income securities with a weighted average of five years or less.

Blanchard Flexible Income (1992) Jack Burks	BLFIX	1.56	431	6.59	6.51	N/A	N/A	N/A	FJMSW

Objective: Attempts to provide high current income while seeking opportunities for capital appreciation.

Blanchard ST Flexible Income (1993) Jack Burks	BSTBX	1.44	291	5.58	6.73	N/A	N/A	N/A	FJMSW

Objective: Seeks a high level of current income and principal stability by investing in a broad range of short-term debt securities with maturities of three years or less.

Dreyfus Short-Term Income (1992) Gerald Thunelius	DSTIX	0.80	291	6.29	6.67	N/A	N/A	N/A	AFJMS

Objective: Invests in a broad range of foreign and domestic debt securities with a dollar weighted average portfolio maturity of three years or less.

Federated ST Income (1992) D. Cunningham	FSISX	0.56	77	6.60	5.78	N/A	5.19	6.49	FJS

Objective: Seeks current income primarily by investing in a diversified portfolio of short- and intermediate-term high grade debt securities.

Hotchkis & Wiley Low Dur. (1993) Rivelle/Landmann	HWLDX	0.58	50	6.40	7.37	N/A	N/A	N/A	FJMSW

Objective: Seeks to maximize total return, consistent with preservation of capital, by investing primarily in investment-grade fixed-income securities, including corporate bonds and Treasuries.

Hotchkis & Wiley ST Inst. (1993) Rivelle/Landmann	N/A	0.48	60	5.56	6.61	N/A	N/A	N/A	FJMSW

Objective: Seeks to maximize total return, consistent with preservation of capital, by investing in a diversified mix of fixed-income securities with varying maturities and a portfolio duration of up to one year.

Hotchkis & Wiley Total Return (1994) Team	HWTRX	0.68	51	7.32	6.57	N/A	N/A	N/A	FJMSW

Objective: Seeks to maximize long-term total return by investing in a diversified portfolio of fixed-income securities of varying maturities with a portfolio duration between two years and eight years.

IAI Reserve (1986) Palmer/Douglas	IARVX	0.85	261	5.28	4.33	N/A	4.22	5.76	AFJMS

Objective: Pursues a high level of capital stability and liquidity by investing in high-quality bonds and similar debt securities.

SHORT/INTERMEDIATE-TERM GENERAL CORPORATES

Fund Name/ Start Date/ Manager	Symbol	Expense Ratio %	Portfolio Turnover %	Dividend Yield %	1-Year Annual Return	3-Year Annual Return	5-Year Annual Return	10-Year Annual Return	Broker Availability
Invesco Short-Term Bond (1993) Team Managed	INIBX	0.46	68	5.84	5.02	N/A	N/A	N/A	AJSW
Objective: Invests primarily in short-term debt securities with maturities of three years or less.										
Janus Short-Term Bond (1992) Sandy Rufenacht	JASBX	0.65	337	5.98	5.74	N/A	N/A	N/A	FMS
Objective: Tries to provide a high level of current income primarily by investing in short and intermediate fixed-income securities, with maturities of three years to five years.										
Loomis Sayles Short-Term Bond (1992) John Hyll	LSSTX	1.00	214	5.89	5.01	N/A	N/A	N/A	FJMSW
Objective: To achieve highest total return of current income and capital appreciation with relatively low fluctuation in net asset value by investing in bonds with maturities of five years or less.										
Merriman Flexible Bond (1988) Merriman/Notaro	MTFYX	1.50	291	5.84	7.62	5.45	8.07	N/A	JSW
Objective: To provide income, preservation of capital, and secondarily, growth of capital by investing, either directly or through other mutual funds, in all types of debt securities.										
Neuberger & Berman Ltd. Mat. Bond^ (1993) T. Wolfe	NLMBX	0.70	88	6.47	5.18	N/A	5.74	6.81	FMS
Objective: Seeks high current income and low risk to principal by investing in a diversified portfolio of short- to intermediate-term debt securities with average maturities of less than five years.										
Neuberger & Ber. Ultra ST Bond^ (1993) J. Mahoney	NBMMX	0.65	148	5.40	4.90	N/A	4.22	N/A	FMS
Objective: Seeks a higher return than money market funds by investing in a wide array of short-term bonds.										
Rainier Int. Fixed Income (1994) Frost/Raney	RIMFX	0.95	15	5.20	4.50	N/A	N/A	N/A	AFJMS
Objective: Tries to provide investors with a modest degree of current income.										
Sit Bond (1993) Team Managed	N/A	0.80	159	6.89	5.03	N/A	N/A	N/A	FJMS
Objective: Seeks to maximize total return, consistent with the preservation of capital.										
Stein Roe Intermediate Bond (1978) M. Kennedy	SRBFX	0.70	202	6.43	5.51	N/A	7.31	7.94	FJMSW
Objective: Pursues high current income primarily by investing in marketable debt securities.										
Strong Advantage (1988) Jeffrey Koch	STADX	0.80	17	6.31	6.35	N/A	7.06	N/A	FJMSW
Objective: Seeks a high level of current income, consistent with minimum fluctuation in principal, by investing in money market instruments and other debt securities.										

^=with some discount brokers, Neuberger & Berman funds are operated as Trust accounts. In essence, these are a separate share class of funds with the exact same name. Trust funds are different in that they charge slightly higher management fees and are offered exclusively through select brokers, including Fidelity.

SHORT/INTERMEDIATE-TERM
GENERAL CORPORATES

Fund Name/ Start Date/ Manager	Symbol	Expense Ratio %	Portfolio Turnover %	Dividend Yield %	1-Year Annual Return	3-Year Annual Return	5-Year Annual Return	10-Year Annual Return	Broker Availability
Strong Short-Term Bond (1987) Tank/Fitterer	SSTBX	0.90	250	7.44	7.11	N/A	7.01	N/A	FJMSW

Objective: Seeks the highest level of income consistent with minimum fluctuation in principal value and current liquidity by investing in short- and intermediate-term debt securities with maturities between one and three years.

| **UAM Chicago Interm. Bond** (1995) W. ZImmer | N/A | 0.80 | 24 | 5.78 | 4.74 | N/A | N/A | N/A | JS |

Objective: Seeks a high level of current income consistent with moderate interest rate exposure.

| **UAM Sirach Fixed-Income** (1993) Team Managed | N/A | 0.76 | 165 | 6.47 | 3.43 | N/A | N/A | N/A | JS |

Objective: Seeks total return with reasonable risk to principal by investing most of its assets in investment-grade fixed-income securities.

| **Warburg Pincus Fixed Income** (1987) Team Managed | CUFIX | 0.75 | 183 | 6.54 | 6.10 | N/A | 7.86 | N/A | FJMSW |

Objective: Invests at least 80 percent of assets in fixed-income securities, and can invest up to 20 percent of the portfolio in money market instruments.

| **Westwood Int. Bond** (1991) Byrne/Fraze | WEIBX | 1.17 | 165 | 0.00 | 4.48 | N/A | 6.29 | N/A | FMSW |

Objective: Seeks a maximum total return by investing in intermediate-term fixed-income securities.

LONG-TERM GENERAL CORPORATES

Fund Name/ Start Date/ Manager	Symbol	Expense Ratio %	Portfolio Turnover %	Dividend Yield %	1-Year Annual Return	3-Year Annual Return	5-Year Annual Return	10-Year Annual Return	Broker Availability
Blanchard Flexible Income (1992) Jack Burks	BLFIX	1.56	431	6.47	6.69	4.86	N/A	N/A	FJMSW
Objective: Seeks high income and capital appreciation by investing in a broad range of fixed-income securities according to market conditions.									
Federated Managed Income (1994) Charles Ritter	FMIFX	0.75	165	5.59	6.04	N/A	N/A	N/A	FJS
Objective: Attempts to provide current income primarily by moving money between stocks, bonds, and cash reserves.									
Hotchkis & Wiley Total Return (1994) Team Managed	HWTRX	0.68	51	7.28	6.63	N/A	N/A	N/A	FJMSW
Objective: Seeks to maximize long-term total return by investing in a diversified portfolio of fixed-income securities of varying maturities with a portfolio duration of two years to eight years.									
Invesco Select Income (1976) J. Paul	FBDSX	1.00	181	7.70	5.72	6.86	9.23	8.44	JS
Objective: Invests at least 50 percent of the portfolio in debt securities rated medium and higher.									
Janus Flexible Income (1987) Speaker/Rufenacht	JAFIX	0.96	250	8.19	9.17	N/A	10.57	N/A	FMS
Objective: Seeks maximum total return, while preserving capital, by actively managing a portfolio of income producing securities.									
Loomis Sayles Bond (1991) Daniel Fuss	LSBDX	0.79	35	7.83	11.29	10.96	13.94	N/A	FJMSW
Objective: To achieve high total return through a combination of current income and capital appreciation by investing at least 65 percent of total assets in bonds.									
Wasatch-Hosington U.S. Treasury (1986) Samuel Stewart	N/A	1.00	43	6.34	4.42	N/A	5.67	N/A	FMSW
Objective: Seeks to receive current income and secondarily capital appreciation at low risk by investing in fixed-income securities.									

HIGH QUALITY CORPORATES

Fund Name/ Start Date/ Manager	Symbol	Expense Ratio %	Portfolio Turnover %	Dividend Yield %	1-Year Annual Return	3-Year Annual Return	5-Year Annual Return	10-Year Annual Return	Broker Availability
Babson Bond Trust "L" (1945) Edward Martin	BABIX	0.97	50	N/A	3.78	4.11	7.09	7.88	FJMSW

Objective: Contains a diversified portfolio of fixed-income securities with the primary emphasis placed on producing current regular income.

Fund Name/ Start Date/ Manager	Symbol	Expense Ratio %	Portfolio Turnover %	Dividend Yield %	1-Year Annual Return	3-Year Annual Return	5-Year Annual Return	10-Year Annual Return	Broker Availability
Crabbe Huson Income (1989) Huson/Nesbit	CHINX	0.80	543	6.46	4.49	3.98	5.92	N/A	AFJMSW

Objective: Seeks to provide the highest level of current income that is consistent with preservation of capital by investing in a diversified mix of fixed-income securities, convertible bonds, and debentures.

Fund Name/ Start Date/ Manager	Symbol	Expense Ratio %	Portfolio Turnover %	Dividend Yield %	1-Year Annual Return	3-Year Annual Return	5-Year Annual Return	10-Year Annual Return	Broker Availability
Dreyfus A Bonds Plus (1976) Garitt Kono	DRBDX	0.93	166	6.15	4.33	3.75	8.25	8.46	FJMSW

Objective: Invests at least 80 percent of the portfolio in bonds rated A or better by S&P or Moody's with the overall goal of generating a maximum amount of income.

Fund Name/ Start Date/ Manager	Symbol	Expense Ratio %	Portfolio Turnover %	Dividend Yield %	1-Year Annual Return	3-Year Annual Return	5-Year Annual Return	10-Year Annual Return	Broker Availability
IAI Bond (1977) Hill/Bettin/Douglas	IAIBX	1.09	425	6.29	4.10	3.23	7.20	8.00	AFJMS

Objective: Seeks a high level of current income by investing in investment-grade bonds and other debt securities considered to be of similar quality.

Fund Name/ Start Date/ Manager	Symbol	Expense Ratio %	Portfolio Turnover %	Dividend Yield %	1-Year Annual Return	3-Year Annual Return	5-Year Annual Return	10-Year Annual Return	Broker Availability
Stein Roe Income (1986) Ann Benjamin	SRHBX	0.82	135	7.28	5.64	5.43	8.72	8.65	FJMSW

Objective: Pursues high current income by investing principally in medium quality debt securities.

Fund Name/ Start Date/ Manager	Symbol	Expense Ratio %	Portfolio Turnover %	Dividend Yield %	1-Year Annual Return	3-Year Annual Return	5-Year Annual Return	10-Year Annual Return	Broker Availability
Strong Corporate Bond (1985) Koch/Bender	STCBX	1.00	621	7.23	7.02	8.39	10.66	7.73	FJMSW

Objective: Seeks to obtain a high level of current income by investing in a diversified portfolio of fixed-income securities and dividend paying common stocks.

Fund Name/ Start Date/ Manager	Symbol	Expense Ratio %	Portfolio Turnover %	Dividend Yield %	1-Year Annual Return	3-Year Annual Return	5-Year Annual Return	10-Year Annual Return	Broker Availability
UAM DSI Limited Maturity Bond (1989) D. Gray	DSILX	0.87	126	6.30	5.33	N/A	5.80	N/A	JS

Objective: To generate maximum total return through investing in investment-grade fixed-income securities.

Fund Name/ Start Date/ Manager	Symbol	Expense Ratio %	Portfolio Turnover %	Dividend Yield %	1-Year Annual Return	3-Year Annual Return	5-Year Annual Return	10-Year Annual Return	Broker Availability
Wright Total Return Bond (1993) Team Managed	WTRBX	0.80	50	6.22	2.89	3.16	6.83	7.03	AFJMSW

Objective: Attempts to provide a superior rate of total return with a high level of income.

HIGH-YIELD CORPORATES

Fund Name/ Start Date/ Manager	Symbol	Expense Ratio %	Portfolio Turnover %	Dividend Yield %	1-Year Annual Return	3-Year Annual Return	5-Year Annual Return	10-Year Annual Return	Broker Availability
Federated High-Yield Trust (1984) Mark Durbiano	FHYTX	0.88	87	10.12	13.19	10.09	12.40	10.50	FJSW
	Objective: Seeks high current income by investing in a professionally managed, diversified portfolio of fixed-income securities.								
Invesco High-Yield (1984) J. Paul	FHYPX	1.00	201	9.37	14.00	8.49	11.32	8.95	AJSW
	Objective: Invests in fixed-income securities rated in lower categories by recognized services.								
Janus High-Yield Fund (1994) Ronald Speaker	JAHYX	N/A	N/A	9.19	N/A	N/A	N/A	N/A	FMS
	Objective: Seeks to obtain high current income and capital appreciation by investing at least 65 percent of the portfolio in high-yield, high-risk, fixed-income securities.								
Strong High-Yield Bond Fund (1995) Jeffrey Koch	STHYX	N/A	N/A	10.25	N/A	N/A	N/A	N/A	FJMSW
	Objective: Pursues high current income and capital appreciation by investing in higher yielding and lower quality fixed-income securities.								

SHORT/INTERMEDIATE-TERM GOVERNMENT

Fund Name/ Start Date/ Manager	Symbol	Expense Ratio %	Portfolio Turnover %	Dividend Yield %	1-Year Annual Return	3-Year Annual Return	5-Year Annual Return	10-Year Annual Return	Broker Availability
Benham ST Treas. & Agcy. (1992) D. Schroeder	BSTAX	0.67	224	5.66	4.61	N/A	N/A	N/A	JS

Objective: Invests exclusively in securities issued or guaranteed by the U.S. Treasury and other U.S. government agencies with average maturities from 13 months to three years.

| Crabbe Huson US Govt. Income (1989) Huson/Nesbit | CHUSX | 0.75 | 230 | 5.61 | 4.89 | N/A | 5.36 | N/A | AFJMSW |

Objective: Seeks to provide a high level of current income, while preserving capital, by investing most of its assets in short- and intermediate-term debt U.S. government obligations.

| Dreyfus Short-Int. Govt. (1987) Gerald Thunelius | DSIGX | 0.66 | 387 | 5.66 | 5.26 | N/A | 6.60 | N/A | AFJMS |

Objective: Invests in securities issued or guaranteed by the U.S. government in the pursuit of a high-level of current income consistent with the preservation of capital.

| Federated Int. Govt. Trust (1992) Nason/Balestrino | FIGIX | 0.79 | N/A | 5.73 | 4.37 | N/A | N/A | N/A | FJW |

Objective: Seeks current income by investing in U.S. government securities with maturities of five years or less.

| Federated Short-Int. Govt. (1992) Nason/Balestrino | FSGIX | 0.79 | N/A | 5.35 | 4.91 | N/A | N/A | N/A | FJW |

Objective: Seeks current income by investing in U.S. government securities with maturities of 3.5 years or less.

| Founders Govt. Securities (1988) Team Managed | FGVSX | 1.30 | 141 | 4.60 | 2.85 | N/A | 4.55 | N/A | AFMSW |

Objective: Seeks current income by investing primarily in obligations of the U.S. government.

| IAI Government (1991) Bettin/Coleman | SPSIX | 1.10 | 284 | 5.87 | 3.73 | N/A | 5.73 | N/A | AFJMS |

Objective: Pursues as high a level of current income as is consistent with preservation of capital by investing in securities backed by the U.S. government, with dollar-weighted average maturities of two to five years.

| Janus Intermediate Govt. Secs. (1991) S. Rufenacht | JAIGX | 0.65 | 252 | 5.80 | 1.66 | N/A | 4.21 | N/A | FMS |

Objective: Seeks to provide a high level of current income by investing in obligations issued by the U.S. government and its agencies with an average maturity of less than ten years.

| Managers Short Govt. (1992) W. Stevens | MGSGX | 1.25 | 238 | 4.94 | 4.41 | N/A | 3.08 | N/A | JS |

Objective: Seeks high current income while preserving capital by investing primarily in U.S. government securities with an average maturity not exceeding three years.

| Montgomery Short Govt. Bond (1992) Wm. Stevens | MNSGX | 1.55 | 350 | 5.69 | 5.70 | N/A | N/A | N/A | FJMSW |

Objective: Invests in obligations issued or guaranteed by the U.S. government with an average portfolio duration similar to that of three-year U.S. Treasury Notes in an effort to manage interest rate risk.

| Sit U.S. Govt. Securities (1987) Team Managed | SNGVX | 0.80 | 51 | 6.10 | 5.83 | N/A | 6.55 | N/A | FJMS |

Objective: Invests in debt issued, guaranteed or insured by the U.S. government or its agencies.

SHORT/INTERMEDIATE-TERM GOVERNMENT

Fund Name/ Start Date/ Manager	Symbol	Expense Ratio %	Portfolio Turnover %	Dividend Yield %	1-Year Annual Return	3-Year Annual Return	5-Year Annual Return	10-Year Annual Return	Broker Availability
Smith Breeden Sht. Dur. U.S. Govt. (1992) D. Dektar	SBSHX	0.78	225	5.60	5.73	N/A	N/A	N/A	JS

Objective: Seeks a high level of current income, consistent with low volatility, by investing in high-quality securities of the U.S. government.

Fund Name/ Start Date/ Manager	Symbol	Expense Ratio %	Portfolio Turnover %	Dividend Yield %	1-Year Annual Return	3-Year Annual Return	5-Year Annual Return	10-Year Annual Return	Broker Availability
Stein Roe Income (1993) Steve Luetger	SRLIX	0.82	135	7.26	5.65	N/A	8.73	8.91	FJMSW

Objective: Invests for high current income, primarily from U.S. government and other high-quality debt securities with a dollar-weighted average portfolio maturity of less than three years.

Fund Name/ Start Date/ Manager	Symbol	Expense Ratio %	Portfolio Turnover %	Dividend Yield %	1-Year Annual Return	3-Year Annual Return	5-Year Annual Return	10-Year Annual Return	Broker Availability
Warburg Pincus Int. Mat. Govt. (1988) Team	CUIGX	0.60	106	6.19	4.70	N/A	6.75	N/A	FJMSW

Objective: Seeks to achieve a high level of current income consistent with the preservation of capital.

LONG-TERM GOVERNMENT CORPORATES

Fund Name/ Start Date/ Manager	Symbol	Expense Ratio %	Portfolio Turnover %	Dividend Yield %	1-Year Annual Return	3-Year Annual Return	5-Year Annual Return	10-Year Annual Return	Broker Availability
Benham LT Treasury & Agcy (1992) D. Schroeder	BLAGX	0.67	112	6.48	1.73	N/A	N/A	N/A	JS

Objective: Invests exclusively in securities issued or guaranteed by the U.S. Treasury and agencies of the U.S. government with average maturities of 20 to 30 years.

Bull & Bear U.S. Govt. Secs. (1986) Steven Landis	BBUSX	N/A	N/A	N/A	N/A	N/A	N/A	N/A	AJMW

Objective: Designed for long-term investors who want to invest in securities for a high level of income and liquidity that are backed by the U.S. government.

Federated U.S. Govt. Bond (1985) S. Nason	FEDBX	0.85	37	6.17	7.72	N/A	7.72	7.58	JS

Objective: Invests in investment-grade bonds, with total return as a secondary objective.

Heartland U.S. Govt. Secs. (1987) Retzer/Nasgovitz	HRUSX	1.07	97	6.59	3.09	N/A	7.59	N/A	AFJMSW

Objective: Invests in government securities to generate an attractive current income while protecting principal.

Invesco U.S. Govt. Securities (1986) R. Hinderlie	FBDGX	1.00	99	5.79	2.26	N/A	6.32	6.52	AJSW

Objective: Invests in obligations issued or guaranteed by the U.S. government or its agencies.

Loomis Sayles U.S. Govt. (1991) Kent Newmark	LSGSX	1.00	169	6.17	2.21	N/A	8.66	N/A	FJMSW

Objective: Invests at least 65 percent of total assets in U.S. government securities to achieve the highest total return of current income and capital appreciation.

Managers Bond (1984) D. Fuss	MGFIX	1.34	46	6.79	4.34	6.52	8.76	9.41	JS

Objective: Seeks income primarily through investment in fixed-income securities.

Rushmore U.S. Govt. Bond (1985) Team Managed	RSGVX	0.80	63	6.28	124	N/A	7.51	8.07	FJSW

Objective: Seeks to invest in U.S. government securities with maturities of up to 30 years.

Stein Roe Govt. Income (1986) Michael Kennedy	SRGPX	1.00	73	6.01	4.22	N/A	6.30	7.40	FJMSW

Objective: Seeks high current income by investing in debt securities backed by the U.S. government, such as Treasury obligations and GNMA certificates.

Strong Government (1986) Bradley Tank	STVSX	0.90	479	6.72	3.69	N/A	8.55	N/A	FJMSW

Objective: Seeks a high level of current income from a diversified portfolio of securities issued or guaranteed by the U.S. government.

MORTGAGE-BACKED GOVERNMENT

Fund Name/ Start Date/ Manager	Symbol	Expense Ratio %	Portfolio Turnover %	Dividend Yield %	1-Year Annual Return	3-Year Annual Return	5-Year Annual Return	10-Year Annual Return	Broker Availability
Benham Adj. Rate Govt. (1991) N. Rankin	BARGX	0.60	221	5.55	5.70	N/A	4.59	N/A	JS
		Objective: Invests primarily in adjustable rate mortgage securities issued by the U.S. government or its agencies.							
Benham GNMA Income (1985) Team Managed	BGNMX	0.58	64	7.02	5.01	N/A	6.89	8.31	JS
		Objective: Invests in GNMA instruments.							
Dreyfus GNMA (1985) Garritt Kono	DRGMX	0.96	144	6.74	5.34	N/A	6.31	7.46	AFJMSW
		Objective: Seeks to provide high current income by investing predominately in GNMAs.							
Federated ARMs (1992) Malus/Nason	FASSX	0.55	65	5.94	6.30	N/A	5.42	6.61	FJSW
		Objective: Seeks current income consistent with minimal volatility of principal by investing at least 65 percent of all assets in a professionally managed portfolio of U.S. government securities.							
Federated GNMA Trust (1992) Kathy Malus	FGSSX	0.56	136	6.41	4.62	N/A	6.44	8.20	FJSW
		Objective: Seeks current income by investing in U.S. government securities, mostly instruments of the Government National Mortgage Association.							
Federated Income Trust (1992) Kathy Malus	FITSX	0.56	217	6.23	5.19	N/A	6.16	7.81	FJS
		Objective: Pursues current income by investing in U.S. government securities and certain collateralized mortgage obligations.							
Lexington GNMA Income (1973) Denis Jamison	LEXNX	1.01	31	7.17	6.10	N/A	6.91	8.21	FJMS
		Objective: Seeks a high level of current income consistent with liquidity and safety of principal by investing primarily in mortgage-backed GNMA certificates.							
Managers Int. Mortgage (1986) Team Managed	MGIGX	1.17	506	6.13	4.16	N/A	2.88	6.69	JS
		Objective: Seeks to produce high current income through investing in mortgage-related securities with maturities of less than 15 years from the date of purchase.							
Smith Breeden Int. Dur. U.S. Govt. (1995) D. Dektar	SBIDX	0.88	193	6.50	5.29	N/A	N/A	N/A	AJS
		Objective: Seeks to exceed the total return of intermediate bond indexes by investing in high-quality U.S. government and related mortgage-backed securities.							
Wright Current Income (1987) Team Managed	WCIFX	0.90	26	N/A	4.79	N/A	N/A	N/A	AFJMSW
		Objective: Seeks a high level of current income consistent with moderate fluctuations of principal by constructing a portfolio of quality mortgage-related securities.							

SHORT/INTERMEDIATE U.S. TREASURIES

Fund Name/ Start Date/ Manager	Symbol	Expense Ratio %	Portfolio Turnover %	Dividend Yield %	1-Year Annual Return	3-Year Annual Return	5-Year Annual Return	10-Year Annual Return	Broker Availability
Benham Target Mat. 2000 (1985) D. Schroeder	BTMTX	0.63	53	6.10	4.02	3.37	8.71	9.35	JS
		Objective: Invests principally in zero-coupon U.S. Treasury securities maturing in 2000.							
Benham Target Mat. 2005 (1985) D. Schroeder	BTFIX	0.71	34	6.54	2.16	3.71	10.48	10.34	JS
		Objective: Invests principally in zero-coupon U.S. Treasury securities maturing in 2005.							
Benham Target Mat. 2010 (1985) D. Schroeder	BTTNX	0.71	26	6.81	0.78	3.67	11.11	10.37	JS
		Objective: Invests primarily in zero-coupon U.S. Treasury securities maturing in 2010.							
Benham Target Mat. 2015 (1986) D. Schroeder	BTFTX	0.71	70	7.06	−0.75	3.25	11.63	9.38	JS
		Objective: Invests primarily in zero-coupon U.S. Treasury securities maturing in 2015.							
Benham Target Mat. 2020 (1989) D. Schroeder	BTTTX	0.72	78	7.48	−2.09	2.02	11.9	N/A	JS
		Objective: Invests primarily in zero-coupon U.S. Treasury securities maturing in 2020.							
Benham Target Mat. 2025 (1996) D. Schroeder	BTTRX	N/A	N/A	7.26	N/A	N/A	N/A	N/A	JS
		Objective: Invests primarily in zero-coupon U.S. Treasury securities maturing in 2025.							
Benham Treasury Note (1980) D. Schroeder	CPTNX	0.53	168	6.15	4.77	N/A	6.32	6.77	JS
		Objective: Invests at least 65 percent of total assets in U.S. Treasury Notes.							
Federated U.S. Govt.: **1–3 Yrs.** (1984) S. Nason	FSGVX	0.54	142	5.76	5.15	N/A	5.18	6.49	JS
		Objective: Invests only in U.S. government securities with remaining maturities less than 3 1/2 years.							
Federated U.S. Govt.: **2–5 Yrs.** (1995) Team	FIGTX	0.54	163	6.10	4.62	N/A	6.19	7.21	JS
		Objective: Invests in U.S. government securities with remaining maturities of five years or less.							
Federated U.S. Govt.: **5–10 Yrs.** (1995) Team	FGVIX	0.11	29	6.62	N/A	N/A	N/A	N/A	JS
		Objective: Invests in U.S. government securities with remaining maturities of ten years or less.							
Founders Government **Securities** (1988) Team Managed	FGVSX	1.30	141	4.60	2.85	N/A	4.55	N/A	AFMSW
		Objective: Seeks current income primarily by investing in obligations of the U.S. government, but may also invest up to 30 percent of assets in debt issued or guaranteed by foreign governments.							
Wright U.S. Treasury (1993) Team Managed	WGOBX	0.90	8	5.69	2.39	N/A	8.12	8.13	AFJMSW
		Objective: Seeks a high total return including capital appreciation and income.							
Wright U.S. Treasury **Near-Term** (1993) Team Managed	WNTBX	0.80	21	5.25	4.91	N/A	5.86	6.75	AFJMSW
		Objective: Seeks a high level of income above short-term money market rates and subject to only modest fluctuations in principal value.							

INTERNATIONAL/GLOBAL BOND

Fund Name/ Start Date/ Manager	Symbol	Expense Ratio %	Portfolio Turnover %	Dividend Yield %	1-Year Annual Return	3-Year Annual Return	5-Year Annual Return	10-Year Annual Return	Broker Availability
Benham European Govt. Bond (1992) Team Managed	BEGBX	0.82	167	N/A	7.63	8.91	N/A	N/A	JS

Objective: Invests primarily in European government debt securities of the highest quality.

Brinson Global Bond (1995) G. Brinson	BPGBX	0.90	184	N/A	11.00	7.64	N/A	N/A	JS

Objective: Attempts to maximize total return (capital appreciation and current income) while controlling risk by investing in a globally diverse portfolio of fixed-income securities.

Bull & Bear Global Inc. (1983) Steven Landis	BBGLX	2.21	385	8.19	8.22	1.28	7.67	4.41	AFMW

Objective: Seeks to achieve a high level of income by investing in a diversified portfolio of investment-grade fixed-income debt securities.

Guinness Flt. Glo. Govt. Bond (1994) P. Saunders	N/A	1.89	203	4.53	5.26	N/A	N/A	N/A	FJMSW

Objective: Seeks to provide investors with both current income and capital appreciation through a globally diverse portfolio of fixed-income securities.

Lexington Ramirez Glo. Inc. (1994) Jamison/Ramirez	LEBDX	2.75	165	8.82	13.34	N/A	N/A	N/A	FJMSW

Objective: Pursues high current income by investing in a combination of foreign and domestic high-yield, lower-rated debt securities.

Loomis Sayles Global Bond (1991) E. John de Beer	LSGBX	1.50	148	6.53	17.8	8.18	9.66	N/A	FJMSW

Objective: Seeks high current income and capital appreciation from investment-grade, fixed-income obligations (including convertibles) denominated in various currencies.

Managers Global Bond (1994) O. Rogge	MGGBX	1.55	214	5.04	5.62	N/A	N/A	N/A	JS

Objective: Seeks high total return by investing primarily in domestic and foreign fixed-income securities.

Strong International Bond (1994) Shirish Maleker	SIBUX	0.00	473	N/A	7.67	N/A	N/A	N/A	FJMSW

Objective: Seeks a high total return by investing in fixed-income securities around the world.

Strong ST Global Bond (1994) Shirish Maleker	STGBX	0.00	437	8.05	10.04	N/A	N/A	N/A	FJMSW

Objective: Seeks a high total return by investing in fixed-income securities around the world.

Vontobel International Bond (1994) Sven Rump	VIBDX	1.76	19	N/A	7.32	N/A	N/A	N/A	FJMSW

Objective: Seeks to maximize total return from both capital growth and income by investing in a global portfolio of fixed-income instruments.

Warburg Pincus Glo. Fixed Inc. (1990) Team Managed	CGFIX	0.95	129	5.78	11.06	6.13	9.2	N/A	FJMSW

Objective: Seeks to maximize total investment return with a combination of prudent global investment management, interest income, currency gains, and capital appreciation.

SHORT/INTERMEDIATE MUNICIPALS

Fund Name/ Start Date/ Manager	Symbol	Expense Ratio %	Portfolio Turnover %	Dividend Yield %	1-Year Annual Return	3-Year Annual Return	5-Year Annual Return	10-Year Annual Return	Broker Availability
Babson Tax-Free "S" (1980) Joel Vernick	BASTX	1.01	41	N/A	3.49	3.27	5.01	5.66	FJMSW

Objective: Invests in municipal debt issues with dollar-weighted average maturities of less than five years.

Fund Name/ Start Date/ Manager	Symbol	Expense Ratio %	Portfolio Turnover %	Dividend Yield %	1-Year Annual Return	3-Year Annual Return	5-Year Annual Return	10-Year Annual Return	Broker Availability
Benham Natl. T/F Int. Term (1984) Team Managed	BNTIX	0.70	46	4.20	4.55	3.78	6.20	6.58	JS

Objective: Seeks a high level of current income exempt from federal taxes by investing in municipal debt issues with maturities from four to 12 years.

Fund Name/ Start Date/ Manager	Symbol	Expense Ratio %	Portfolio Turnover %	Dividend Yield %	1-Year Annual Return	3-Year Annual Return	5-Year Annual Return	10-Year Annual Return	Broker Availability
Dreyfus Intermediate Muni (1983) Monica Wieboldt	DITEX	0.71	49	4.76	4.27	3.84	6.70	7.02	FJMS

Objective: Invests in municipal debt issues with dollar-weighted average maturities of three to ten years.

Fund Name/ Start Date/ Manager	Symbol	Expense Ratio %	Portfolio Turnover %	Dividend Yield %	1-Year Annual Return	3-Year Annual Return	5-Year Annual Return	10-Year Annual Return	Broker Availability
Dreyfus Sh-Int. Tax Exempt (1987) S. Weinstock	DSIBX	0.68	44	3.83	4.57	3.63	5.06	N/A	AJMS

Objective: Seeks to provide investors with a high level of current income exempt from Federal income taxes through investment in medium and lower grade municipal securities.

Fund Name/ Start Date/ Manager	Symbol	Expense Ratio %	Portfolio Turnover %	Dividend Yield %	1-Year Annual Return	3-Year Annual Return	5-Year Annual Return	10-Year Annual Return	Broker Availability
Federated Intermediate Muni (1985) J. Conley	FIMTX	0.57	19	4.45	4.24	3.33	5.80	6.09	FJS

Objective: Seeks to provide a high level of current income exempt from Federal income taxes through investments in medium and lower grade municipal securities.

Fund Name/ Start Date/ Manager	Symbol	Expense Ratio %	Portfolio Turnover %	Dividend Yield %	1-Year Annual Return	3-Year Annual Return	5-Year Annual Return	10-Year Annual Return	Broker Availability
Federated ST Muni Trust (1993) Jonathan Conley	FSHSX	0.46	33	3.83	4.07	3.81	4.4	4.98	FJS

Objective: Seeks to provide investors with a high level of current income exempt from Federal income taxes through investment in medium and lower grade municipal securities.

Fund Name/ Start Date/ Manager	Symbol	Expense Ratio %	Portfolio Turnover %	Dividend Yield %	1-Year Annual Return	3-Year Annual Return	5-Year Annual Return	10-Year Annual Return	Broker Availability
Invesco Tax-Free Int. Bond (1993) J. Grabovac	N/A	0.70	23	4.13	3.87	N/A	N/A	N/A	AJS

Objective: Invests in a diversified portfolio of intermediate-term obligations that pay interest exempt from Federal taxes.

Fund Name/ Start Date/ Manager	Symbol	Expense Ratio %	Portfolio Turnover %	Dividend Yield %	1-Year Annual Return	3-Year Annual Return	5-Year Annual Return	10-Year Annual Return	Broker Availability
Neuberger & Berman Municipal^ (1987) C. Del Villar	NBMUX	0.65	0	4.17	4.23	3.53	5.79	N/A	FS

Objective: A short-to-intermediate-term bond fund seeking high current tax-exempt income with low risk to principal.

Fund Name/ Start Date/ Manager	Symbol	Expense Ratio %	Portfolio Turnover %	Dividend Yield %	1-Year Annual Return	3-Year Annual Return	5-Year Annual Return	10-Year Annual Return	Broker Availability
Stein Roe Intermediate Muni (1985) J. Costopoulos	SRIMX	0.70	66	4.41	4.48	3.95	6.56	6.67	FJMSW

Objective: Seeks to provide a high level of current income exempt from Federal income taxes through investment in medium and lower grade municipal securities.

Fund Name/ Start Date/ Manager	Symbol	Expense Ratio %	Portfolio Turnover %	Dividend Yield %	1-Year Annual Return	3-Year Annual Return	5-Year Annual Return	10-Year Annual Return	Broker Availability
Strong Municipal Adv. (1995) Steven Harrop	SMUAX	N/A	N/A	4.93	N/A	N/A	N/A	N/A	FJMSW

Objective: Seeks to provide investors with a high level of current income exempt from Federal income taxes through investment in medium and lower grade municipal securities.

Fund Name/ Start Date/ Manager	Symbol	Expense Ratio %	Portfolio Turnover %	Dividend Yield %	1-Year Annual Return	3-Year Annual Return	5-Year Annual Return	10-Year Annual Return	Broker Availability
Strong ST Municipal (1991) Steven Harrop	STSMX	0.80	227	5.12	4.42	2.58	N/A	N/A	FJMSW

Objective: Pursues total return by investing for a high level of federal tax-exempt current income with minimal share price fluctuation through buying investment-grade municipal bonds with maturities of three years or less.

Fund Name/ Start Date/ Manager	Symbol	Expense Ratio %	Portfolio Turnover %	Dividend Yield %	1-Year Annual Return	3-Year Annual Return	5-Year Annual Return	10-Year Annual Return	Broker Availability
Warburg Pincus Tax-Free (1988) S. Parente	N/A	0.48	38	4.73	5.10	4.31	7.96	N/A	FJMSW

Objective: Seeks to maximize current interest income exempt from Federal income taxes, consistent with the preservation of capital.

LONG-TERM MUNICIPALS

Fund Name/ Start Date/ Manager	Symbol	Expense Ratio %	Portfolio Turnover %	Dividend Yield %	1-Year Annual Return	3-Year Annual Return	5-Year Annual Return	10-Year Annual Return	Broker Availability
Babson Tax-Free "L" (1980) Joel Vernick	BALTX	1.01	39	N/A	5.12	3.25	6.57	6.95	FJMSW
Objective: Invests at least 65 percent of assets in municipal debt issues in the top four credit ratings.									
Benham National T/F Long-Term (1984) G. MacEwen	BTFLX	0.70	49	4.82	6.27	3.75	7.59	7.00	JS
Objective: Invests in municipal debt issues with average weighted maturities of 12 years or more.									
Blanchard Flex. Tax-Free Bond (1993) Ken McAlley	BTFBX	1.05	275	4.88	7.24	N/A	N/A	N/A	FJMSW
Objective: Pursues a high level of current interest income exempt from Federal income tax by investing in municipal bonds of various maturities according to prevailing market conditions.									
Bull & Bear Muni Income (1984) Steven Landis	BTFBX	1.78	172	3.85	4.47	1.64	4.81	6.18	AFJMW
Objective: Invests for the maximum possible income that is exempt from Federal income tax consistent with the preservation of principal.									
Dreyfus General Muni Bond (1984) Paul Disdier	GMBDX	0.88	115	5.27	4.90	3.39	7.13	7.57	FJMW
Objective: Seeks to invest at least 65 percent of total assets in municipal debt issues falling within the top four credit ratings.									
Dreyfus Insured Muni Bond (1985) L. Troutman	DTBDX	0.85	83	5.01	4.83	2.07	5.85	6.40	AFJMSW
Objective: Seeks to provide a high level of current income exempt from Federal income taxes primarily through investing in medium and lower grade municipal securities.									
Dreyfus Municipal Bond (1976) Richard Moynihan	DRTAX	0.70	52	5.26	5.36	3.23	6.56	7.11	FJMS
Objective: Seeks to provide a high level of current income exempt from Federal income taxes through investing in medium and lower grade municipal securities.									
Invesco Tax-Free LT Bond (1981) J. Grabovac	FTIFX	0.92	99	4.51	6.19	3.54	6.82	7.65	AJSW
Objective: Invests primarily in municipal bonds or short-term notes rated BBB or better.									
Janus Tax Exempt Federal (1993) Darrell Watters	JATEX	0.70	164	5.31	7.45	3.59	N/A	N/A	FMS
Objective: Diversified fund seeking a high level of current income exempt from Federal income tax by investing at least 80 percent of assets in municipal obligations.									
Loomis Sayles Muni Bond (1991) Martha Hodgman	N/A	1.00	41	4.66	5.12	3.63	6.90	N/A	FJMSW
Objective: Seeks a high level of current interest income exempt from Federal income tax consistent with capital preservation by using municipal securities.									

LONG-TERM MUNICIPALS

Fund Name/ Start Date/ Manager	Symbol	Expense Ratio %	Portfolio Turnover %	Dividend Yield %	1-Year Annual Return	3-Year Annual Return	5-Year Annual Return	10-Year Annual Return	Broker Availability
Stein Roe Managed Muni (1977) M. Jane McCart	SRMMX	0.72	40	5.08	5.99	4.05	6.82	7.44	FJMSW

Objective: Seeks to provide a high level of current income exempt from Federal income taxes through investing in medium and lower grade municipal securities.

Fund Name/ Start Date/ Manager	Symbol	Expense Ratio %	Portfolio Turnover %	Dividend Yield %	1-Year Annual Return	3-Year Annual Return	5-Year Annual Return	10-Year Annual Return	Broker Availability
Strong Municipal Bond (1986) Mary Bourbulas	SXFIX	0.80	514	5.49	3.63	2.31	6.49	N/A	FJMSW

Objective: Seeks total return and moderate price fluctuations by investing in investment-grade obligations capable of producing current income exempt from Federal taxation.

HIGH-YIELD MUNICIPALS

Fund Name/ Start Date/ Manager	Symbol	Expense Ratio %	Portfolio Turnover %	Dividend Yield %	1-Year Annual Return	3-Year Annual Return	5-Year Annual Return	10-Year Annual Return	Broker Availability
Stein Roe High-Yield Muni (1984) M. Jane McCart	SRMFX	0.85	34	5.70	6.47	5.10	6.44	7.60	FJMSW

Objective: Seeks to provide a high level of current income exempt from Federal income taxes by investing in medium and lower grade municipal securities.

Strong High-Yield Municipal Bond (1993) Tom Conlin	SHYLX	0.40	114	6.90	5.38	N/A	N/A	N/A	FJMSW

Objective: Pursues total return by investing in long-term, medium and lower quality municipal obligations offering a high level of current income that is exempt from Federal taxation.

CALIFORNIA MUNICIPALS

Fund Name/ Start Date/ Manager	Symbol	Expense Ratio %	Portfolio Turnover %	Dividend Yield %	1-Year Annual Return	3-Year Annual Return	5-Year Annual Return	10-Year Annual Return	Broker Availability
Dreyfus CA Intermediate Muni (1992) L. Troutman	DCIMX	0.65	41	4.23	4.07	3.38	N/A	N/A	FJMS

Objective: Invests at least 65 percent of assets in California obligations that are exempt from Federal and California state taxation with dollar-weighted average maturities of three to ten years.

Dreyfus CA Tax Exempt Bond (1983) Joseph Darcy	DRCAX	0.69	56	5.02	5.06	2.61	5.64	6.25	FJMS

Objective: Seeks to provide a high level of current income exempt from California state and Federal taxation by investing in medium and lower grade municipal securities.

Dreyfus General Calif. Muni (1989) Paul Disdier	GCABX	0.76	83	4.91	6.85	3.89	7.31	N/A	FJMW

Objective: Pursues current income by investing in municipal obligations that are free of California state and Federal taxation.

Montgomery Cal Tax-Free Sh-Int (1993) W. Stevens	MNCTX	0.61	58	4.36	5.25	N/A	N/A	N/A	FJMSW

Objective: Invests at least 80 percent of total assets in debt securities that are exempt from Federal and California personal income taxes with an average portfolio duration comparable to three-year U.S. Treasuries.

NEW YORK MUNICIPALS

Fund Name/ Start Date/ Manager	Symbol	Expense Ratio %	Portfolio Turnover %	Dividend Yield %	1-Year Annual Return	3-Year Annual Return	5-Year Annual Return	10-Year Annual Return	Broker Availability
Dreyfus General NY Muni Bond (1984) M. Wieboldt	GNYMX	0.86	66	5.13	5.38	3.19	7.13	7.07	FJM

Objective: Pursues current income by investing in municipal obligations that are free of New York state and Federal taxation.

Dreyfus NY Ins. Tax Ex. Bond (1987) L. Troutman	DNYBX	0.99	31	4.75	4.05	2.74	6.13	N/A	AFJMSW

Objective: Invests primarily in securities insured as to timely payment of principal and interest that provide income free of New York state and Federal taxation.

Dreyfus NY Intermediate Tax Ex. (1987) M. Wieboldt	DRNIX	0.84	47	4.49	4.63	3.74	6.74	N/A	AFJMS

Objective: Invests at least 65 percent of assets in New York obligations that are exempt from Federal and New York state taxation with dollar-weighted average maturities of three to ten years.

Dreyfus NY Tax Exempt (1983) Monica Wieboldt	DRNYX	0.71	82	4.95	4.90	3.05	6.52	6.72	FJMSW

Objective: Seeks to provide a high level of current income exempt from New York state and Federal taxation by investing in medium and lower grade municipal securities.

Neuberger & Berman NY Ins. Int.^ (1994) C. Del Villar	N/A	0.66	0	4.05	3.49	N/A	N/A	N/A	FS

Objective: Seeks a high level of current income exempt from Federal and New York state and city income taxes, consistent with the preservation of capital.

Warburg Pincus NY Int. Muni (1987) Christensen	CNMBX	0.60	105	4.13	5.07	4.19	6.29	N/A	FJMSW

Objective: Seeks double tax-free income from New York intermediate tax-free municipal bonds.

---

^=with some discount brokers, Neuberger & Berman funds are operated as Trust accounts. In essence, these are a separate share class of funds with the exact same name. Trust funds are different in that they charge slightly higher management fees and are offered exclusively through select brokers, including Fidelity.

OTHER STATE MUNICIPALS

Fund Name/ Start Date/ Manager	Symbol	Expense Ratio %	Portfolio Turnover %	Dividend Yield %	1-Year Annual Return	3-Year Annual Return	5-Year Annual Return	10-Year Annual Return	Broker Availability
Benham AZ Muni Int. Term (1994) Team Managed	BEAMX	0.14	36	4.06	4.39	N/A	N/A	N/A	JS
Objective: Seeks to provide a high level of current income exempt from Arizona state and Federal income taxes.									
Benham FL Muni Int. Term (1994) G. MacEwen	N/A	0.13	66	4.13	4.46	N/A	N/A	N/A	JS
Objective: Seeks to obtain a high level of current income exempt from Florida state and Federal income taxes.									
Crabbe Huson Oregon Muni. Bond (1984) Huson	ORBFX	0.98	23	4.05	3.43	3.56	5.75	6.14	AFJMSW
Objective: Seeks to provide a high level of income exempt from Oregon and Federal income taxation by investing in municipal bonds issued by the state of Oregon.									
Dreyfus CT Intermediate Muni (1992) Stephen Kris	DCTIX	0.72	20	4.29	3.92	3.83	N/A	N/A	FJMS
Objective: Pursues income by investing in securities exempt from Connecticut state and Federal income taxation with weighted average maturities of three years to ten years.									
Dreyfus FL Intermediate Muni (1992) Stephen Kris	DFLIX	0.69	25	4.16	3.72	3.54	N/A	N/A	FJMS
Objective: Pursues income by investing in securities exempt from Florida state and Federal income taxation with weighted average maturities of three to ten years.									
Dreyfus MA Intermediate (1992) Lawrence Troutman	DMAIX	0.75	32	4.24	3.76	3.35	N/A	N/A	FJMS
Objective: Pursues income by investing in securities exempt from Massachusetts state and Federal income taxation with weighted average maturities of three to ten years.									
Dreyfus MA Tax Exempt (1985) Joseph Darcy	DMEBX	0.79	61	5.27	6.16	3.68	6.73	6.62	FJMS
Objective: Seeks to provide a high level of current income exempt from Federal and state income taxes through investing in medium and lower grade municipal securities issued by the state of Massachusetts.									
Dreyfus NJ Intermediate Muni (1992) Stephen Kris	DNJIX	0.72	14	4.23	3.51	3.39	N/A	N/A	FJMSW
Objective: Pursues income by investing in securities exempt from New Jersey state and Federal income taxation with weighted average maturities of three to ten years.									
Dreyfus NJ Muni (1987) Samuel Weinstock	DRNJX	0.80	24	5.10	4.88	3.30	6.78	N/A	AFJMSW
Objective: Seeks to provide a high level of current income exempt from Federal and state income taxes through investing in medium and lower grade municipal securities issued by the state of New Jersey.									
Dreyfus PA Intermediate Muni (1993) M. Weiboldt	DPABX	0.48	5	4.60	4.73	N/A	N/A	N/A	AJS
Objective: Seeks to maximize current income exempt from Federal income taxes and taxes imposed by the Commonwealth of Pennsylvania.									
IAI MN Tax-Free (1992) Coleman/Douglas	N/A	0.25	94	4.51	N/A	N/A	N/A	N/A	AFJMS
Objective: Seeks a high level of current income exempt from Federal and Minnesota state income taxation by investing in investment-grade municipal bonds.									

OTHER STATE MUNICIPALS

Fund Name/ Start Date/ Manager	Symbol	Expense Ratio %	Portfolio Turnover %	Dividend Yield %	1-Year Annual Return	3-Year Annual Return	5-Year Annual Return	10-Year Annual Return	Broker Availability
Rushmore MD Tax-Free (1983) Team Managed	RSXLX	0.77	37	4.98	4.83	N/A	6.37	6.16	FJS

Objective: Seeks tax-exempt Federal and Maryland state income by investing in municipal bonds issued by the state of Maryland.

Fund Name/ Start Date/ Manager	Symbol	Expense Ratio %	Portfolio Turnover %	Dividend Yield %	1-Year Annual Return	3-Year Annual Return	5-Year Annual Return	10-Year Annual Return	Broker Availability
Rushmore VA Tax-Free (1983) Team Managed	RSXIX	0.77	55	4.72	4.97	3.36	6.41	N/A	FJS

Objective: Seeks tax-exempt Federal and Virginia state income by investing in municipal bonds issued by the state of Virginia.

Fund Name/ Start Date/ Manager	Symbol	Expense Ratio %	Portfolio Turnover %	Dividend Yield %	1-Year Annual Return	3-Year Annual Return	5-Year Annual Return	10-Year Annual Return	Broker Availability
Sit MN Tax-Free Income (1993) Team Managed	SMTFX	0.80	16	5.68	7.08	N/A	N/A	N/A	FJMS

Objective: Seeks to provide a high level of current income exempt from Federal and Minnesota state income taxes.

Getting More Information

Once you have identified possible fund picks for your portfolio, you will want to order a prospectus and annual report. After you've set up your account with a discount broker, you can make this request one of two ways: by calling your broker or contacting the fund company. Either way is fine, though you can get more specific information by calling the fund. That's because representatives at the brokerage firms are not trained to know the ins and outs of every fund. Therefore, below you will find the toll-free contact number for each fund family listed in the preceding directory.

Mutual Fund Contact Numbers

American AAdvantage
800-388-3344

American Heritage
800-828-5050

Ariel Funds
800-292-7435

Artisan Funds
800-344-1770

ASM Fund
800-445-2763

Babson Funds
800-422-2766

Baron Funds
800-992-2766

Benham Funds
800-321-8321

Berger Funds
800-333-1001

Blanchard Funds
800-922-7771

Bonnel Growth Fund
800-426-6635

Bramwell Fund
800-272-6227

Brinson Funds
800-448-2430

Bull & Bear Funds
800-847-4200

Cappiello-Rushmore Funds
800-621-7874

Century Shares Trust
800-321-1928

Cohen & Steers Realty Shares
800-437-9912

Crabbe Huson Funds
800-541-9732

Dreyfus Funds
800-645-6561

FAM Value Fund
800-932-3271

Federated Funds
800-341-7400

Founders Funds
800-525-2440

Fremont Funds
800-548-4539

Gabelli/Westwood Funds
800-422-3554

Gateway Funds
800-354-6339

Guinness Flight Funds
800-915-6565

Heartland Funds
800-432-7856

Hotchkis and Wiley Funds
800-236-4479

IAI Funds
800-945-3863

Invesco Funds
800-525-8085

Janus Funds
800-525-8983

Kaufmann Fund
800-666-4943

Lexington Funds
800-526-0056

Loomis Sayles Funds
800-633-3330

Managers Funds
800-835-3879

Matthews International Funds
800-789-2742

Merger Fund
800-343-8959

Merriman Funds
800-423-4893

Midas Fund
800-400-6432

Monetta Funds
800-666-3882

Montag & Caldwell Funds
800-992-8151

Montgomery Funds
800-572-3863

Navellier Funds
800-887-8671

Neuberger & Berman Funds
800-877-9700

Oakmark Funds
800-625-6275

Oberweis Funds
800-323-6166

PBHG Funds
800-809-8008

Rainier Funds
800-248-6314

Robertson Stephens Funds
800-766-3863

Royce Funds
800-221-4268

Selected American Funds
800-279-0279

Sit Funds
800-332-5580

Skyline Funds
800-458-5222

Smith Breeden Funds
800-221-3138

Stein Roe Funds
800-338-2550

Strong Funds
800-368-1030

Third Avenue Value Fund
800-443-1021

Turner Funds
800-224-6312

UAM Funds
800-638-7983

United Services Funds
800-873-8637

Value Line Funds
800-223-0818

Van Wagoner Funds
800-228-2121

Vontobel Funds
800-527-9500

Warburg Pincus Funds
800-927-2874

Wasatch Funds
800-551-1700

William Blair Funds
800-742-7272

Wright Funds
800-888-9471

Yacktman Fund
800-525-8258

GLOSSARY
of Investment Terms

adviser—Organization hired by a mutual fund to provide professional guidance and management

aggressive growth fund—Mutual fund that seeks high growth through aggressive investment strategies. Such funds typically hold shares of small, emerging companies and offer the potential for rapid growth.

annual report—Yearly summary sent by a mutual fund to its shareholders showing which securities it holds and discussing its performance over the period in question

ask or offer price—The lowest amount a seller is willing to take for shares of a stock or mutual fund. It represents the net asset value plus any sales charges.

assets—The investment holdings owned by a fund

asset allocation—Act of spreading investment money across various categories, such as stock, bond, and money market funds

automatic reinvestment—The shareholder-authorized purchase of additional shares using fund dividends and capital gains distributions

average maturity—Refers to the length of time before a bond issuer must return the holder's principal. Bonds are issued for a variety of maturities, from 30 days to more than 30 years. Bond mutual funds attempt to maintain a portfolio of bonds with different maturities. When taken together, you can measure the fund's average maturity.

balanced fund—Mutual fund that equalizes its portfolio by holding a blend of stocks, bonds, and cash

bear market—Period in which stock market prices are generally falling

beta—Coefficient measure of a stock or mutual fund's relative volatility in relation to the Standard & Poor's 500 index, which has a beta of 1

bid price—The highest amount a buyer is willing to pay for shares of a stock or mutual fund (also referred to as the redemption price). Except for funds with a back-end sales load, this is the same as *net asset value.*

blue chip—Common stock of a nationally known company with a long record of profit growth, dividend payments, and a reputation for quality products and services

blue-sky laws—A body of state laws governing registration and distribution of mutual fund shares. All 50 states and the District of Columbia regulate mutual funds.

bond—Any interest-bearing or discounted government or corporate obligation to pay a specified sum of money, usually at regular intervals

bond fund—Mutual fund that holds bonds of various maturities and safety ratings

book value—What a company would be worth if all assets were sold (assets minus liabilities). Also, the price at which an asset is carried on the balance sheet.

bottom-up investing—The search for outstanding individual stocks with little regard for overall economic trends

broker—Person who acts as an intermediary between a buyer and seller

bull market—Period in which security prices are generally rising

buy and hold strategy—Technique that calls for accumulating and keeping shares in a mutual fund over many years, regardless of price swings

call—An option contract that gives the holder the right to purchase a specified security at a stated price during a specific period of time

capital appreciation—Increase in the market value of a mutual fund's securities. This is reflected in the increased net asset value of a fund's shares.

capital depreciation—Decline in the value of a given investment

capital gains distribution—Payment to shareholders of profits realized by a fund for securities sold at a premium to their original cost. For tax purposes, gains held more than one year can be distributed as long-term capital gains. However, gains from securities held less than one year are taxed as ordinary income by the Internal Revenue Service.

cash equivalent—Investment that can easily be turned into cash. Examples include certificates of deposit and money market funds.

cash position—Figure that shows what percentage of a fund's portfolio is invested in cash; includes cash plus cash equivalents minus current liabilities.

certificate of deposit—Instrument issued by a bank or savings and loan that pays a specific amount of interest for a set time period. If you take your money out before the maturity date, you are assessed an early-withdrawal penalty.

check writing privilege—Service offered by most discount brokers and some mutual funds that allows shareholders to write checks against their fund holdings. The money in cash accounts continues to earn interest until a check clears.

closed-end fund—Investment company that issues a limited number of shares and is traded on a stock exchange. The value of such funds is determined by market supply and demand, meaning shares do not necessarily trade at net asset value.

commercial paper—Short-term, unsecured promissory notes issued by corporations to finance immediate credit needs

commission—Fee paid by investors to a broker or other sales agent for the purchase of investment products

common stock—Security representing ownership of a corporation's assets that generally carries voting rights. Common stock dividends, however, are always paid after the company has met its obligations for bonds, debentures, and preferred stock.

compounding—Earnings on top of earnings

contrarian—Investor who does the opposite of the majority at any particular time

convertible securities—Securities that can be exchanged for other securities of the issuer (under certain conditions), usually from preferred stock or bonds into common stock

credit risk—Risk that a bond issuer will default on the payment of interest and return of principal. Risk is minimized by investing in bonds issued through large blue-chip corporations or government agencies.

current assets—In a mutual fund, this includes cash plus cash equivalents minus current liabilities.

current liabilities—Obligations due within one year or less

custodian—Organization, usually a bank or trust company, that holds the securities and other assets of a mutual fund

debenture—A bond secured only by the general credit of a corporation

distributions—Dividends paid from net investment income plus realized capital gains

diversification—Spreading risk by putting assets into several different investment categories (i.e., stocks, bonds, and cash)

diversified investment company—Under the Investment Company Act, this represents a company that, with respect to 75 percent of total assets, has not invested more than 5 percent in any one company and holds no more than 10 percent of the outstanding voting securities of any one company.

dividend—Distribution of earnings to shareholders

dividend yield—The cash dividend paid per share each year divided by the current share price

dollar-cost-averaging—The process of accumulating positions in mutual funds over time by investing a set amount of money each month, thus buying more shares when prices are down, less when they are up

Dow Jones Industrial Average—The oldest and most widely quoted stock market indicator. Represents the price direction of 30 blue chip stocks on the New York Stock Exchange. (Doesn't always give an accurate view of what's happening with the market as a whole.)

earnings—Net income after all charges divided by the number of outstanding shares

equity income fund—Mutual fund that seeks to produce a high level of income without undue risk by investing primarily in a combination of dividend-paying stocks, corporate bonds, and convertibles

exchange privilege—Option enabling fund shareholders to shift investments from one fund to another

expense ratio—Percent of assets taken from a fund to cover all operating costs

fixed-income security—A preferred stock or debt instrument (i.e., a bond) with a stated percentage or dollar amount of income paid at regular intervals

401(k) plan—Employer-sponsored retirement plan enabling employees to defer taxes on a portion of their salaries by making a contribution

front-end load—Sales fee charged to investors of some mutual funds at the time shares are purchased

fund family—Group of mutual funds managed and distributed by the same company

fund symbol—Letter code used to identify a fund on the exchange

general government bond fund (short/intermediate term)—Mutual fund that seeks to provide current income and stability of principal by investing in a blend of U.S. government-backed securities. The average maturity of bonds in this type of portfolio is usually ten years or less.

global stock fund—Mutual fund that seeks growth by investing primarily in stocks of companies located around the world, including the United States

government agency issues—Debt securities issued by governmental enterprises, federal agencies, and international institutions

growth and income fund—Mutual fund that seeks both growth of capital and current income by investing in dividend-paying stocks with the potential for growth.

growth fund—Mutual fund that seeks long-term growth without undue risk by investing in the stocks of solid U.S.-based companies.

growth stock—Stock of a corporation that shows greater-than-average gains in earnings.

hedge fund—Mutual fund that hedges its market commitments by holding securities likely to increase in value while "shorting" other securities likely to decrease with the sole objective of capital appreciation.

income—Dividends, interest, and/or short-term capital gains paid to a mutual fund's shareholders.

income fund—Mutual fund whose primary objective is to generate current income.

index fund—Mutual fund that seeks to match the returns of a particular market index, such as the Standard & Poor's 500 or Russell 2000. These funds essentially allow you to "buy the market," but never outperform it.

individual retirement account (IRA)—Tax-deferred account established to hold funds until retirement

inflation—A persistent upward movement in the general price level of goods and services that reduces the purchasing power of money

institutional investor—Organization that trades a large volume of securities (i.e., a mutual fund, bank, or insurance company)

interest rate risk—Refers to the chance that market rates will rise above the fixed rate of your bond, thus reducing your principal value and total return. (The opposite is also true, and if rates fall, the principal value of your bond will rise.) Interest rate risk is minimized by investing in short-term bond funds.

international equity fund—Mutual fund that seeks growth by investing in securities of companies located in developed markets outside of the United States, such as Japan, New Zealand, Australia, Canada, and Western Europe. International equity funds entail an added degree of risk because of political instability, currency fluctuations, foreign taxes, and differences in financial reporting standards.

Investment Company Act of 1940—Federal statute enacted by Congress in 1940 requiring the registration and regulation of investment companies (mutual funds)

investment management company—Organization hired to advise the directors and trustees of a mutual fund in selecting and supervising assets in a fund's portfolio

investment objective—An investor's long-term goal and reason for placing money into a mutual fund in the first place

Keogh plan—A tax-favored retirement program for the self-employed and their employees

liquidity—The ability to redeem all or part of your mutual fund shares on any business day for the posted net asset value

load—Sales commission assessed by some mutual funds to compensate the person who sells them (usually a stockbroker or financial planner). There are two types of loads: Front-end loads are taken out when a fund is purchased. Back-end loads are collected when a fund is sold. Loads typically range from 2 to 8 percent.

long-term funds—Mutual fund designed for capital appreciation over an extended period of time

management fee—Amount paid by a mutual fund for the services of an investment adviser

market capitalization—Calculated by multiplying the number of shares outstanding by the per share price of a stock. One can also categorize equities into several different classes, including micro-cap, small-cap, mid-cap, and large-cap. The general guidelines for these classifications are as follows:

- **micro-cap**—Stock market capitalizations of $0 to $100 million
- **small-cap**—Stock market capitalizations of $100 to $750 million
- **mid-cap**—Stock market capitalizations of $750 million to $2 billion
- **large-cap**—Stock market capitalizations of $2 billion or more

market order—Order to buy or sell a security at the best available price

money market fund—Highly liquid mutual fund that invests in short-term securities and seeks to maintain a stable net asset value of $1 per share (although this is not guaranteed)

municipal fund—Bond issued by a state, city, municipality, or revenue district. Municipal bonds, also known as *munis,* are exempt from federal, and in some cases, state and local income taxes.

mutual fund—An investment company that raises money from shareholders and puts it to work in stocks, options, bonds, or money market securities. Offers investors diversification and professional management.

Nasdaq Composite—An index (formerly the National Association of Securities Dealers Automated Quotation System) weighted by market value and representing domestic companies that are sold over-the-counter

net asset value (NAV)—Market worth of one share of a mutual fund. It is calculated by adding up a fund's total assets, subtracting any liabilities, and dividing the resulting figure by the number of outstanding shares.

no-load fund—Mutual fund whose shares are bought and sold at the prevailing net asset value, without any sales charges or commissions

open-end fund—A mutual fund ready to issue and redeem an unlimited number of shares as requested by investors

operating expenses—Costs paid from a fund's assets before earnings are distributed to shareholders for overhead and operations

pension plan—Retirement program based on a defined formula providing employees with benefits paid during the remainder of their lifetime upon reaching a stated age

pension rollover—Opportunity to take distributions from a qualified pension or profit-sharing plan and reinvest them in an individual retirement account (IRA) within 60 days from the date of distribution

performance record—A statistical record of what kind of returns a fund and/or fund manager has produced over a stated period of time

pooling—Concept behind mutual funds whereby the assets of various investors with common goals are brought together and invested in one diversified portfolio

portfolio—Collection of investment securities owned by an individual or institution that might include stocks, bonds, and money market instruments

portfolio manager—Person responsible for investing a fund's pool of assets in accordance with the provisions set out in the prospectus

portfolio turnover—Measure of trading activity in a fund. Shows how frequently securities are bought and sold.

preferred stock—Equity security that generally carries a fixed dividend that must be satisfied before dividends are paid to holders of common shares

price-earnings ratio (PE)—Price of a stock divided by its earnings per share

principal—The initial amount of money invested in a fund, before reinvested dividends and capital gains

professional management—Major advantage to mutual fund investing. Stands for the ability to hire an experienced professional to decide which securities to buy and sell in an investor's fund portfolio.

prospectus—Official document describing a mutual fund's investment objectives, policies, services, fees, and past performance history

proxy statement—Information about fund matters sent annually to shareholders of record to be voted on. (Sadly, many fund investors don't even bother to vote, meaning fund trustees often get their way no matter what.)

prudent man rule—Law governing the investment of trust funds in states that give broad discretion to trustees

qualified plans—Retirement plans that meet the requirements of sections 401(a), 403(a), or 403(b) of the Internal Revenue Code or the Self-Employed Individuals Tax Retirement Act

record date—Date of ownership determining a shareholder's eligibility to receive announced distributions

redemption—The act of selling shares of a mutual fund

redemption-in-kind—Redemption of investment company shares for which payment is made in portfolio securities rather than cash

registered investment company—Investment company that has filed a registration statement with the Securities and Exchange Commission (SEC) under the requirements of the Investment Company Act of 1940

reinvestment—Act of using mutual fund dividends and capital gains distributions to automatically buy additional shares, thus increasing an investor's overall holdings

return on investment—Amount of money an investment earns over a given period of time. It is often expressed as a percentage.

risk—Accepted possibility that an investment will fluctuate in value

rollover—Shifting of assets from one qualified retirement plan to another without penalty

sales load—Amount charged for the sales of mutual fund shares by a stockbroker or other sales professional, usually added to the net asset value

sector fund—Mutual fund that invests in the securities of a single industry or country-specific region

Securities and Exchange Commission (SEC)—Federal agency that regulates the registration and distribution of mutual fund shares

senior securities—Notes, bonds, debentures, or preferred stocks that have a claim to assets and earnings ahead of holders of common stock

shareholder—Investor who owns shares in a mutual fund

short sale—The sale of a security that is not owned but rather borrowed with the hope that the price will go down so it can be repurchased at a lower price and therefore generate a profit

short-term funds—Mutual funds that invest in securities with the intention of holding them for one year or less (i.e., money market funds)

small company fund—Mutual fund that seeks capital appreciation by investing in the stocks of small, fast-growing companies

Standard & Poor's Composite Index of 500 Stocks (S&P 500)—Tracks the performance of 500 widely held common stocks. It includes most blue chip names and represents almost two-thirds of the U.S. stock market's total value. It is weighted by market value.

statement of additional information (SAI)—Supplement to a prospectus that contains updated or more complete information about a mutual fund. (Also referred to as "Part B" of the registration statement.)

stock—Represents ownership in a corporation. Usually listed in terms of shares.

systematic withdrawal plan—Program in which a fund shareholder receives regular automatic distributions from their investments. Shares are redeemed to meet the shareholder's income needs, and payments are sent out monthly, quarterly, or annually, as specified.

tax-deferred income—Refers to dividends, interest, and capital gains received from investments held in qualified retirement plans, such as IRAs, Keoghs, 401(k)s, and 403(b)s. This income is not subject to current taxation, but will be taxed when withdrawn.

time horizon—Length of time you plan to keep your money invested. This helps to pinpoint which types of investments should be included in your portfolio. That's because the longer your time horizon, the more risk you can take because you will be able to weather any short-term declines in the market.

total return—Measure of a fund's overall performance during a given period of time that encompasses all aspects affecting its return, including dividends, capital gains distributions, and changes in net asset value

transfer agent—Organization hired by a mutual fund to prepare and maintain records on shareholder accounts

Treasury bill—Noninterest-bearing security issued at a discount to its value by the U.S. Treasury with a maturity of one year or less

turnover rate—Measure of how frequently a fund manager buys and sells securities in the portfolio

12b-1 fee—Mutual fund expense used to pay for marketing and distribution costs

U.S. government bond—Bond issued by the U.S. Treasury or other government agency. These are considered to be the safest of all investments, since they're backed by the full faith and credit of the U.S. government.

U.S. government securities—Refers to the various types of marketable securities issued by the U.S. Treasury, including bills, notes, and bonds

value fund—Mutual fund with the objective of buying stocks in companies whose shares are priced below book or intrinsic value

volatility—Measure of risk that refers to how a fund's share price moves up or down compared to its benchmark market index

warrant—Option to buy a specific number of shares of stock at a stated price during a limited time period

wash sale—Purchase and sale of a security either simultaneously or within a short period of time. Wash sales taking place within 30 days of the underlying purchase do not qualify for a tax loss deduction under Internal Revenue Service rules.

withdrawal plan—Program in which shareholders receive income or principal payments at regular intervals from their mutual fund investments

yield—Measure of the net income (dividends and interest minus expenses) earned by the securities in a fund's portfolio during a specified period of time

yield to maturity—The rate of return on a debt security held to maturity

INDEX

2. **Access to the *FUND CONNECTION* TELEPHONE HOTLINE**

   Each Friday, and whenever the market moves up or down more than 100 points, you can call in and hear Kirk's late-breaking market commentary and asset allocation advice. You'll find out about new funds and program updates before anyone else. (Similar hotlines cost more than $100 a year!)

3. **Special Report: "THE TOP FUND FOR THE 21ST CENTURY"**

   There are more than 6,000 mutual funds on the market, but only one is good enough to be crowned Kirk's "Top Fund for the 21st Century." This fund is so good, you can buy it and relax through the turn of the century, knowing your money is in very good (and profitable) hands.

Don't wait to reap the mutual fund rewards waiting for you. Subscribe to Kirk Kazanjian's *Fund Connection* today!

SUBSCRIPTION SAVINGS CERTIFICATE

Yes, Kirk! I want to earn more from my NTF funds with less risk. Send me 12 months of *Fund Connection* at the introductory price of just $99. *(That's a savings of almost 60% off the regular rate.)* I'll also receive your FREE tape on "The Secrets to Successful Mutual Fund Investing," unlimited access to your telephone hotline, and your special report "The Top Fund for the 21st Century." Plus, I'm protected by your unconditional money-back guarantee.

Payment Options

___My check made payable to *Fund Connection* is enclosed.

___Charge my credit card.   ❏ Visa   ❏ MasterCard   ❏ Diner's Club

Card # _____ Exp. ___/____

Signature _____

Telephone _____

Name _____

Address _____

City _____ State____ Zip_____

Please Return This Form To:

Kirk Kazanjian's
FUND CONNECTION

PO Box 778
Tulare, CA 93275-0778